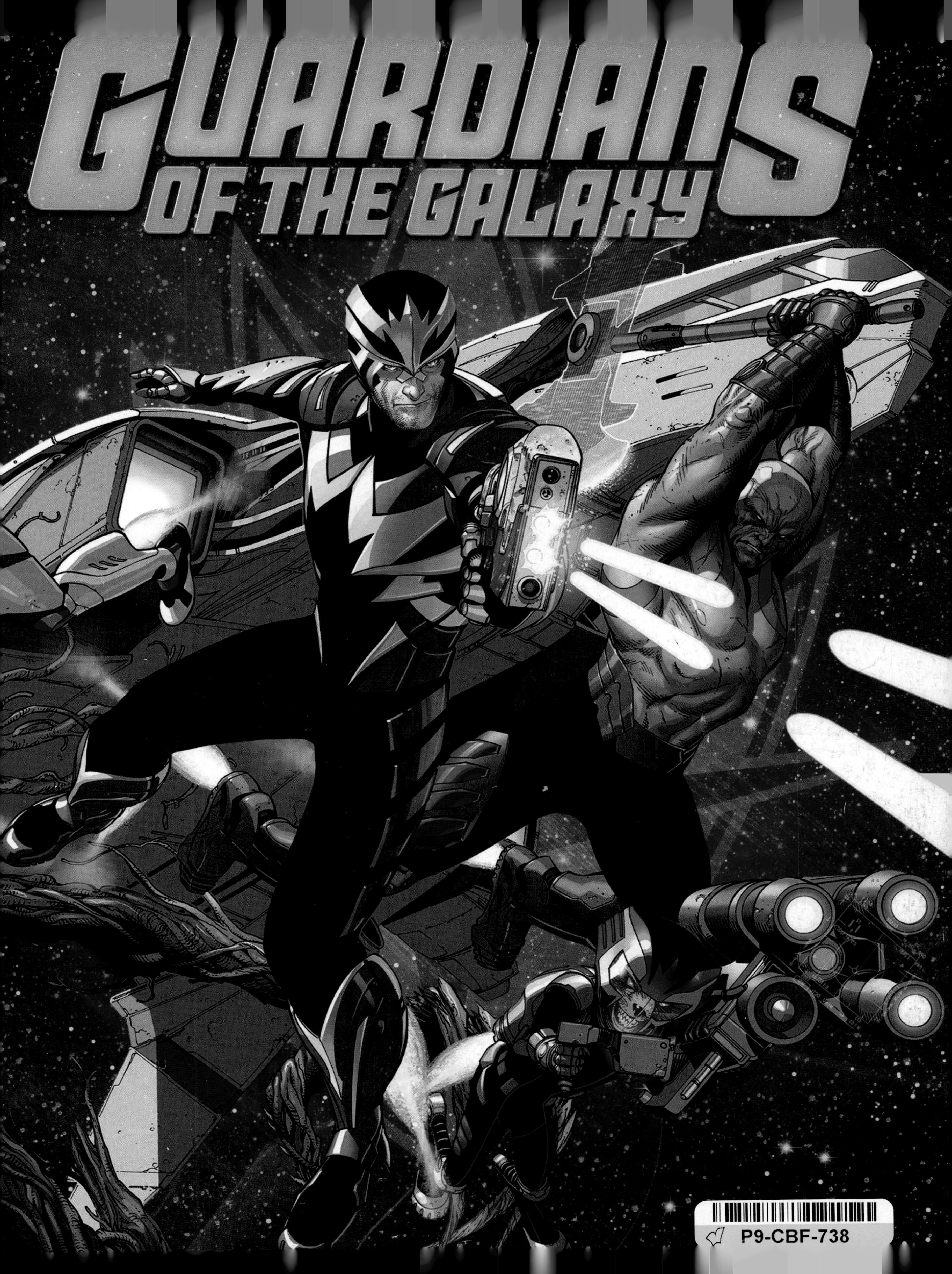
GUARDIANS
OF THE GALAXY

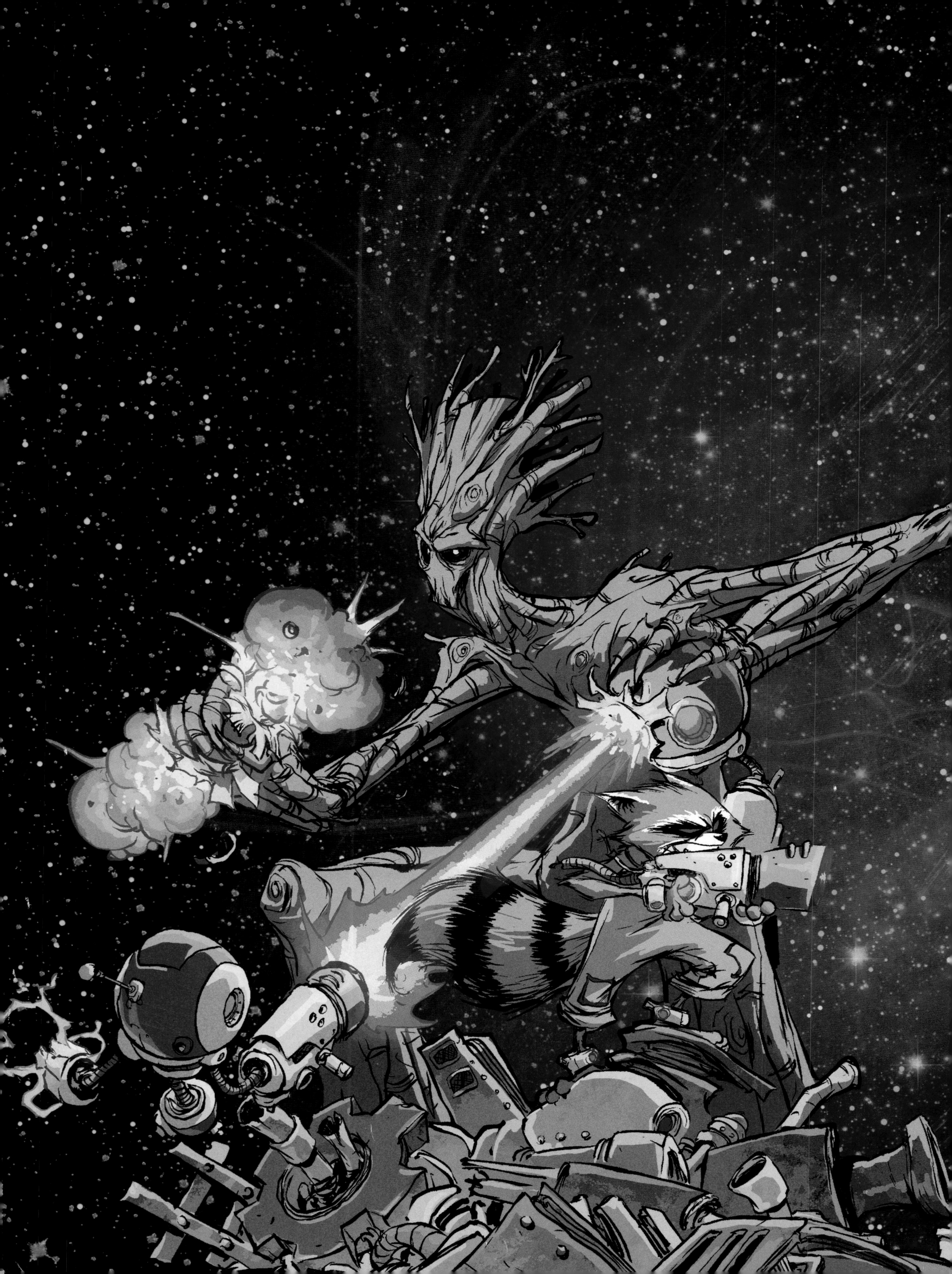

GUARDIANS OF THE GALAXY

DAN ABNETT & ANDY LANNING, BRIAN MICHAEL BENDIS AND **SKOTTIE YOUNG**
WRITERS

PAUL PELLETIER, STEVE McNIVEN AND **SKOTTIE YOUNG**
PENCILERS

RICK MAGYAR, JOHN DELL AND **SKOTTIE YOUNG**
INKERS

NATHAN FAIRBAIRN, JUSTIN PONSOR
AND JEAN-FRANÇOIS BEAULIEU
COLORISTS

VC's JOE CARAMAGNA, VC's CORY PETIT
AND JEFF ECKLEBERRY
LETTERERS

CLINT LANGLEY;
STEVE McNIVEN, JOHN DELL & JUSTIN PONSOR;
AND SKOTTIE YOUNG & JEAN-FRANÇOIS BEAULIEU
COVER ART

LAUREN SANKOVITCH, ELLIE PYLE,
DEVIN LEWIS, BILL ROSEMANN, STEPHEN WACKER,
SANA AMANAT AND **NICK LOWE**
EDITORS

...DIANS OF THE GALAXY: ALL-NEW MARVEL TREASURY EDITION. Contains material originally published in magazine form as GUARDIANS ... GALAXY (2013) #0.1 and #1, GUARDIANS OF THE GALAXY (2008) #1, and ROCKET RACCOON #1. First printing 2017. ISBN# 978-1-302-...-8. Published by MARVEL WORLDWIDE, INC., a subsidiary of MARVEL ENTERTAINMENT, LLC. OFFICE OF PUBLICATION: 135 West 50th ... New York, NY 10020. Copyright © 2017 MARVEL No similarity between any of the names, characters, persons, and/or institutions in ...magazine with those of any living or dead person or institution is intended, and any such similarity which may exist is purely coincidental. ...d in the U.S.A. DAN BUCKLEY, President, Marvel Entertainment; JOE QUESADA, Chief Creative Officer; TOM BREVOORT, SVP of Publishing; ... BOGART, SVP of Business Affairs & Operations, Publishing & Partnership; C.B. CEBULSKI, VP of Brand Management & Development, Asia; ...GABRIEL, SVP of Sales & Marketing, Publishing; JEFF YOUNGQUIST, VP of Production & Special Projects; DAN CARR, Executive Director of ...hing Technology; ALEX MORALES, Director of Publishing Operations; SUSAN CRESPI, Production Manager; STAN LEE, Chairman Emeritus. ...ormation regarding advertising in Marvel Comics or on Marvel.com, please contact Vit DeBellis, Integrated Sales Manager, at vdebellis@ ....com. For Marvel subscription inquiries, please call 888-511-5480. **Manufactured between 2/3/2017 and 3/7/2017 by WORZALLA** ...SHING CO., STEVENS POINT, WI, USA.

Collection Editor: JENNIFER GRÜNWALD
Assistant Editor: CAITLIN O'CONNELL
Associate Managing Editor: KATERI WOODY
Editor, Special Projects: MARK D. BEAZLEY
VP Production & Special Projects: JEFF YOUNGQUIST
SVP Print, Sales & Marketing: DAVID GABRIEL
Book Designer: ADAM DEL RE

Editor in Chief: AXEL ALONSO
Chief Creative Officer: JOE QUESADA
President: DAN BUCKLEY
Executive Producer: ALAN FINE

GUARDIANS OF THE GALAXY 1

(2008)

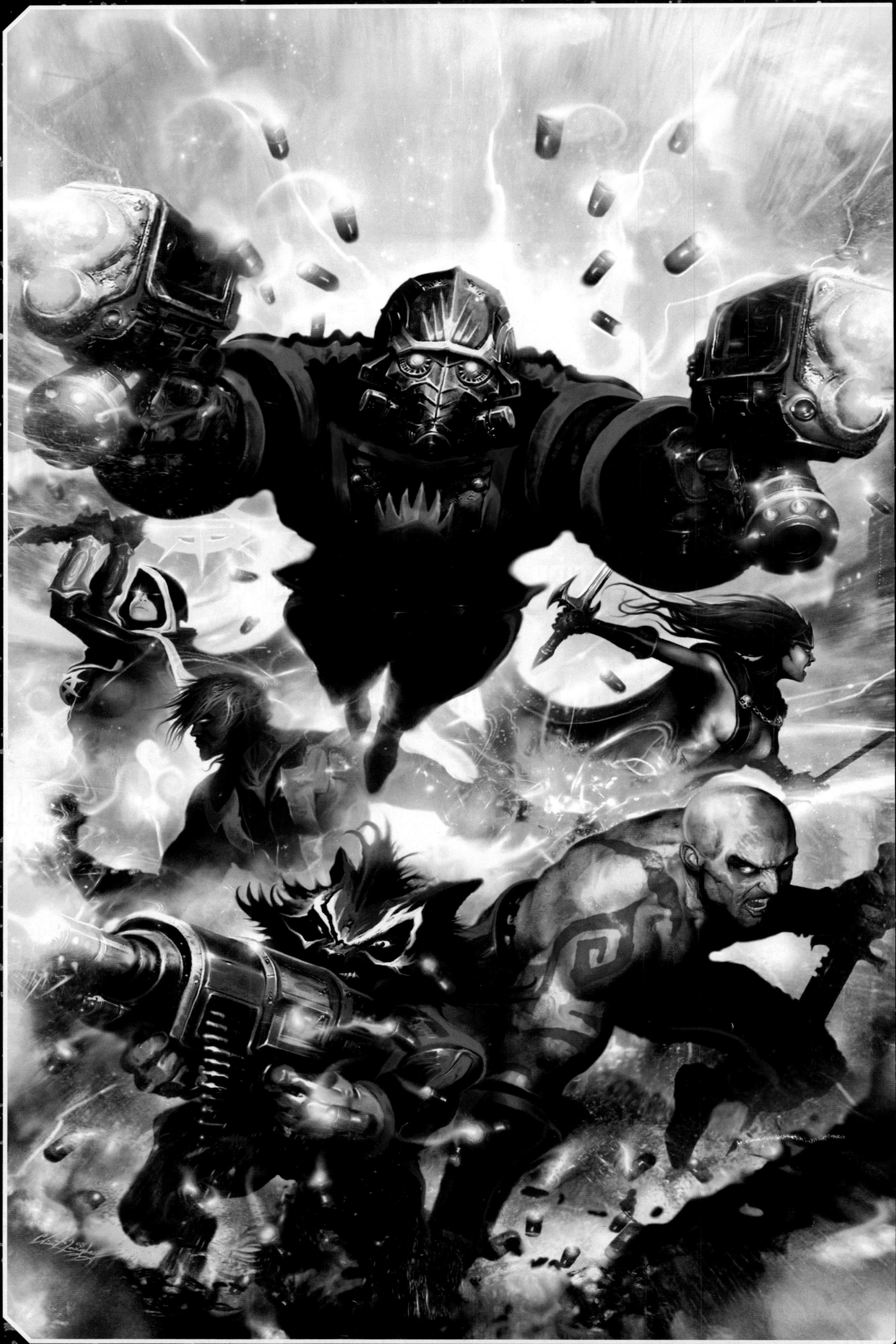

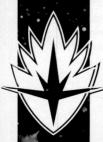

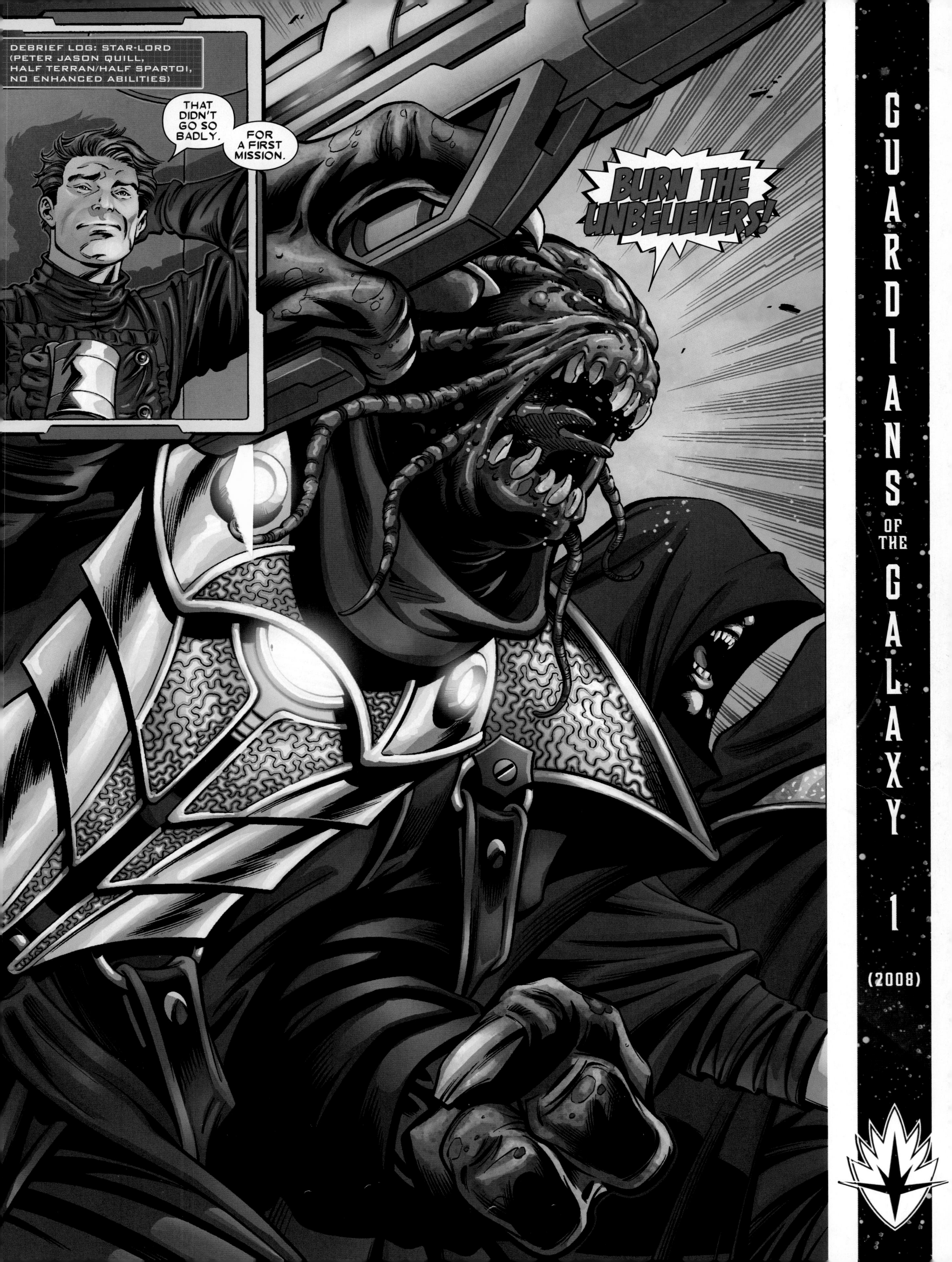

DEBRIEF LOG: STAR-LORD (PETER JASON QUILL, HALF TERRAN/HALF SPARTOI, NO ENHANCED ABILITIES)
THAT DIDN'T GO SO BADLY.
FOR A FIRST MISSION.
BURN THE UNBELIEVERS!
GUARDIANS OF THE GALAXY 1
(2008)

GUARDIANS OF THE GALAXY 1 (2008)

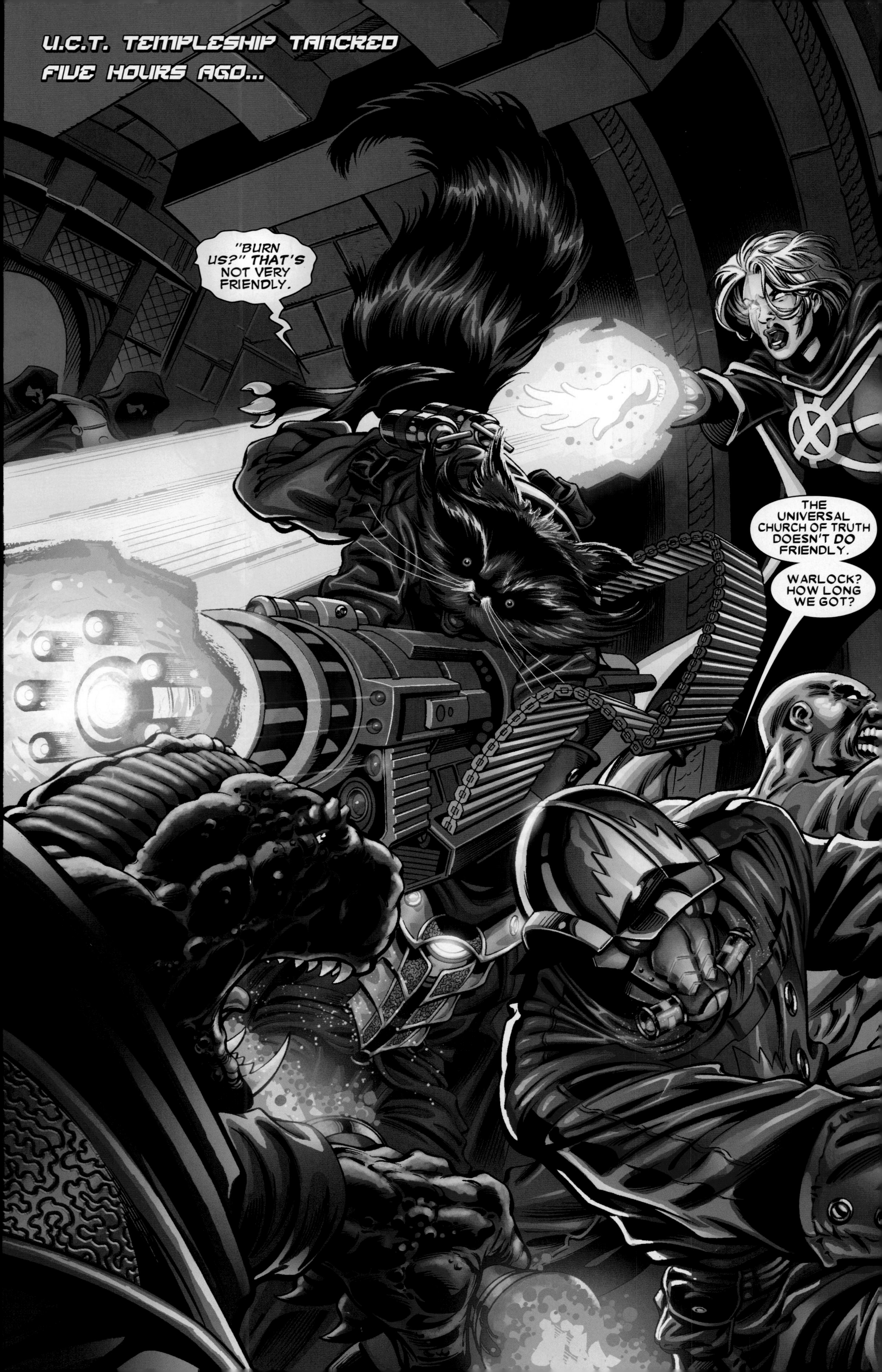
U.C.T. TEMPLESHIP TANCRED
FIVE HOURS AGO...
"BURN US?" THAT'S NOT VERY FRIENDLY.
THE UNIVERSAL CHURCH OF TRUTH DOESN'T DO FRIENDLY.
WARLOCK? HOW LONG WE GOT?

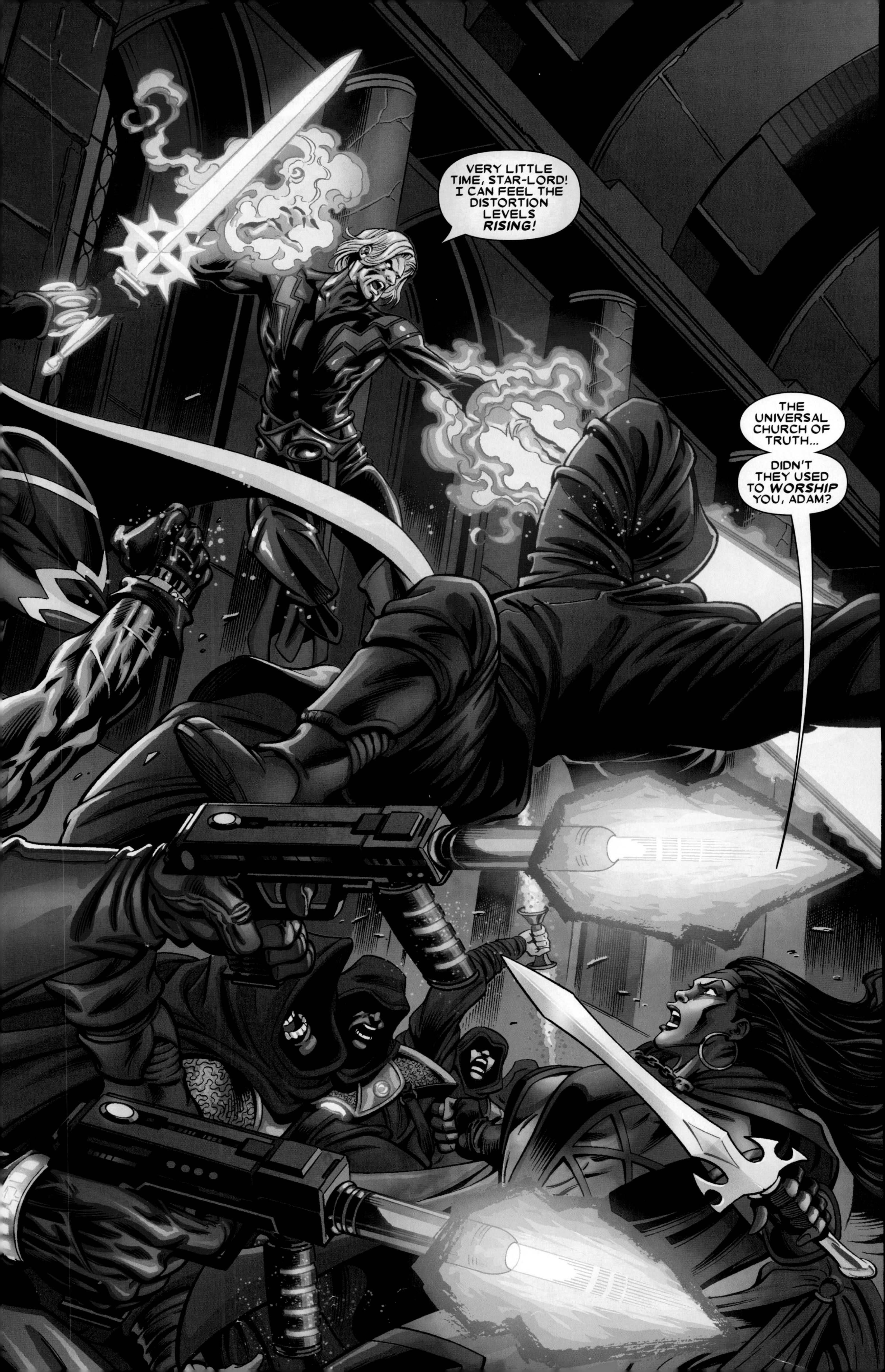
VERY LITTLE TIME, STAR-LORD! I CAN FEEL THE DISTORTION LEVELS *RISING!*
THE UNIVERSAL CHURCH OF TRUTH...
DIDN'T THEY USED TO *WORSHIP* YOU, ADAM?

GUARDIANS OF THE GALAXY 1

(2008)

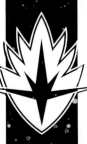

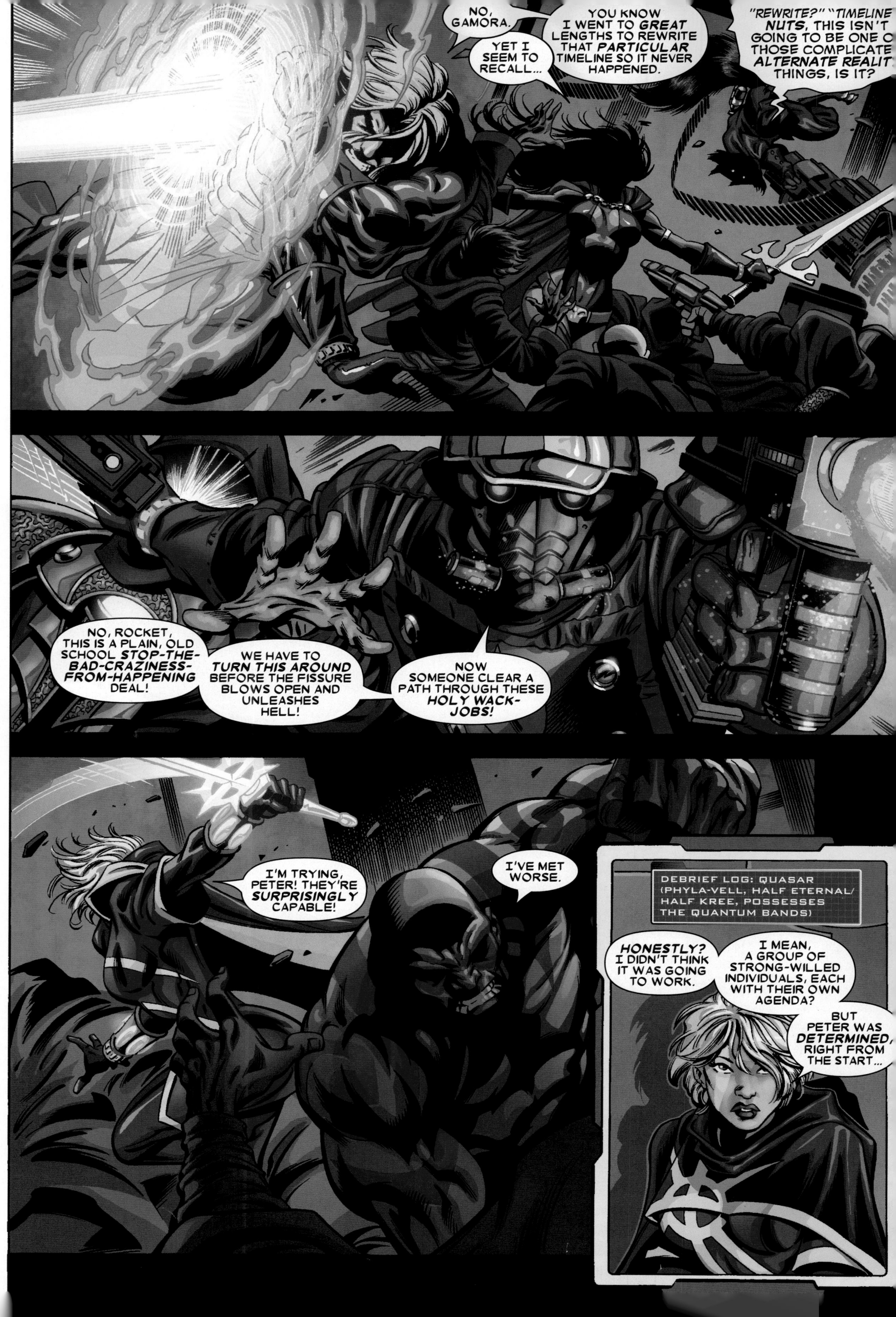

NO, GAMORA.
YET I SEEM TO RECALL...
YOU KNOW I WENT TO GREAT LENGTHS TO REWRITE THAT PARTICULAR TIMELINE SO IT NEVER HAPPENED.
"REWRITE?" "TIMELINE NUTS, THIS ISN'T GOING TO BE ONE O THOSE COMPLICATE ALTERNATE REALIT THINGS, IS IT?
NO, ROCKET, THIS IS A PLAIN, OLD SCHOOL STOP-THE-BAD-CRAZINESS-FROM-HAPPENING DEAL!
WE HAVE TO TURN THIS AROUND BEFORE THE FISSURE BLOWS OPEN AND UNLEASHES HELL!
NOW SOMEONE CLEAR A PATH THROUGH THESE HOLY WACK-JOBS!
I'M TRYING, PETER! THEY'RE SURPRISINGLY CAPABLE!
I'VE MET WORSE.
DEBRIEF LOG: QUASAR (PHYLA-VELL, HALF ETERNAL/ HALF KREE, POSSESSES THE QUANTUM BANDS)
HONESTLY? I DIDN'T THINK IT WAS GOING TO WORK.
I MEAN, A GROUP OF STRONG-WILLED INDIVIDUALS, EACH WITH THEIR OWN AGENDA?
BUT PETER WAS DETERMINED, RIGHT FROM THE START...

GUARDIANS OF THE GALAXY 1 (2008)

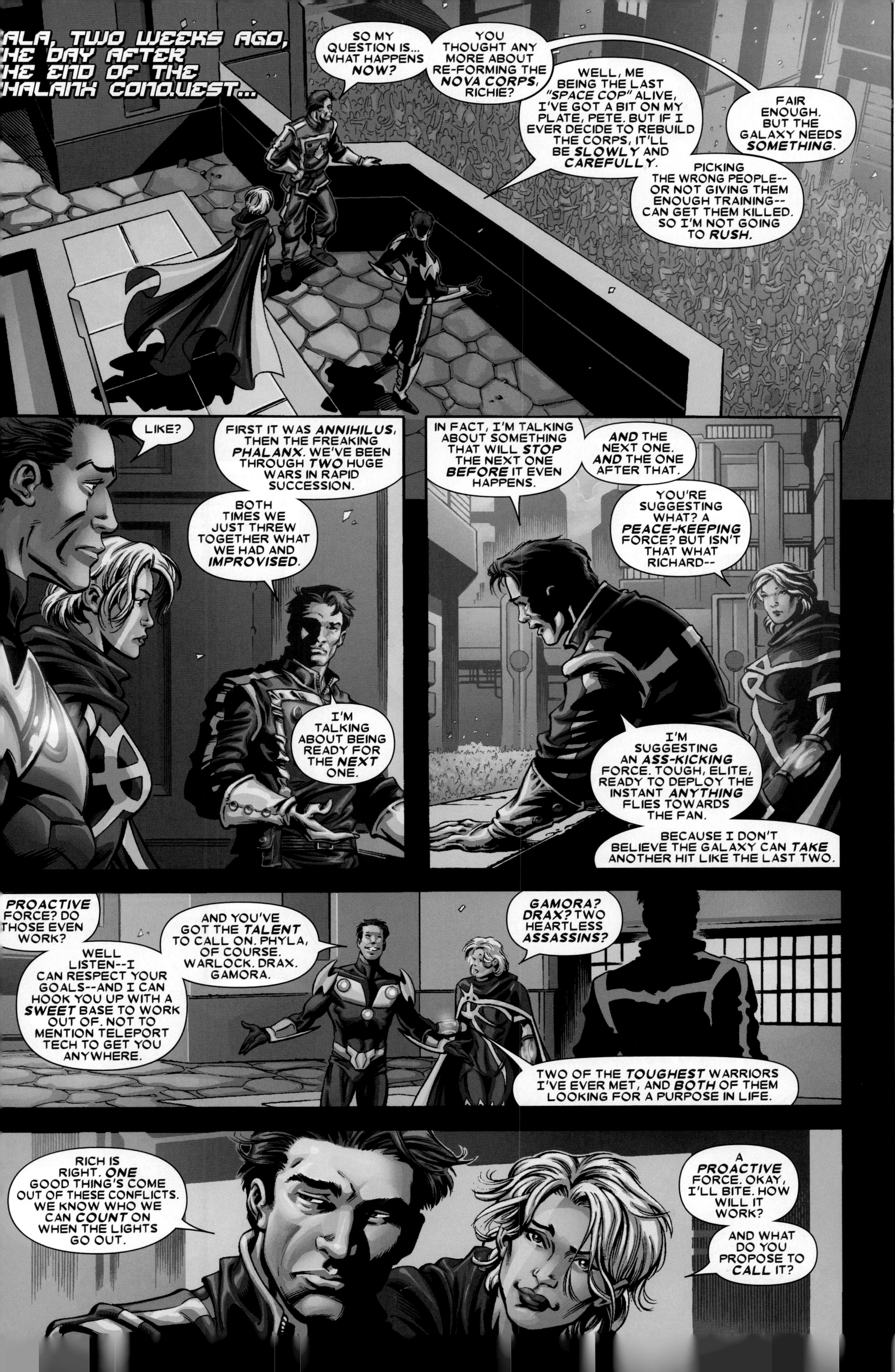

ALA, TWO WEEKS AGO, HE DAY AFTER HE END OF THE HALANX CONQUEST...
SO MY QUESTION IS... WHAT HAPPENS NOW?
YOU THOUGHT ANY MORE ABOUT RE-FORMING THE NOVA CORPS, RICHIE?
WELL, ME BEING THE LAST "SPACE COP" ALIVE, I'VE GOT A BIT ON MY PLATE, PETE. BUT IF I EVER DECIDE TO REBUILD THE CORPS, IT'LL BE SLOWLY AND CAREFULLY.
PICKING THE WRONG PEOPLE-- OR NOT GIVING THEM ENOUGH TRAINING-- CAN GET THEM KILLED. SO I'M NOT GOING TO RUSH.
FAIR ENOUGH. BUT THE GALAXY NEEDS SOMETHING.
LIKE?
FIRST IT WAS ANNIHILUS, THEN THE FREAKING PHALANX. WE'VE BEEN THROUGH TWO HUGE WARS IN RAPID SUCCESSION.
BOTH TIMES WE JUST THREW TOGETHER WHAT WE HAD AND IMPROVISED.
I'M TALKING ABOUT BEING READY FOR THE NEXT ONE.
IN FACT, I'M TALKING ABOUT SOMETHING THAT WILL STOP THE NEXT ONE BEFORE IT EVEN HAPPENS.
AND THE NEXT ONE. AND THE ONE AFTER THAT.
YOU'RE SUGGESTING WHAT? A PEACE-KEEPING FORCE? BUT ISN'T THAT WHAT RICHARD--
I'M SUGGESTING AN ASS-KICKING FORCE. TOUGH, ELITE, READY TO DEPLOY THE INSTANT ANYTHING FLIES TOWARDS THE FAN.
BECAUSE I DON'T BELIEVE THE GALAXY CAN TAKE ANOTHER HIT LIKE THE LAST TWO.
PROACTIVE FORCE? DO THOSE EVEN WORK?
WELL LISTEN--I CAN RESPECT YOUR GOALS--AND I CAN HOOK YOU UP WITH A SWEET BASE TO WORK OUT OF. NOT TO MENTION TELEPORT TECH TO GET YOU ANYWHERE.
AND YOU'VE GOT THE TALENT TO CALL ON. PHYLA, OF COURSE. WARLOCK. DRAX. GAMORA.
GAMORA? DRAX? TWO HEARTLESS ASSASSINS?
TWO OF THE TOUGHEST WARRIORS I'VE EVER MET, AND BOTH OF THEM LOOKING FOR A PURPOSE IN LIFE.
RICH IS RIGHT. ONE GOOD THING'S COME OUT OF THESE CONFLICTS. WE KNOW WHO WE CAN COUNT ON WHEN THE LIGHTS GO OUT.
A PROACTIVE FORCE. OKAY, I'LL BITE. HOW WILL IT WORK?
AND WHAT DO YOU PROPOSE TO CALL IT?

GUARDIANS OF THE GALAXY 1 (2008)

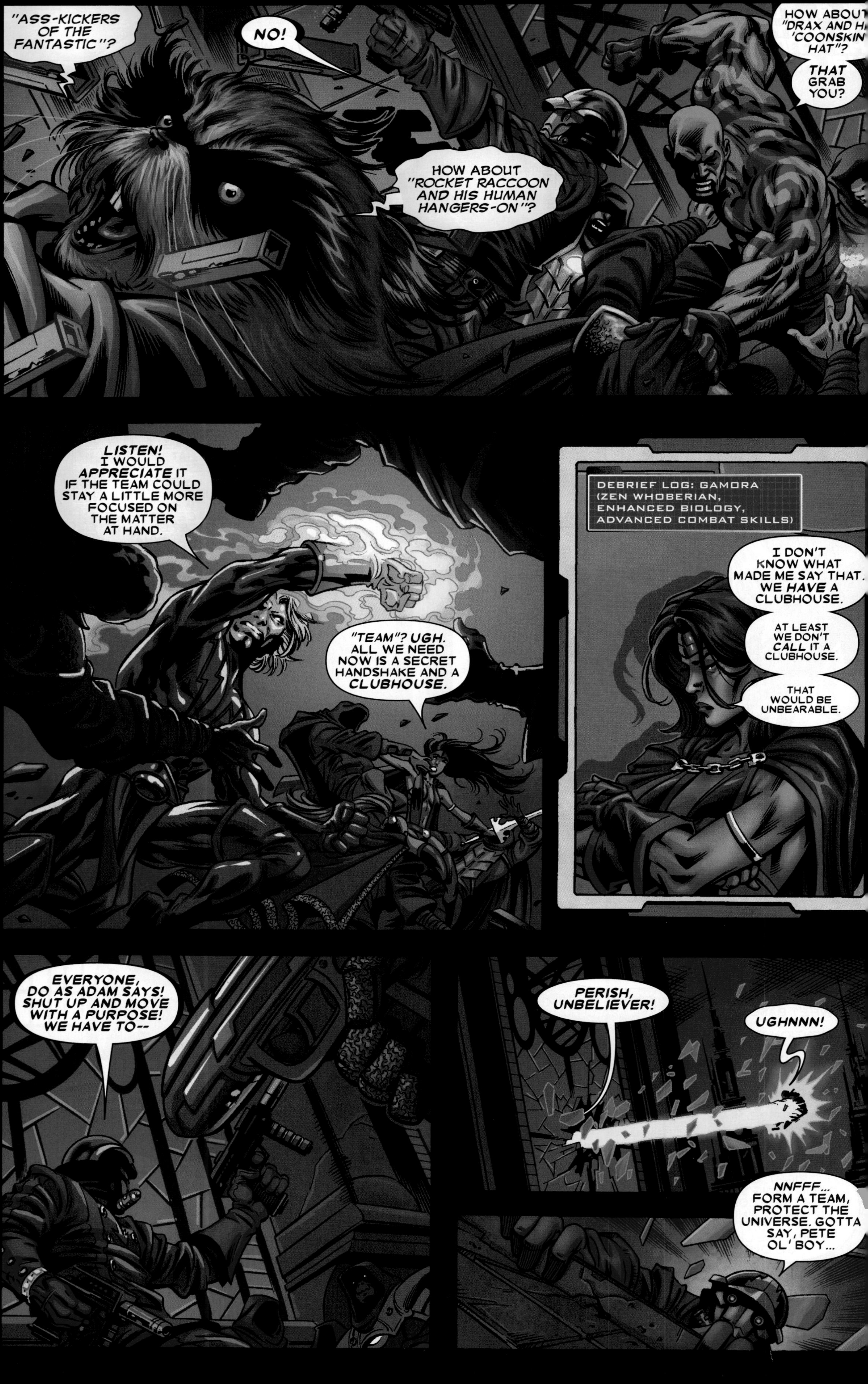
"ASS-KICKERS OF THE FANTASTIC"?
NO!
HOW ABOUT "DRAX AND H 'COONSKIN HAT"?
THAT GRAB YOU?
HOW ABOUT "ROCKET RACCOON AND HIS HUMAN HANGERS-ON"?
LISTEN! I WOULD APPRECIATE IT IF THE TEAM COULD STAY A LITTLE MORE FOCUSED ON THE MATTER AT HAND.
"TEAM"? UGH. ALL WE NEED NOW IS A SECRET HANDSHAKE AND A CLUBHOUSE.
DEBRIEF LOG: GAMORA (ZEN WHOBERIAN, ENHANCED BIOLOGY, ADVANCED COMBAT SKILLS)
I DON'T KNOW WHAT MADE ME SAY THAT. WE HAVE A CLUBHOUSE.
AT LEAST WE DON'T CALL IT A CLUBHOUSE.
THAT WOULD BE UNBEARABLE.
EVERYONE, DO AS ADAM SAYS! SHUT UP AND MOVE WITH A PURPOSE! WE HAVE TO--
PERISH, UNBELIEVER!
UGHNNN!
NNFFF... FORM A TEAM, PROTECT THE UNIVERSE. GOTTA SAY, PETE OL' BOY...

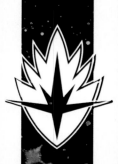

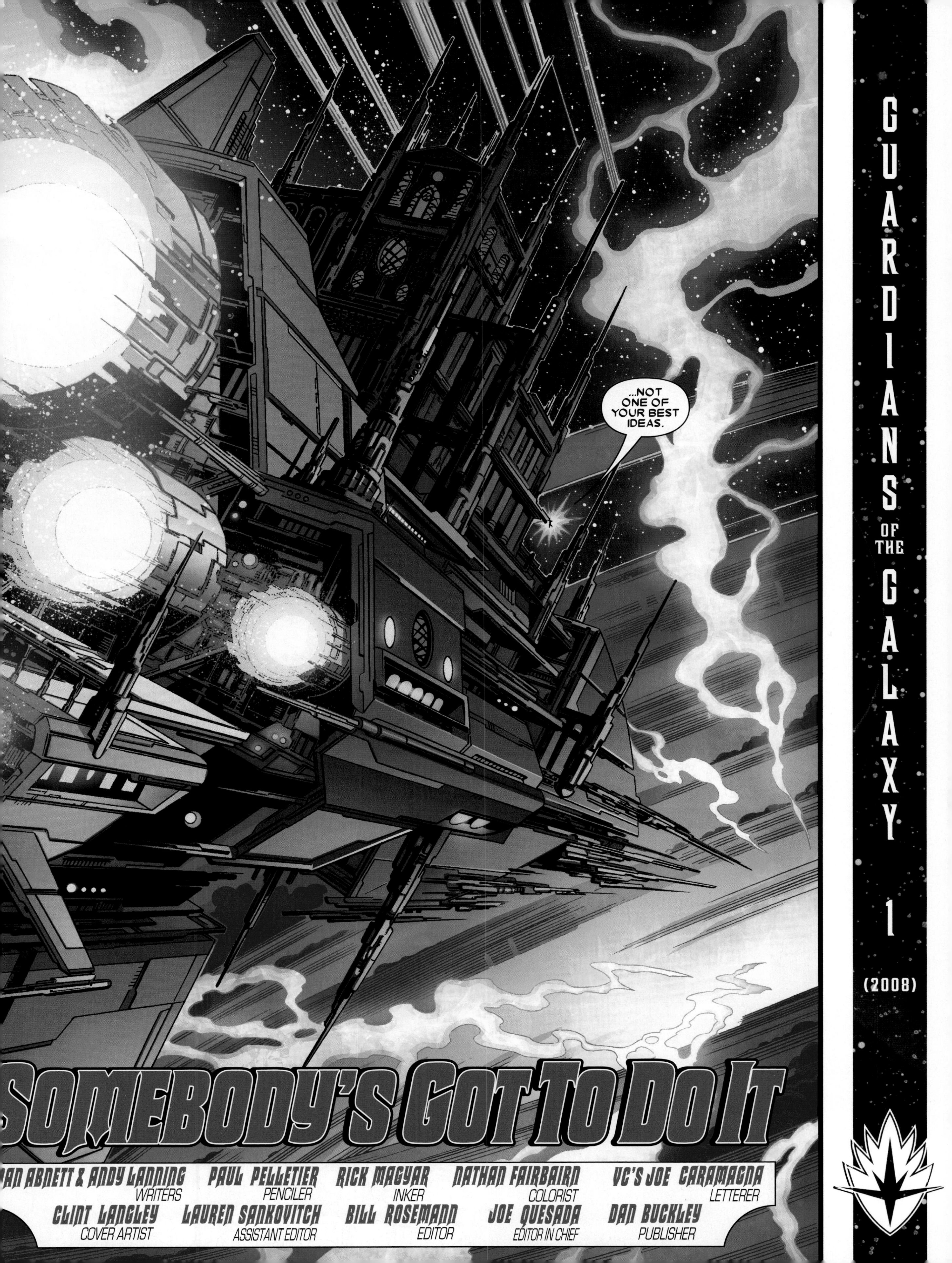
...NOT ONE OF YOUR BEST IDEAS.
SOMEBODY'S GOT TO DO IT
AN ABNETT & ANDY LANNING WRITERS
PAUL PELLETIER PENCILER
RICK MAGYAR INKER
NATHAN FAIRBAIRN COLORIST
VC'S JOE CARAMAGNA LETTERER
CLINT LANGLEY COVER ARTIST
LAUREN SANKOVITCH ASSISTANT EDITOR
BILL ROSEMANN EDITOR
JOE QUESADA EDITOR IN CHIEF
DAN BUCKLEY PUBLISHER
GUARDIANS OF THE GALAXY 1
(2008)

GUARDIANS OF THE GALAXY 1 (2008)

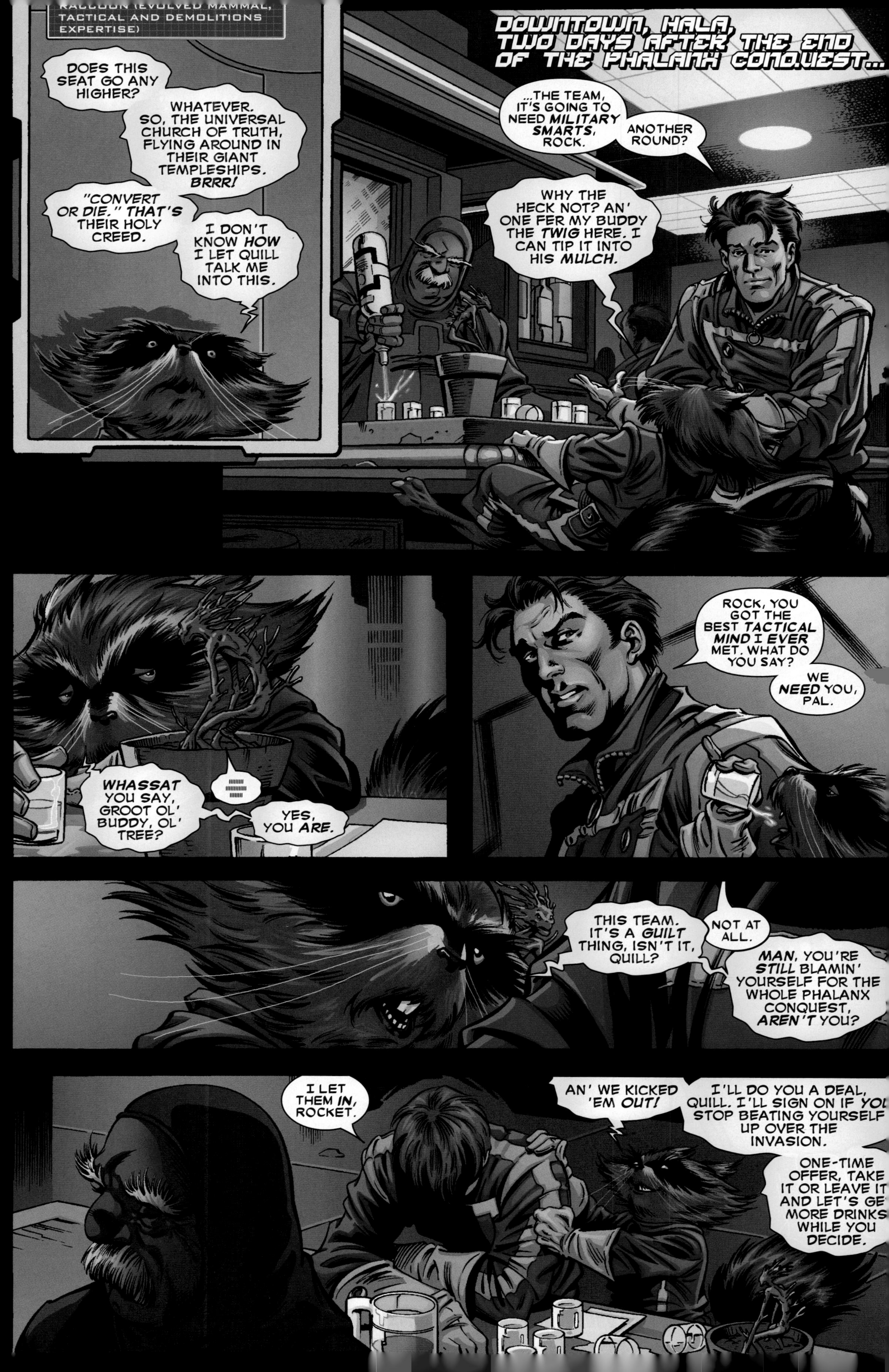
RACCOON (EVOLVED MAMMAL, TACTICAL AND DEMOLITIONS EXPERTISE)
DOES THIS SEAT GO ANY HIGHER?
WHATEVER. SO, THE UNIVERSAL CHURCH OF TRUTH, FLYING AROUND IN THEIR GIANT TEMPLESHIPS. BRRR!
"CONVERT OR DIE." THAT'S THEIR HOLY CREED.
I DON'T KNOW HOW I LET QUILL TALK ME INTO THIS.
DOWNTOWN, HALA, TWO DAYS AFTER THE END OF THE PHALANX CONQUEST...
...THE TEAM, IT'S GOING TO NEED MILITARY SMARTS, ROCK.
ANOTHER ROUND?
WHY THE HECK NOT? AN' ONE FER MY BUDDY THE TWIG HERE. I CAN TIP IT INTO HIS MULCH.
WHASSAT YOU SAY, GROOT OL' BUDDY, OL' TREE?
YES, YOU ARE.
ROCK, YOU GOT THE BEST TACTICAL MIND I EVER MET. WHAT DO YOU SAY?
WE NEED YOU, PAL.
THIS TEAM. IT'S A GUILT THING, ISN'T IT, QUILL?
NOT AT ALL.
MAN, YOU'RE STILL BLAMIN' YOURSELF FOR THE WHOLE PHALANX CONQUEST, AREN'T YOU?
I LET THEM IN, ROCKET.
AN' WE KICKED 'EM OUT!
I'LL DO YOU A DEAL, QUILL. I'LL SIGN ON IF YOU STOP BEATING YOURSELF UP OVER THE INVASION.
ONE-TIME OFFER, TAKE IT OR LEAVE IT AND LET'S GET MORE DRINKS WHILE YOU DECIDE.

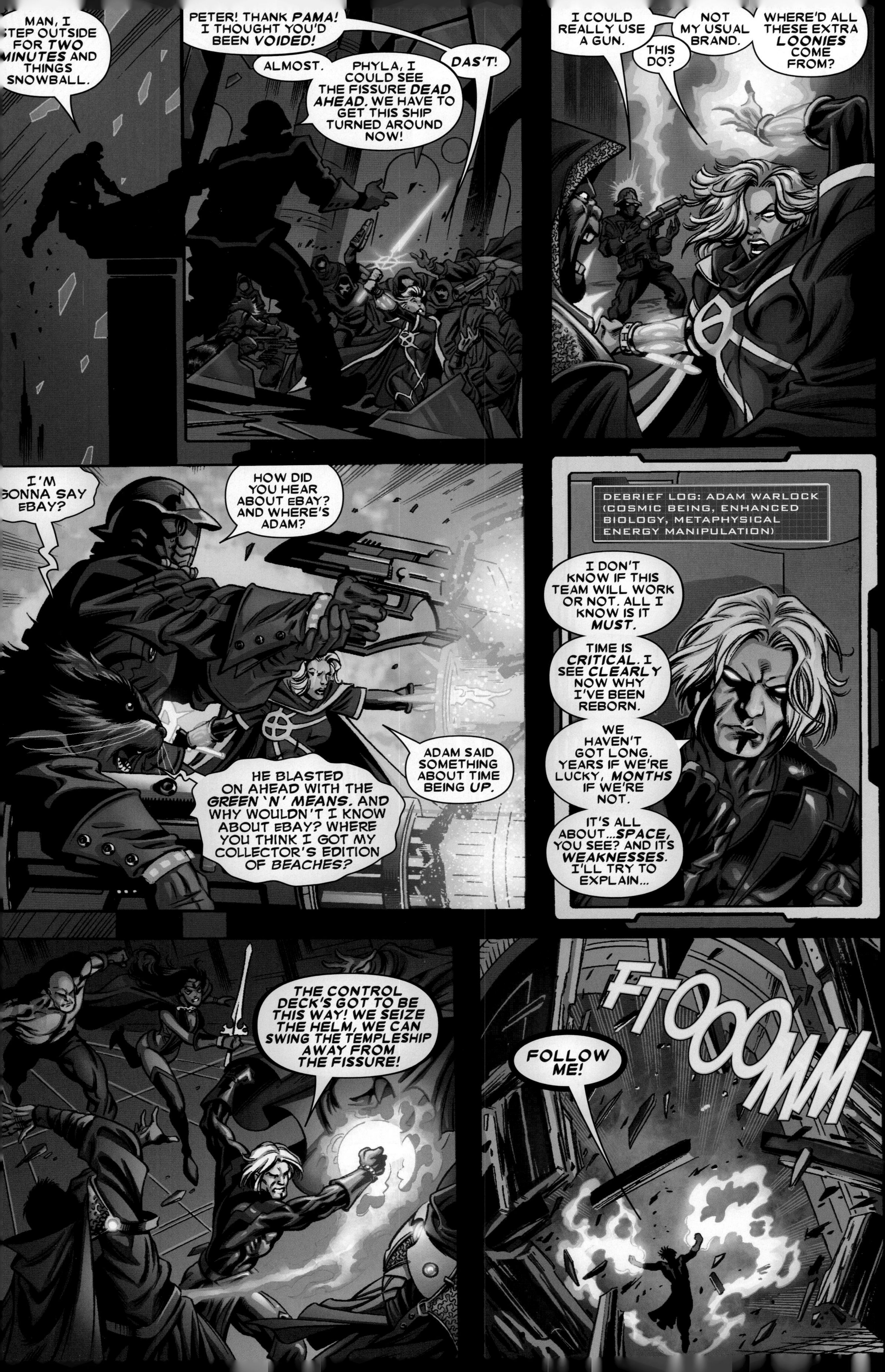
MAN, I STEP OUTSIDE FOR TWO MINUTES AND THINGS SNOWBALL.
PETER! THANK PAMA! I THOUGHT YOU'D BEEN VOIDED!
ALMOST.
PHYLA, I COULD SEE THE FISSURE DEAD AHEAD. WE HAVE TO GET THIS SHIP TURNED AROUND NOW!
DAS'T!
I COULD REALLY USE A GUN.
THIS DO?
NOT MY USUAL BRAND.
WHERE'D ALL THESE EXTRA LOONIES COME FROM?
I'M GONNA SAY EBAY?
HOW DID YOU HEAR ABOUT EBAY? AND WHERE'S ADAM?
HE BLASTED ON AHEAD WITH THE GREEN 'N' MEANS. AND WHY WOULDN'T I KNOW ABOUT EBAY? WHERE YOU THINK I GOT MY COLLECTOR'S EDITION OF BEACHES?
ADAM SAID SOMETHING ABOUT TIME BEING UP.
DEBRIEF LOG: ADAM WARLOCK (COSMIC BEING, ENHANCED BIOLOGY, METAPHYSICAL ENERGY MANIPULATION)
I DON'T KNOW IF THIS TEAM WILL WORK OR NOT. ALL I KNOW IS IT MUST.
TIME IS CRITICAL. I SEE CLEARLY NOW WHY I'VE BEEN REBORN.
WE HAVEN'T GOT LONG. YEARS IF WE'RE LUCKY, MONTHS IF WE'RE NOT.
IT'S ALL ABOUT...SPACE, YOU SEE? AND ITS WEAKNESSES. I'LL TRY TO EXPLAIN...
THE CONTROL DECK'S GOT TO BE THIS WAY! WE SEIZE THE HELM, WE CAN SWING THE TEMPLESHIP AWAY FROM THE FISSURE!
FTOOOMM
FOLLOW ME!

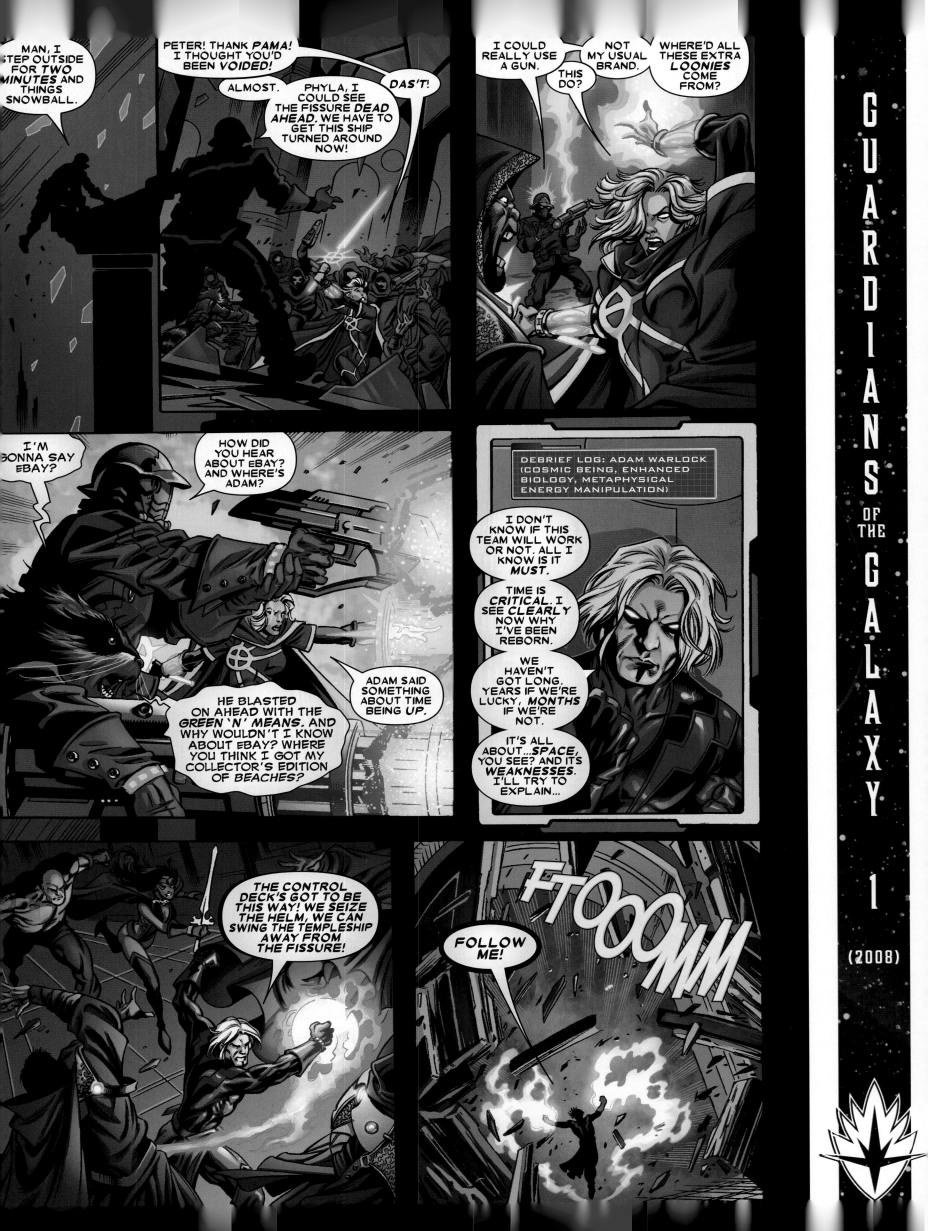

GUARDIANS OF THE GALAXY 1 (2008)

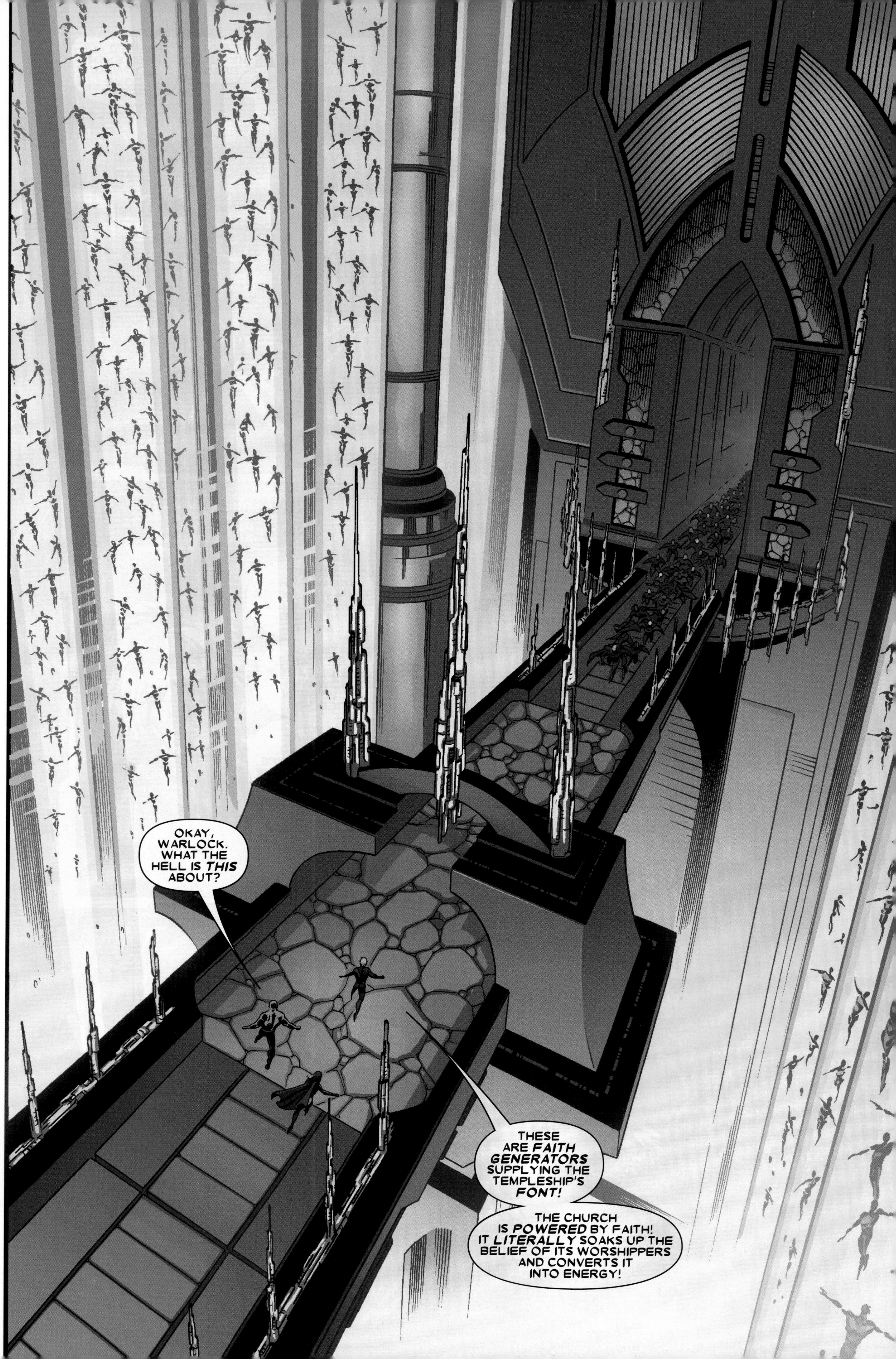

OKAY, WARLOCK. WHAT THE HELL IS *THIS* ABOUT?
THESE ARE *FAITH GENERATORS* SUPPLYING THE TEMPLESHIP'S *FONT!*
THE CHURCH IS *POWERED* BY FAITH! IT *LITERALLY* SOAKS UP THE BELIEF OF ITS WORSHIPPERS AND CONVERTS IT INTO ENERGY!

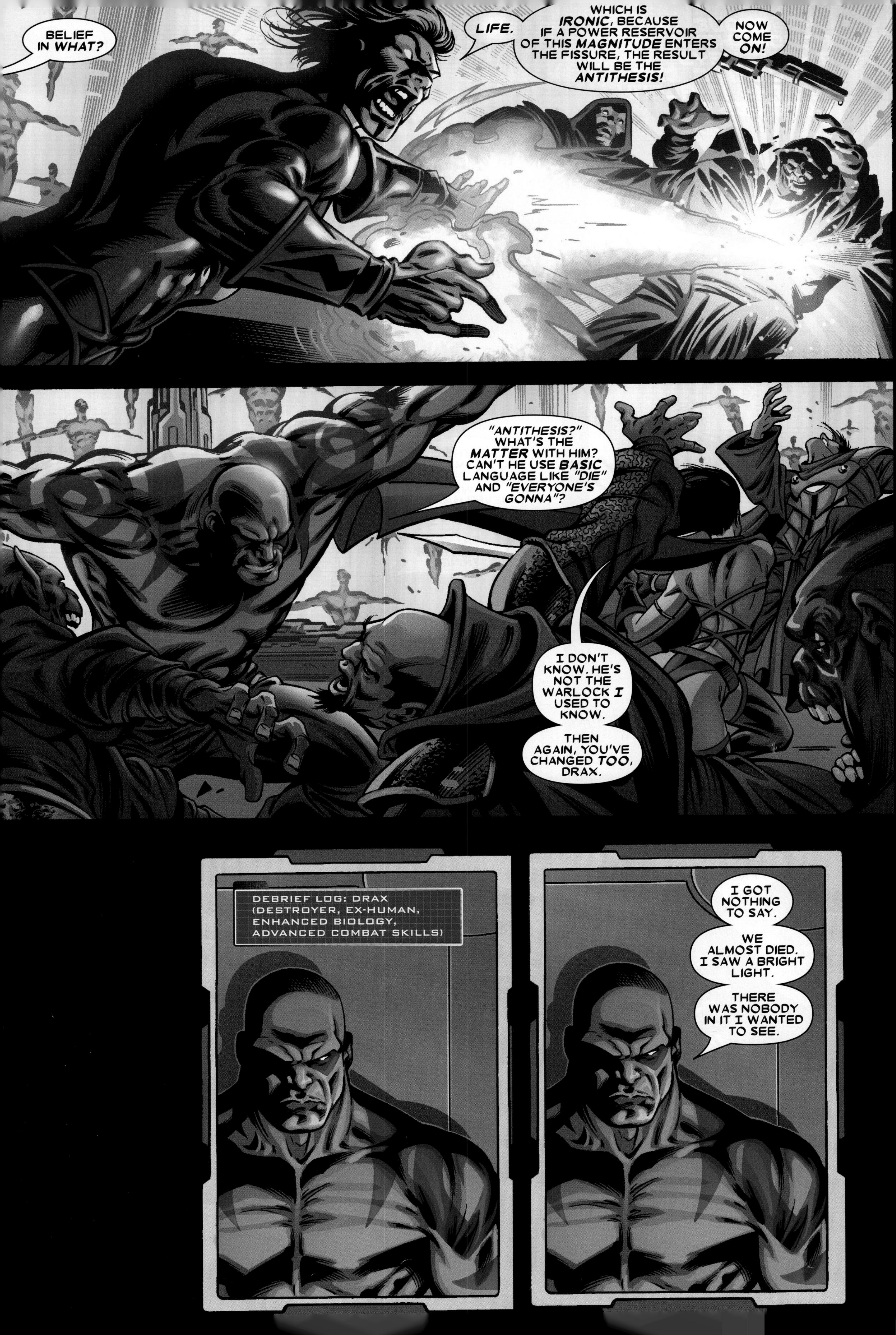
BELIEF IN WHAT?
LIFE.
WHICH IS IRONIC, BECAUSE IF A POWER RESERVOIR OF THIS MAGNITUDE ENTERS THE FISSURE, THE RESULT WILL BE THE ANTITHESIS!
NOW COME ON!
"ANTITHESIS?" WHAT'S THE MATTER WITH HIM? CAN'T HE USE BASIC LANGUAGE LIKE "DIE" AND "EVERYONE'S GONNA"?
I DON'T KNOW. HE'S NOT THE WARLOCK I USED TO KNOW.
THEN AGAIN, YOU'VE CHANGED TOO, DRAX.
DEBRIEF LOG: DRAX (DESTROYER, EX-HUMAN, ENHANCED BIOLOGY, ADVANCED COMBAT SKILLS)
I GOT NOTHING TO SAY.
WE ALMOST DIED. I SAW A BRIGHT LIGHT.
THERE WAS NOBODY IN IT I WANTED TO SEE.

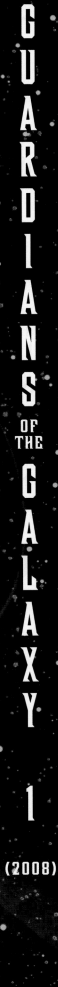

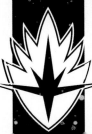

GUARDIANS OF THE GALAXY 1 (2008)

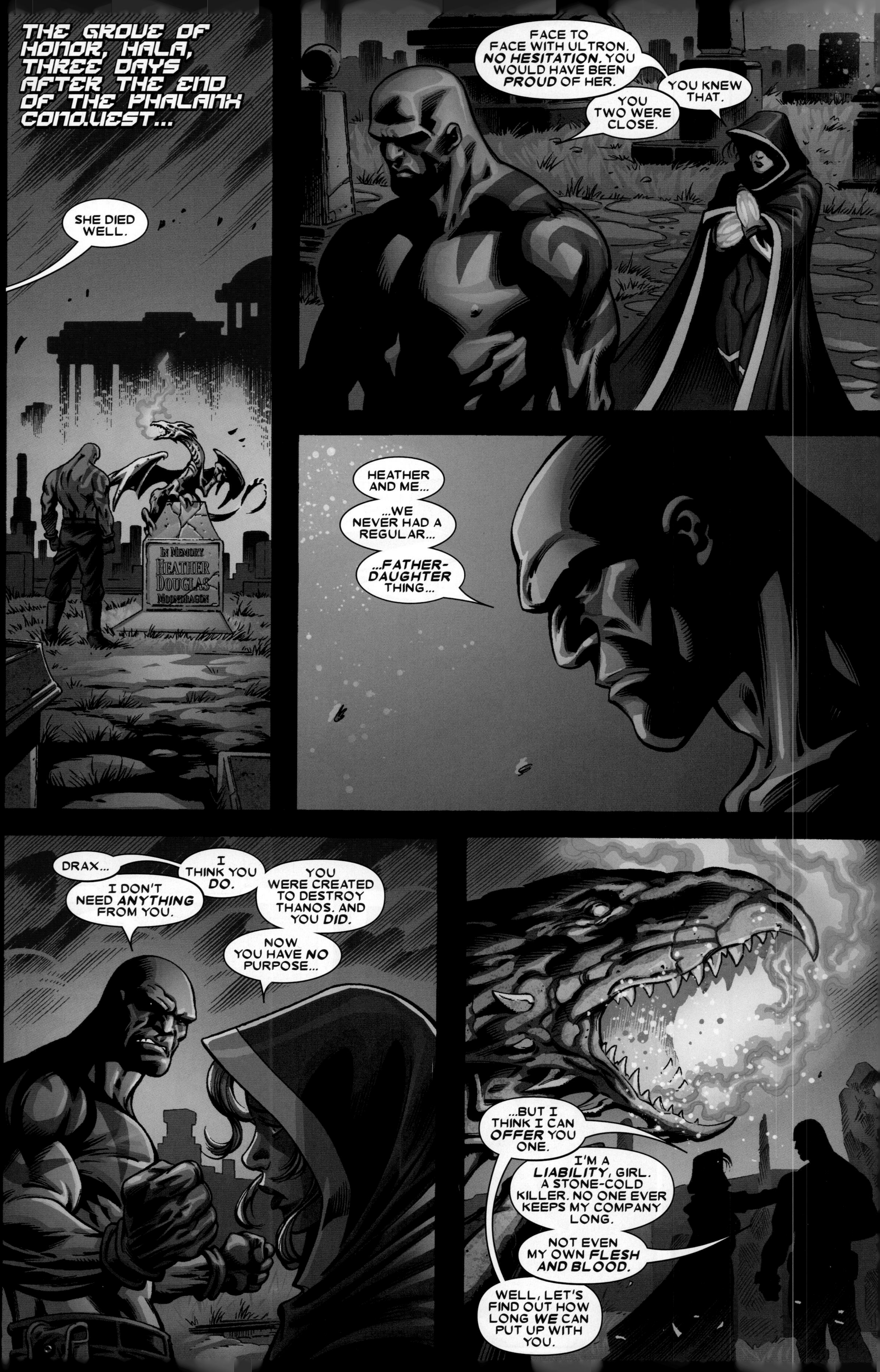
THE GROVE OF HONOR, HALA, THREE DAYS AFTER THE END OF THE PHALANX CONQUEST...
SHE DIED WELL.
IN MEMORY HEATHER DOUGLAS MOONDRAGON
FACE TO FACE WITH ULTRON. NO HESITATION. YOU WOULD HAVE BEEN PROUD OF HER.
YOU TWO WERE CLOSE.
YOU KNEW THAT.
HEATHER AND ME...
...WE NEVER HAD A REGULAR...
...FATHER-DAUGHTER THING...
DRAX...
I DON'T NEED ANYTHING FROM YOU.
I THINK YOU DO.
YOU WERE CREATED TO DESTROY THANOS. AND YOU DID.
NOW YOU HAVE NO PURPOSE...
...BUT I THINK I CAN OFFER YOU ONE.
I'M A LIABILITY, GIRL. A STONE-COLD KILLER. NO ONE EVER KEEPS MY COMPANY LONG.
NOT EVEN MY OWN FLESH AND BLOOD.
WELL, LET'S FIND OUT HOW LONG WE CAN PUT UP WITH YOU.

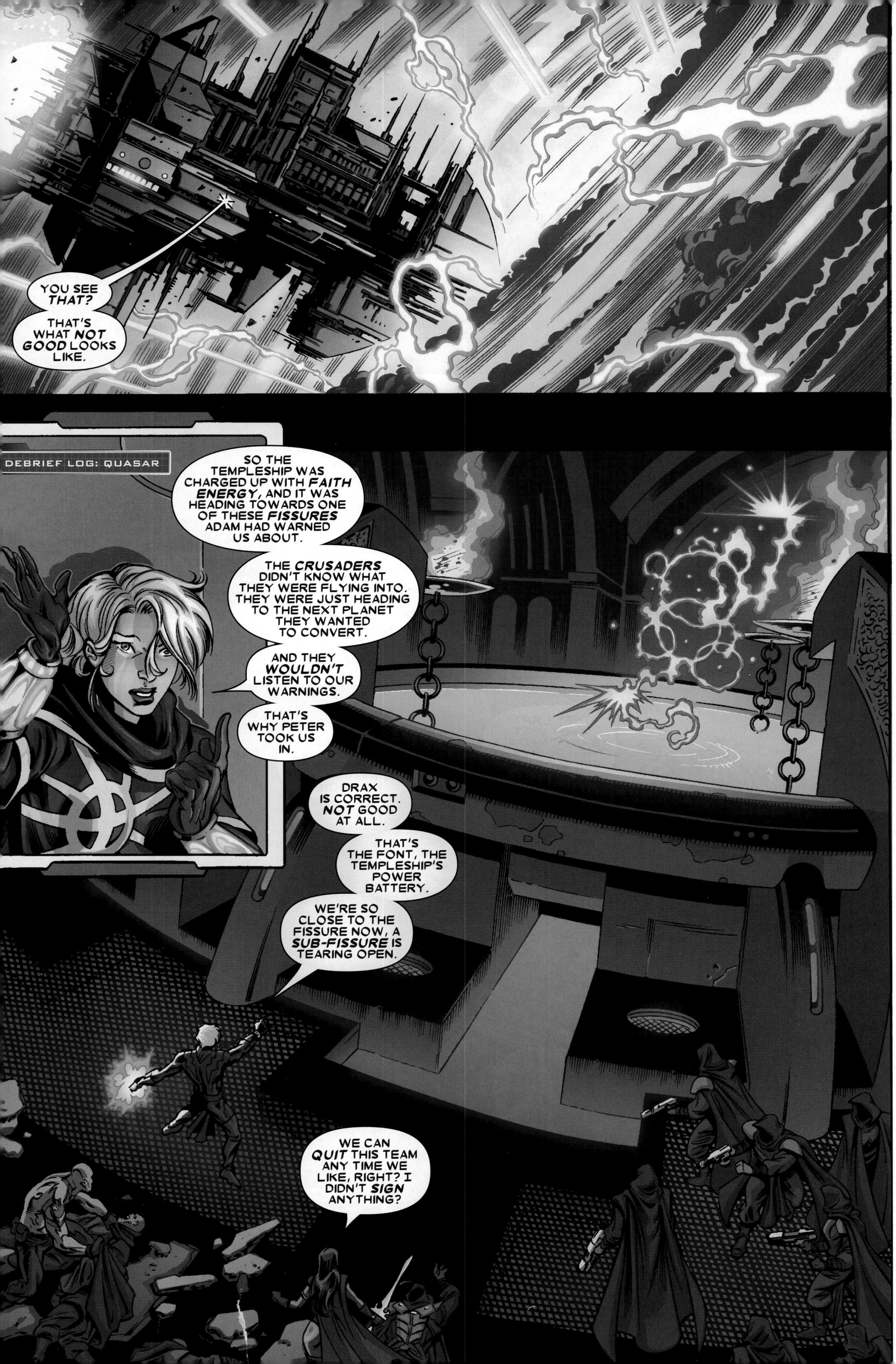

YOU SEE *THAT?*
THAT'S WHAT ***NOT GOOD*** LOOKS LIKE.
DEBRIEF LOG: QUASAR
SO THE TEMPLESHIP WAS CHARGED UP WITH ***FAITH ENERGY***, AND IT WAS HEADING TOWARDS ONE OF THESE ***FISSURES*** ADAM HAD WARNED US ABOUT.
THE ***CRUSADERS*** DIDN'T KNOW WHAT THEY WERE FLYING INTO. THEY WERE JUST HEADING TO THE NEXT PLANET THEY WANTED TO CONVERT.
AND THEY ***WOULDN'T*** LISTEN TO OUR WARNINGS.
THAT'S WHY PETER TOOK US IN.
DRAX IS CORRECT. ***NOT*** GOOD AT ALL.
THAT'S THE FONT, THE TEMPLESHIP'S POWER BATTERY.
WE'RE SO CLOSE TO THE FISSURE NOW, A ***SUB-FISSURE*** IS TEARING OPEN.
WE CAN ***QUIT*** THIS TEAM ANY TIME WE LIKE, RIGHT? I DIDN'T ***SIGN*** ANYTHING?

GUARDIANS OF THE GALAXY 1

(2008)

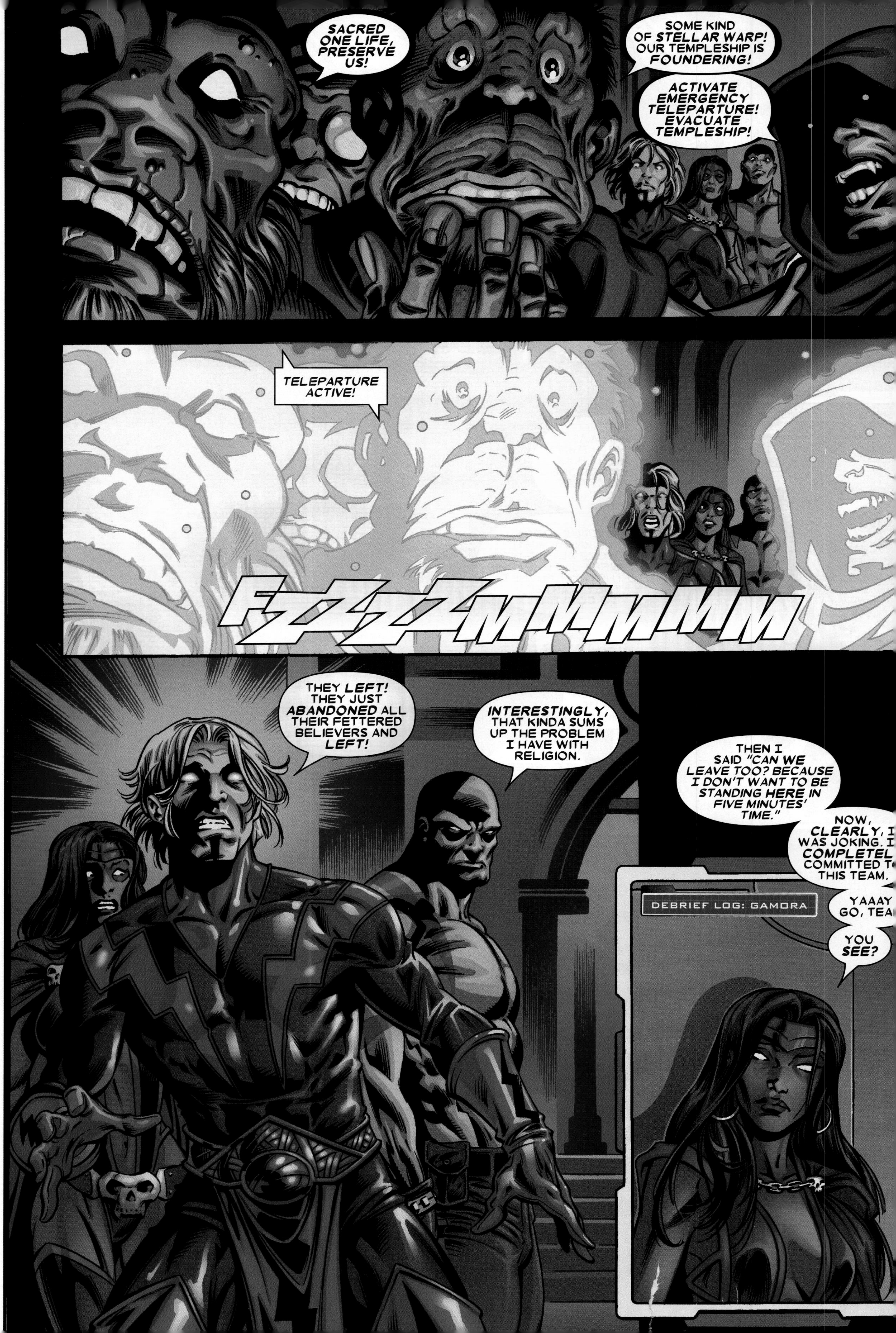
SACRED ONE LIFE, PRESERVE US!
SOME KIND OF STELLAR WARP! OUR TEMPLESHIP IS FOUNDERING!
ACTIVATE EMERGENCY TELEPARTURE! EVACUATE TEMPLESHIP!
TELEPARTURE ACTIVE!
FZZZZMMMMMMM
THEY LEFT! THEY JUST ABANDONED ALL THEIR FETTERED BELIEVERS AND LEFT!
INTERESTINGLY, THAT KINDA SUMS UP THE PROBLEM I HAVE WITH RELIGION.
THEN I SAID "CAN WE LEAVE TOO? BECAUSE I DON'T WANT TO BE STANDING HERE IN FIVE MINUTES' TIME."
DEBRIEF LOG: GAMORA
YOU SEE?

GUARDIANS OF THE GALAXY 1 (2008)

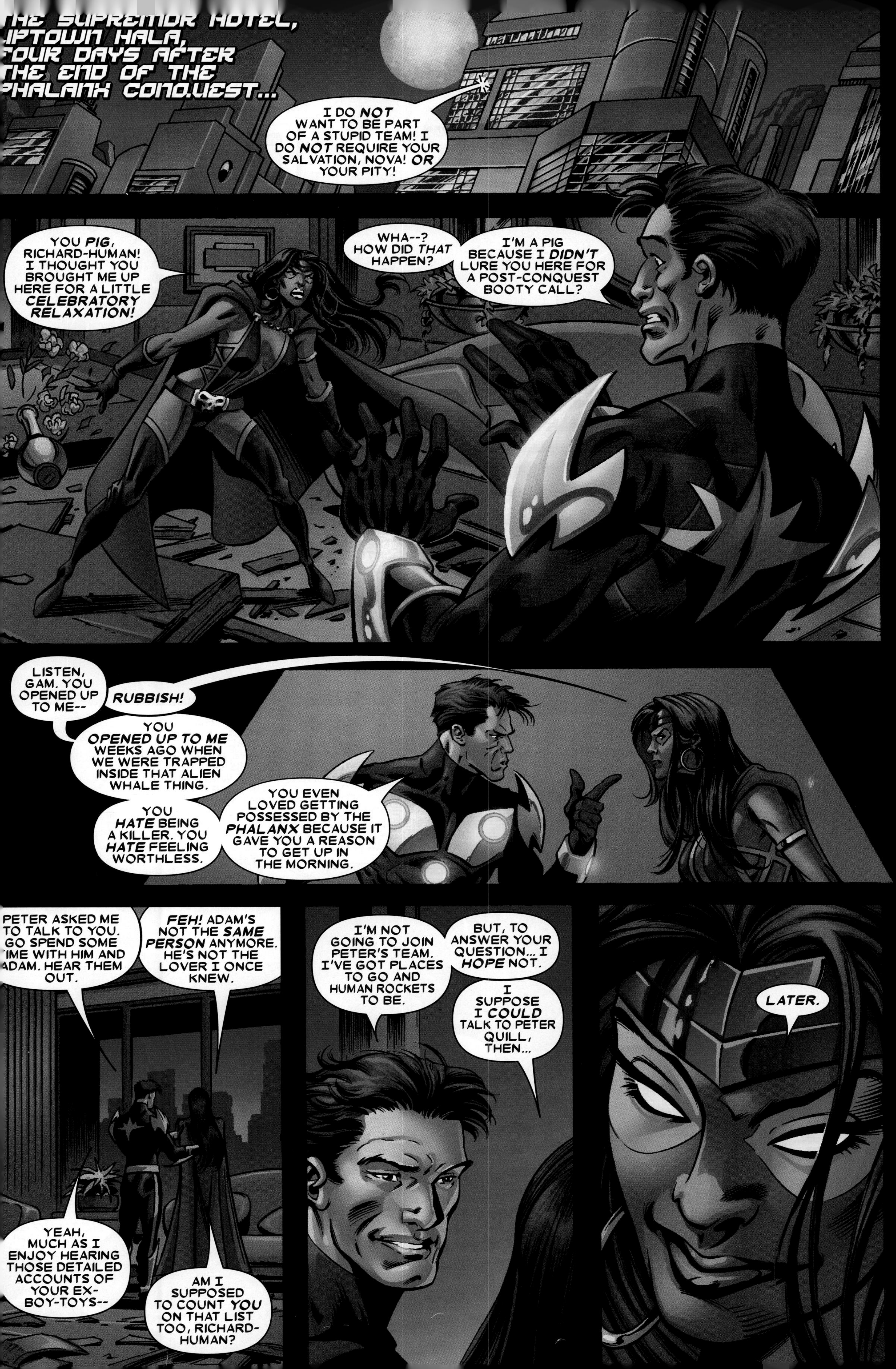
THE SUPREMOR HOTEL, UPTOWN HALA, FOUR DAYS AFTER THE END OF THE PHALANX CONQUEST...
I DO NOT WANT TO BE PART OF A STUPID TEAM! I DO NOT REQUIRE YOUR SALVATION, NOVA! OR YOUR PITY!
YOU PIG, RICHARD-HUMAN! I THOUGHT YOU BROUGHT ME UP HERE FOR A LITTLE CELEBRATORY RELAXATION!
WHA--? HOW DID THAT HAPPEN?
I'M A PIG BECAUSE I DIDN'T LURE YOU HERE FOR A POST-CONQUEST BOOTY CALL?
LISTEN, GAM. YOU OPENED UP TO ME--
RUBBISH!
YOU OPENED UP TO ME WEEKS AGO WHEN WE WERE TRAPPED INSIDE THAT ALIEN WHALE THING.
YOU HATE BEING A KILLER. YOU HATE FEELING WORTHLESS.
YOU EVEN LOVED GETTING POSSESSED BY THE PHALANX BECAUSE IT GAVE YOU A REASON TO GET UP IN THE MORNING.
PETER ASKED ME TO TALK TO YOU. GO SPEND SOME TIME WITH HIM AND ADAM. HEAR THEM OUT.
FEH! ADAM'S NOT THE SAME PERSON ANYMORE. HE'S NOT THE LOVER I ONCE KNEW.
YEAH, MUCH AS I ENJOY HEARING THOSE DETAILED ACCOUNTS OF YOUR EX-BOY-TOYS--
AM I SUPPOSED TO COUNT YOU ON THAT LIST TOO, RICHARD-HUMAN?
I'M NOT GOING TO JOIN PETER'S TEAM. I'VE GOT PLACES TO GO AND HUMAN ROCKETS TO BE.
BUT, TO ANSWER YOUR QUESTION... I HOPE NOT.
I SUPPOSE I COULD TALK TO PETER QUILL, THEN...
LATER.

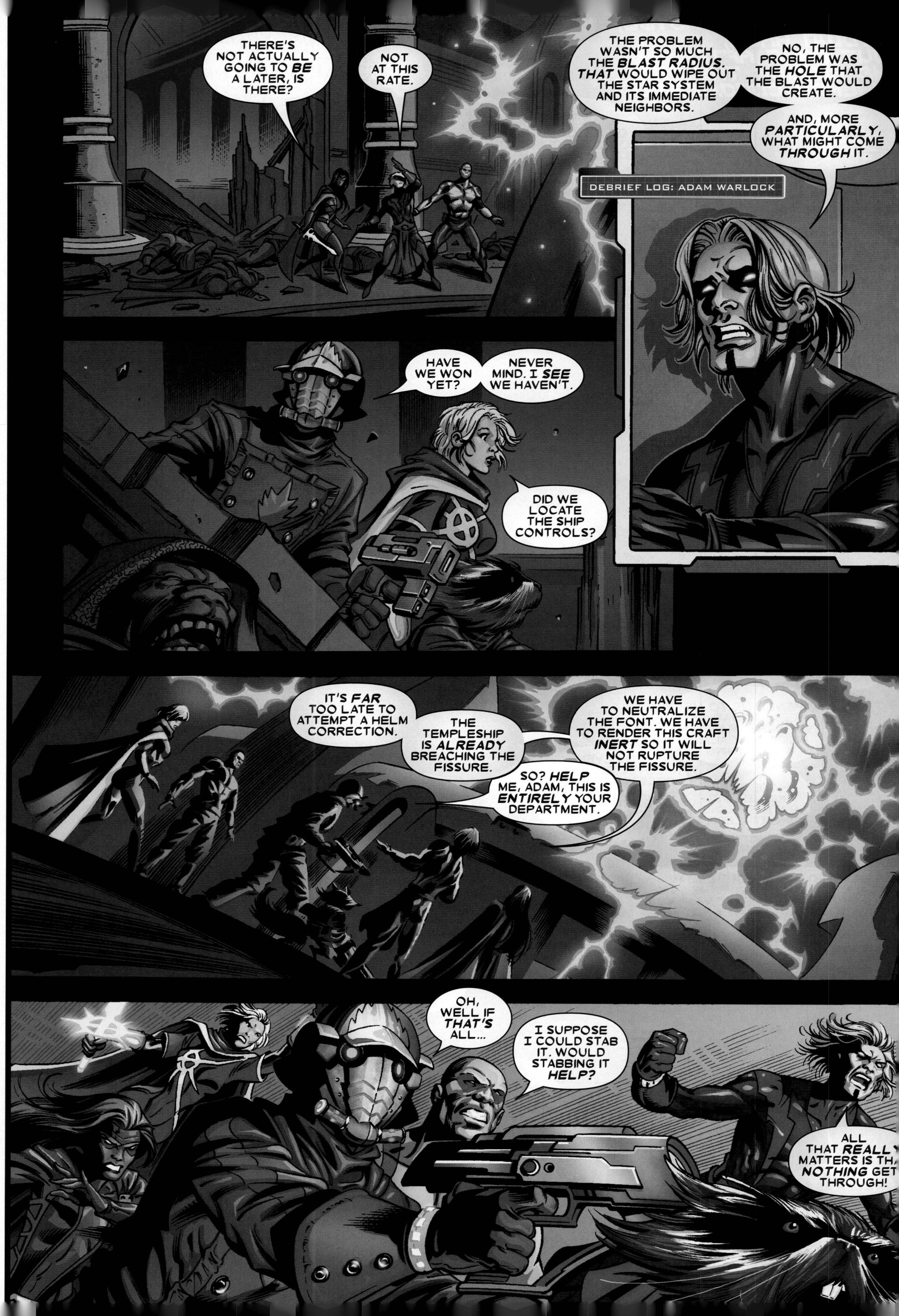
THERE'S NOT ACTUALLY GOING TO BE A LATER, IS THERE?
NOT AT THIS RATE.
THE PROBLEM WASN'T SO MUCH THE BLAST RADIUS, THAT WOULD WIPE OUT THE STAR SYSTEM AND ITS IMMEDIATE NEIGHBORS.
NO, THE PROBLEM WAS THE HOLE THAT THE BLAST WOULD CREATE.
AND, MORE PARTICULARLY, WHAT MIGHT COME THROUGH IT.
DEBRIEF LOG: ADAM WARLOCK
HAVE WE WON YET?
NEVER MIND. I SEE WE HAVEN'T.
DID WE LOCATE THE SHIP CONTROLS?
IT'S FAR TOO LATE TO ATTEMPT A HELM CORRECTION.
THE TEMPLESHIP IS ALREADY BREACHING THE FISSURE.
WE HAVE TO NEUTRALIZE THE FONT. WE HAVE TO RENDER THIS CRAFT INERT SO IT WILL NOT RUPTURE THE FISSURE.
SO? HELP ME, ADAM, THIS IS ENTIRELY YOUR DEPARTMENT.
OH, WELL IF THAT'S ALL...
I SUPPOSE I COULD STAB IT. WOULD STABBING IT HELP?
ALL THAT REALLY MATTERS IS TH NOTHING GET THROUGH!

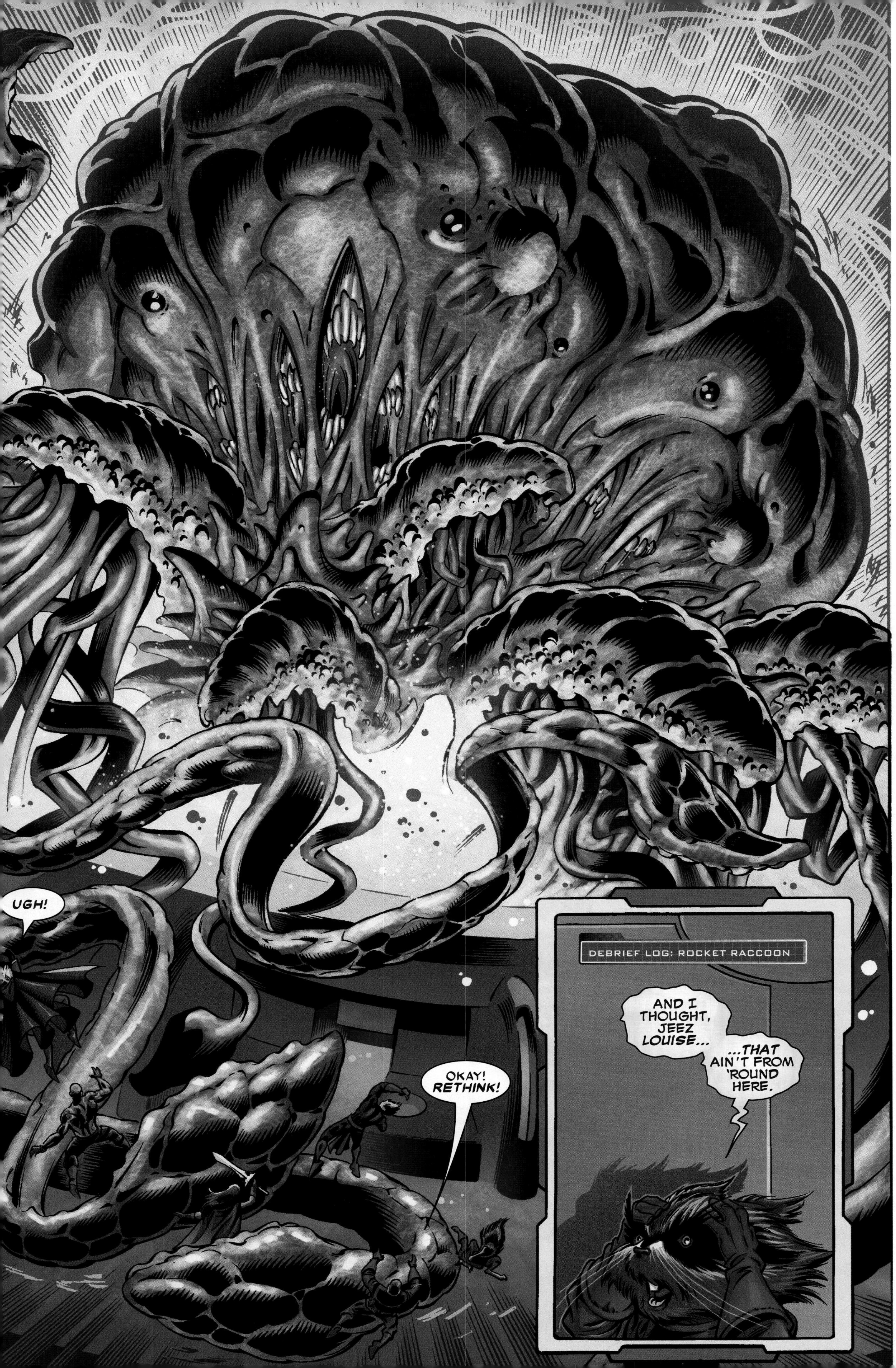
UGH!
OKAY! RETHINK!
DEBRIEF LOG: ROCKET RACCOON
AND I THOUGHT, JEEZ LOUISE...
...THAT AIN'T FROM 'ROUND HERE.

GUARDIANS OF THE GALAXY 1

(2008)

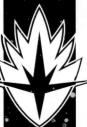

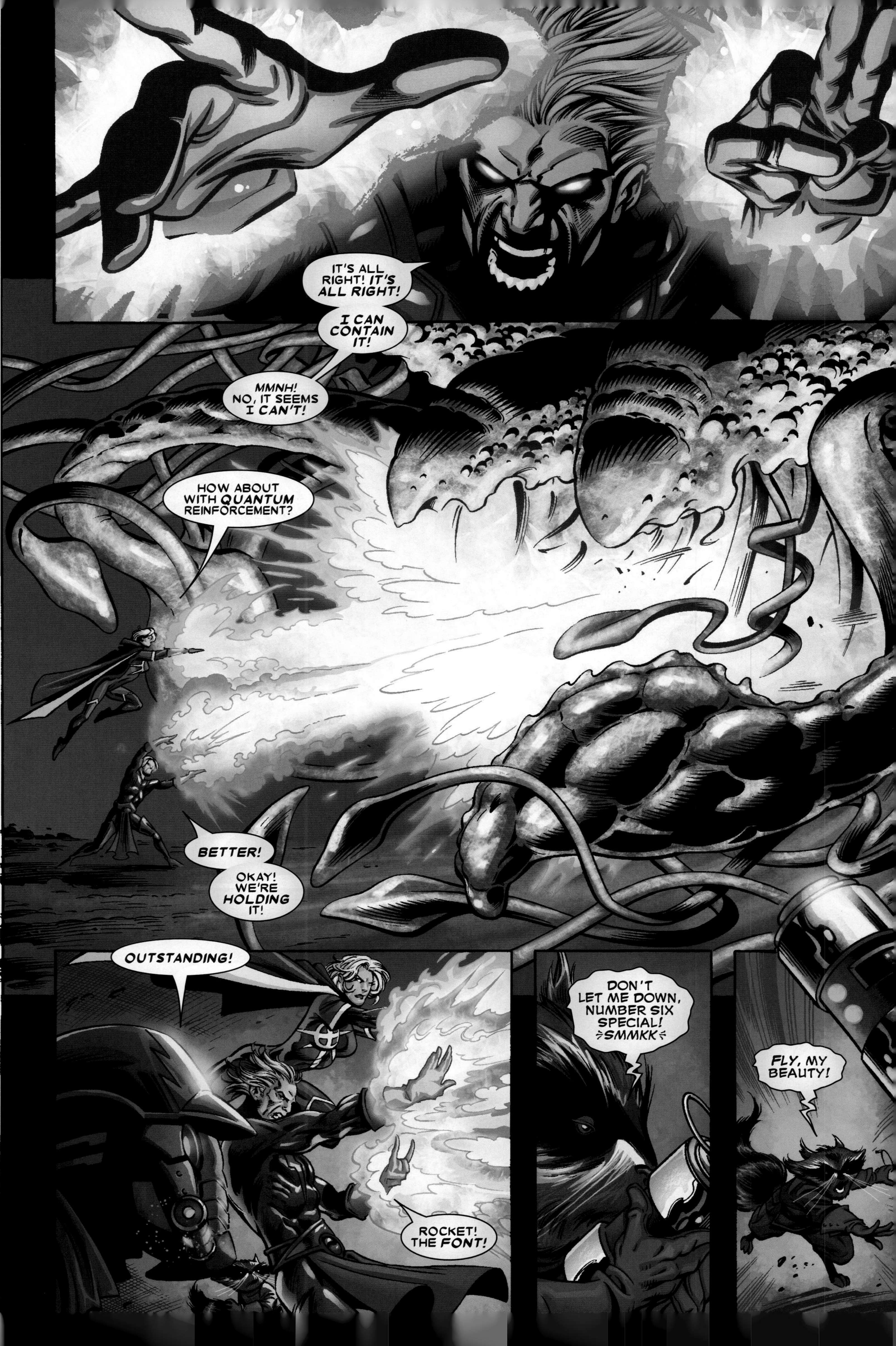
IT'S ALL RIGHT! IT'S ALL RIGHT!
I CAN CONTAIN IT!
MMNH! NO, IT SEEMS I CAN'T!
HOW ABOUT WITH QUANTUM REINFORCEMENT?
BETTER!
OKAY! WE'RE HOLDING IT!
OUTSTANDING!
ROCKET! THE FONT!
DON'T LET ME DOWN, NUMBER SIX SPECIAL! SMMKK
FLY, MY BEAUTY!

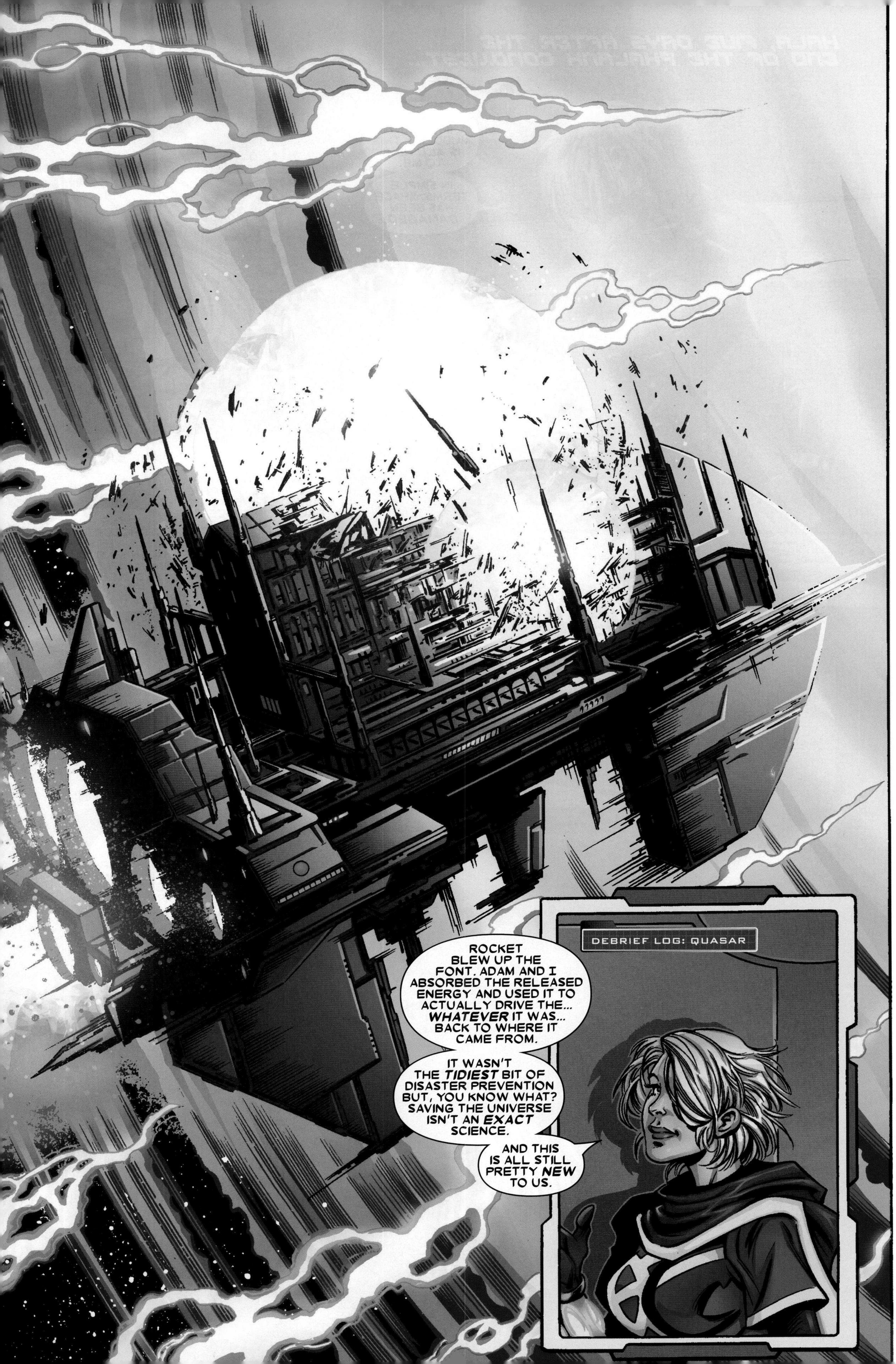
DEBRIEF LOG: QUASAR
ROCKET BLEW UP THE FONT. ADAM AND I ABSORBED THE RELEASED ENERGY AND USED IT TO ACTUALLY DRIVE THE... WHATEVER IT WAS... BACK TO WHERE IT CAME FROM.
IT WASN'T THE TIDIEST BIT OF DISASTER PREVENTION BUT, YOU KNOW WHAT? SAVING THE UNIVERSE ISN'T AN EXACT SCIENCE.
AND THIS IS ALL STILL PRETTY NEW TO US.

GUARDIANS OF THE GALAXY 1

(2008)

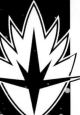

GUARDIANS OF THE GALAXY 1 (2008)

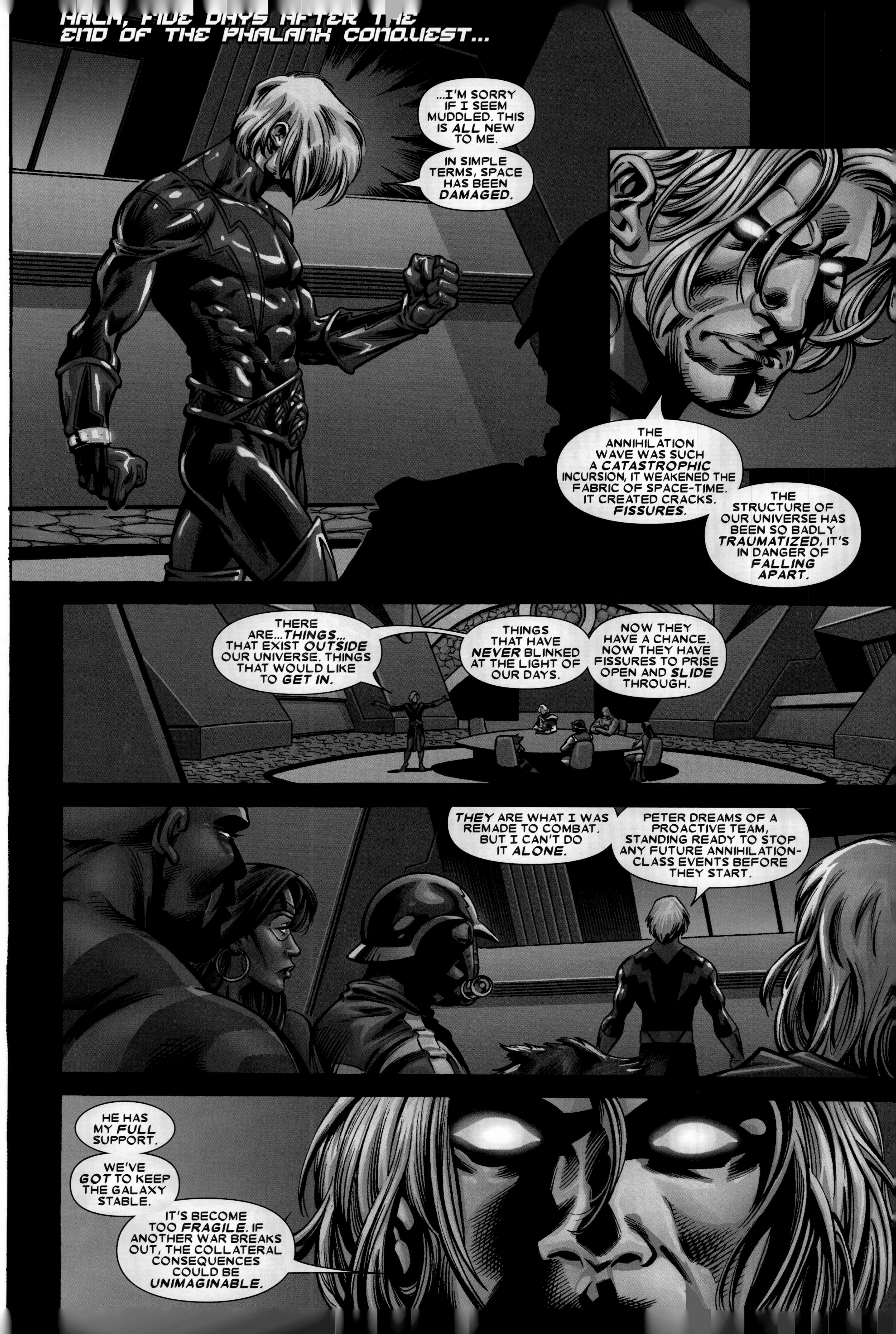
HALA, FIVE DAYS AFTER THE END OF THE PHALANX CONQUEST...
...I'M SORRY IF I SEEM MUDDLED. THIS IS ALL NEW TO ME.
IN SIMPLE TERMS, SPACE HAS BEEN DAMAGED.
THE ANNIHILATION WAVE WAS SUCH A CATASTROPHIC INCURSION, IT WEAKENED THE FABRIC OF SPACE-TIME. IT CREATED CRACKS. FISSURES.
THE STRUCTURE OF OUR UNIVERSE HAS BEEN SO BADLY TRAUMATIZED, IT'S IN DANGER OF FALLING APART.
THERE ARE...THINGS... THAT EXIST OUTSIDE OUR UNIVERSE. THINGS THAT WOULD LIKE TO GET IN.
THINGS THAT HAVE NEVER BLINKED AT THE LIGHT OF OUR DAYS.
NOW THEY HAVE A CHANCE. NOW THEY HAVE FISSURES TO PRISE OPEN AND SLIDE THROUGH.
THEY ARE WHAT I WAS REMADE TO COMBAT. BUT I CAN'T DO IT ALONE.
PETER DREAMS OF A PROACTIVE TEAM, STANDING READY TO STOP ANY FUTURE ANNIHILATION-CLASS EVENTS BEFORE THEY START.
HE HAS MY FULL SUPPORT.
WE'VE GOT TO KEEP THE GALAXY STABLE.
IT'S BECOME TOO FRAGILE. IF ANOTHER WAR BREAKS OUT, THE COLLATERAL CONSEQUENCES COULD BE UNIMAGINABLE.

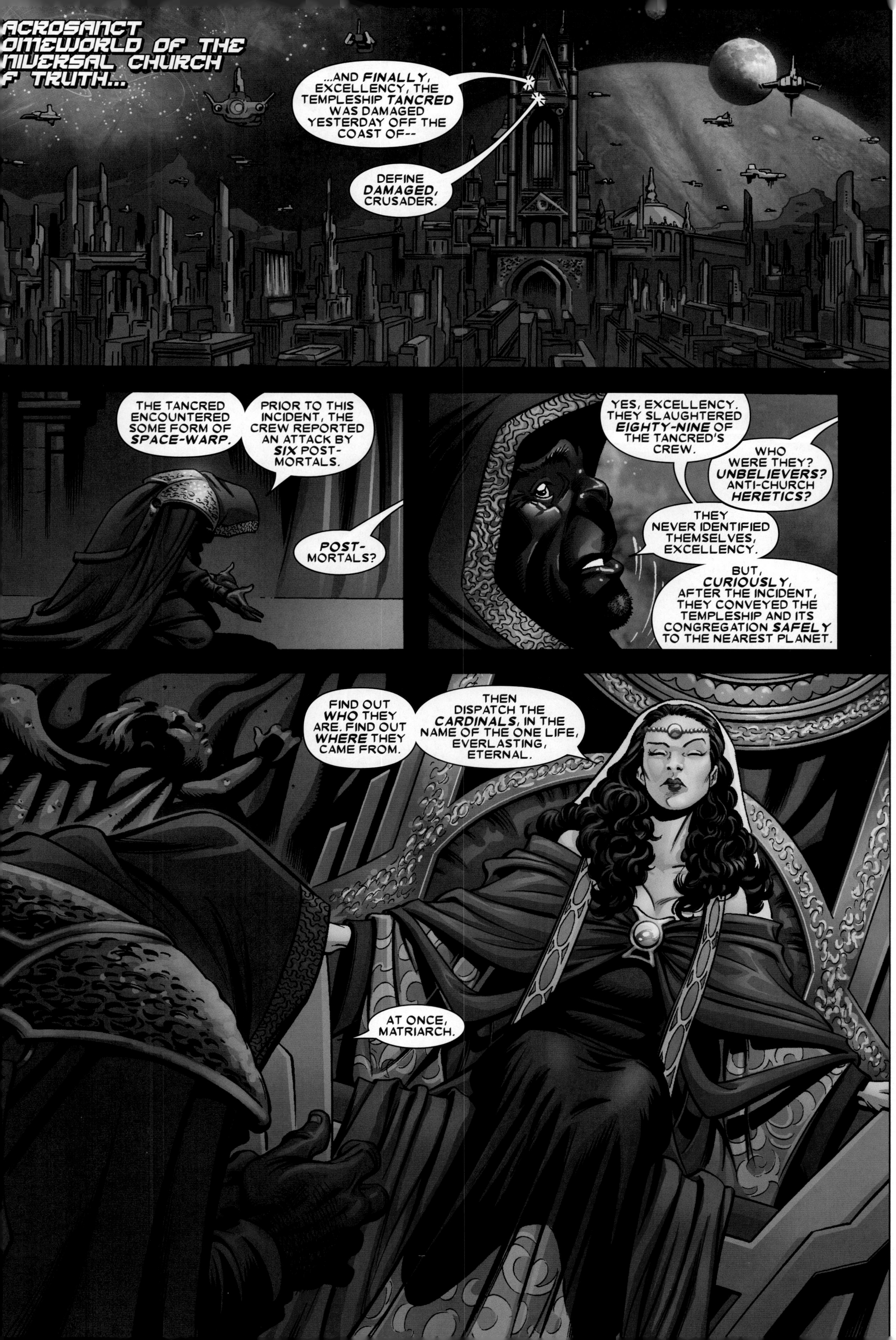

ACROSANCT OMEWORLD OF THE NIVERSAL CHURCH F TRUTH...
...AND FINALLY, EXCELLENCY, THE TEMPLESHIP TANCRED WAS DAMAGED YESTERDAY OFF THE COAST OF--
DEFINE DAMAGED, CRUSADER.
THE TANCRED ENCOUNTERED SOME FORM OF SPACE-WARP.
PRIOR TO THIS INCIDENT, THE CREW REPORTED AN ATTACK BY SIX POST-MORTALS.
POST-MORTALS?
YES, EXCELLENCY. THEY SLAUGHTERED EIGHTY-NINE OF THE TANCRED'S CREW.
WHO WERE THEY? UNBELIEVERS? ANTI-CHURCH HERETICS?
THEY NEVER IDENTIFIED THEMSELVES, EXCELLENCY.
BUT, CURIOUSLY, AFTER THE INCIDENT, THEY CONVEYED THE TEMPLESHIP AND ITS CONGREGATION SAFELY TO THE NEAREST PLANET.
FIND OUT WHO THEY ARE. FIND OUT WHERE THEY CAME FROM.
THEN DISPATCH THE CARDINALS, IN THE NAME OF THE ONE LIFE, EVERLASTING, ETERNAL.
AT ONCE, MATRIARCH.

GUARDIANS OF THE GALAXY 1 (2008)

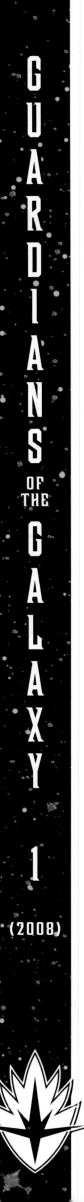

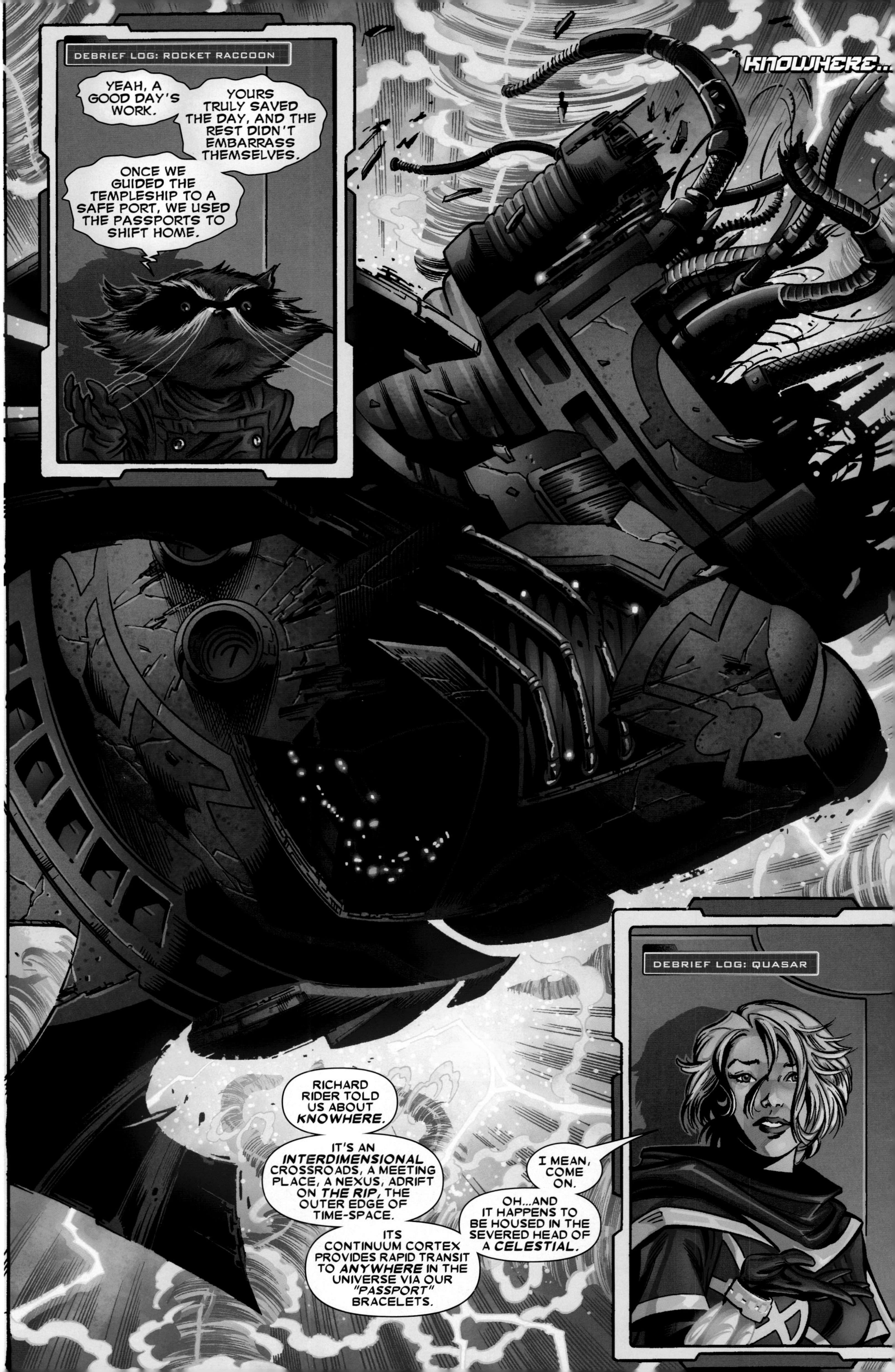
KNOWHERE...
DEBRIEF LOG: ROCKET RACCOON
YEAH, A GOOD DAY'S WORK.
YOURS TRULY SAVED THE DAY, AND THE REST DIDN'T EMBARRASS THEMSELVES.
ONCE WE GUIDED THE TEMPLESHIP TO A SAFE PORT, WE USED THE PASSPORTS TO SHIFT HOME.
DEBRIEF LOG: QUASAR
RICHARD RIDER TOLD US ABOUT *KNOWHERE.*
IT'S AN *INTERDIMENSIONAL* CROSSROADS, A MEETING PLACE, A NEXUS, ADRIFT ON *THE RIP,* THE OUTER EDGE OF TIME-SPACE.
ITS CONTINUUM CORTEX PROVIDES RAPID TRANSIT TO *ANYWHERE* IN THE UNIVERSE VIA OUR *"PASSPORT"* BRACELETS.
I MEAN, COME ON.
OH...AND IT HAPPENS TO BE HOUSED IN THE SEVERED HEAD OF A *CELESTIAL.*

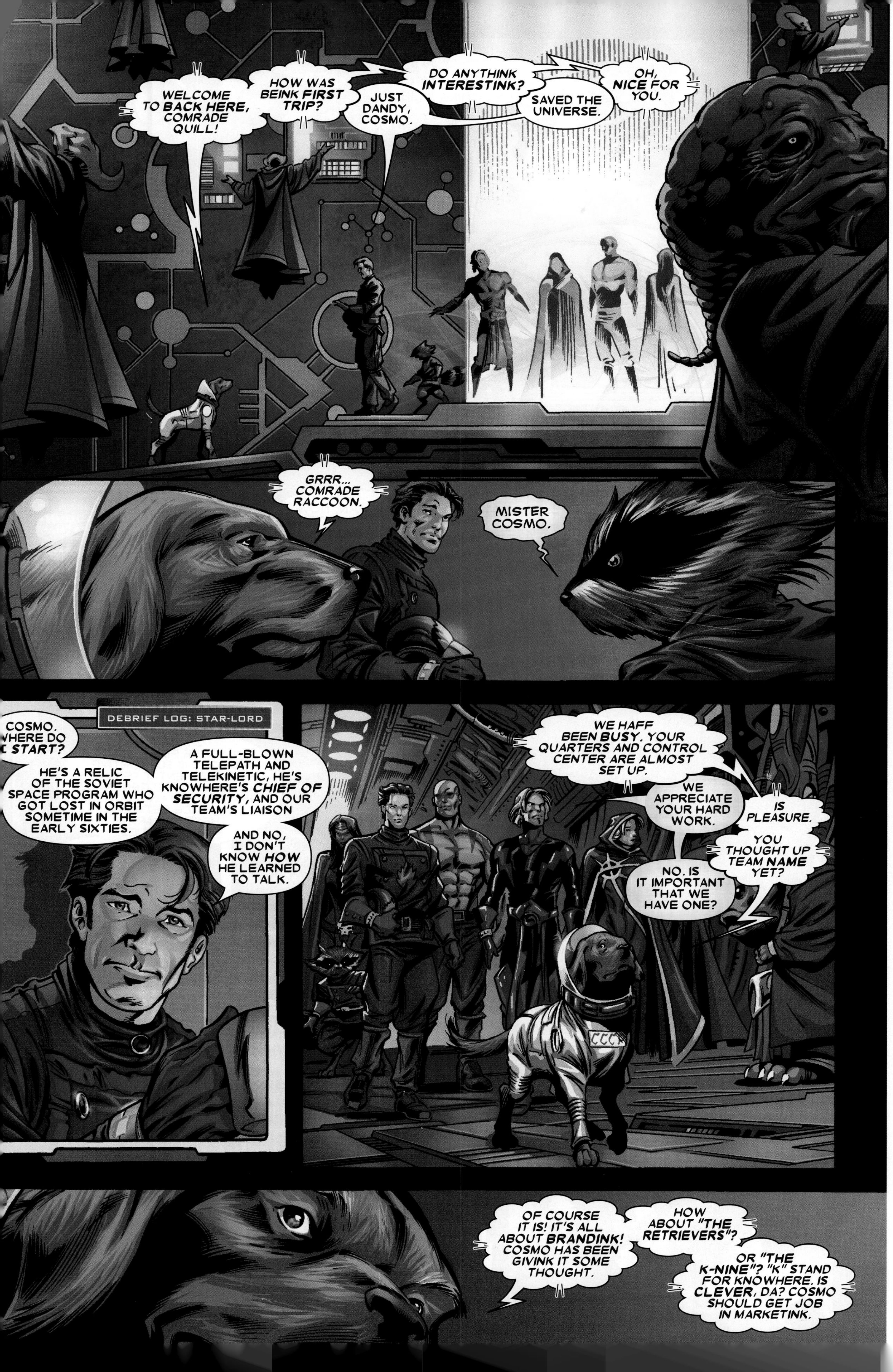
WELCOME TO BACK HERE, COMRADE QUILL!
HOW WAS BEINK FIRST TRIP?
JUST DANDY, COSMO.
DO ANYTHINK INTERESTINK?
SAVED THE UNIVERSE.
OH, NICE FOR YOU.
GRRR... COMRADE RACCOON.
MISTER COSMO.
DEBRIEF LOG: STAR-LORD
COSMO.
START?
HE'S A RELIC OF THE SOVIET SPACE PROGRAM WHO GOT LOST IN ORBIT SOMETIME IN THE EARLY SIXTIES.
A FULL-BLOWN TELEPATH AND TELEKINETIC, HE'S KNOWHERE'S CHIEF OF SECURITY, AND OUR TEAM'S LIAISON
AND NO, I DON'T KNOW HOW HE LEARNED TO TALK.
WE HAFF BEEN BUSY. YOUR QUARTERS AND CONTROL CENTER ARE ALMOST SET UP.
WE APPRECIATE YOUR HARD WORK.
IS PLEASURE.
YOU THOUGHT UP TEAM NAME YET?
NO. IS IT IMPORTANT THAT WE HAVE ONE?
OF COURSE IT IS! IT'S ALL ABOUT BRANDINK! COSMO HAS BEEN GIVINK IT SOME THOUGHT.
HOW ABOUT "THE RETRIEVERS"?
OR "THE K-NINE"? "K" STAND FOR KNOWHERE. IS CLEVER, DA? COSMO SHOULD GET JOB IN MARKETINK.

GUARDIANS OF THE GALAXY 1 (2008)

GUARDIANS OF THE GALAXY 1 (2008)

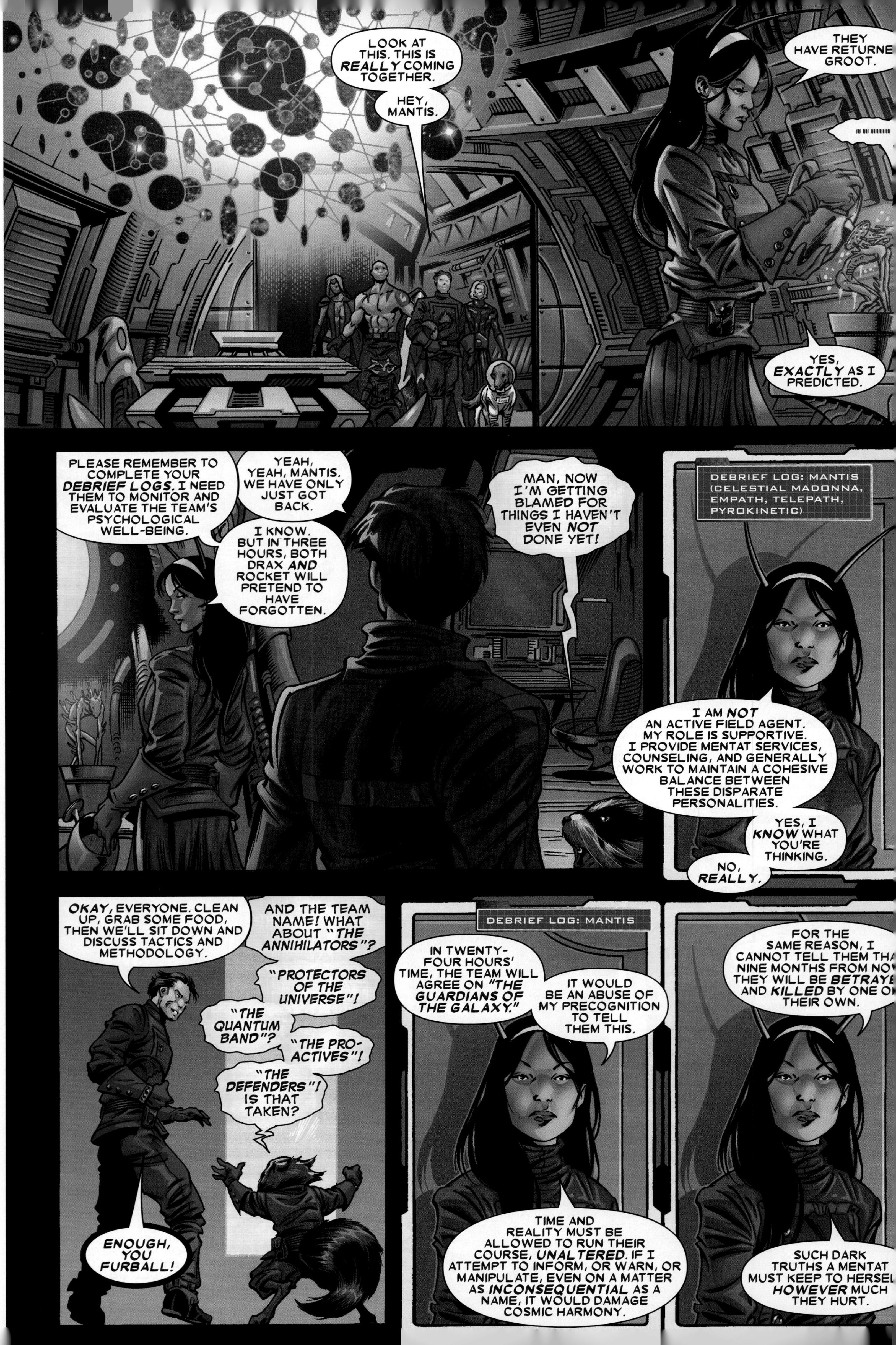

LOOK AT THIS. THIS IS *REALLY* COMING TOGETHER.
HEY, MANTIS.
THEY HAVE RETURNE GROOT.
YES, *EXACTLY* AS I PREDICTED.
PLEASE REMEMBER TO COMPLETE YOUR *DEBRIEF LOGS.* I NEED THEM TO MONITOR AND EVALUATE THE TEAM'S PSYCHOLOGICAL WELL-BEING.
YEAH, YEAH, MANTIS. WE HAVE ONLY JUST GOT BACK.
I KNOW. BUT IN THREE HOURS, BOTH DRAX *AND* ROCKET WILL PRETEND TO HAVE FORGOTTEN.
MAN, NOW I'M GETTING BLAMED FOR THINGS I HAVEN'T EVEN *NOT* DONE YET!
DEBRIEF LOG: MANTIS (CELESTIAL MADONNA, EMPATH, TELEPATH, PYROKINETIC)
I AM *NOT* AN ACTIVE FIELD AGENT. MY ROLE IS SUPPORTIVE. I PROVIDE MENTAT SERVICES, COUNSELING, AND GENERALLY WORK TO MAINTAIN A COHESIVE BALANCE BETWEEN THESE DISPARATE PERSONALITIES.
YES, I *KNOW* WHAT YOU'RE THINKING.
NO, *REALLY.*
OKAY, EVERYONE. CLEAN UP, GRAB SOME FOOD, THEN WE'LL SIT DOWN AND DISCUSS TACTICS AND METHODOLOGY.
AND THE TEAM NAME! WHAT ABOUT *"THE ANNIHILATORS"?*
"PROTECTORS OF THE UNIVERSE"!
"THE QUANTUM BAND"?
"THE PRO-ACTIVES"!
"THE DEFENDERS"! IS THAT TAKEN?
ENOUGH, YOU FURBALL!
DEBRIEF LOG: MANTIS
IN TWENTY-FOUR HOURS' TIME, THE TEAM WILL AGREE ON *"THE GUARDIANS OF THE GALAXY."*
IT WOULD BE AN ABUSE OF MY PRECOGNITION TO TELL THEM THIS.
TIME AND REALITY MUST BE ALLOWED TO RUN THEIR COURSE, *UNALTERED.* IF I ATTEMPT TO INFORM, OR WARN, OR MANIPULATE, EVEN ON A MATTER AS *INCONSEQUENTIAL* AS A NAME, IT WOULD DAMAGE COSMIC HARMONY.
FOR THE SAME REASON, I CANNOT TELL THEM THA NINE MONTHS FROM NO THEY WILL BE *BETRAYE* AND *KILLED* BY ONE O THEIR OWN.
SUCH DARK TRUTHS A MENTAT MUST KEEP TO HERSEL *HOWEVER* MUCH THEY HURT.

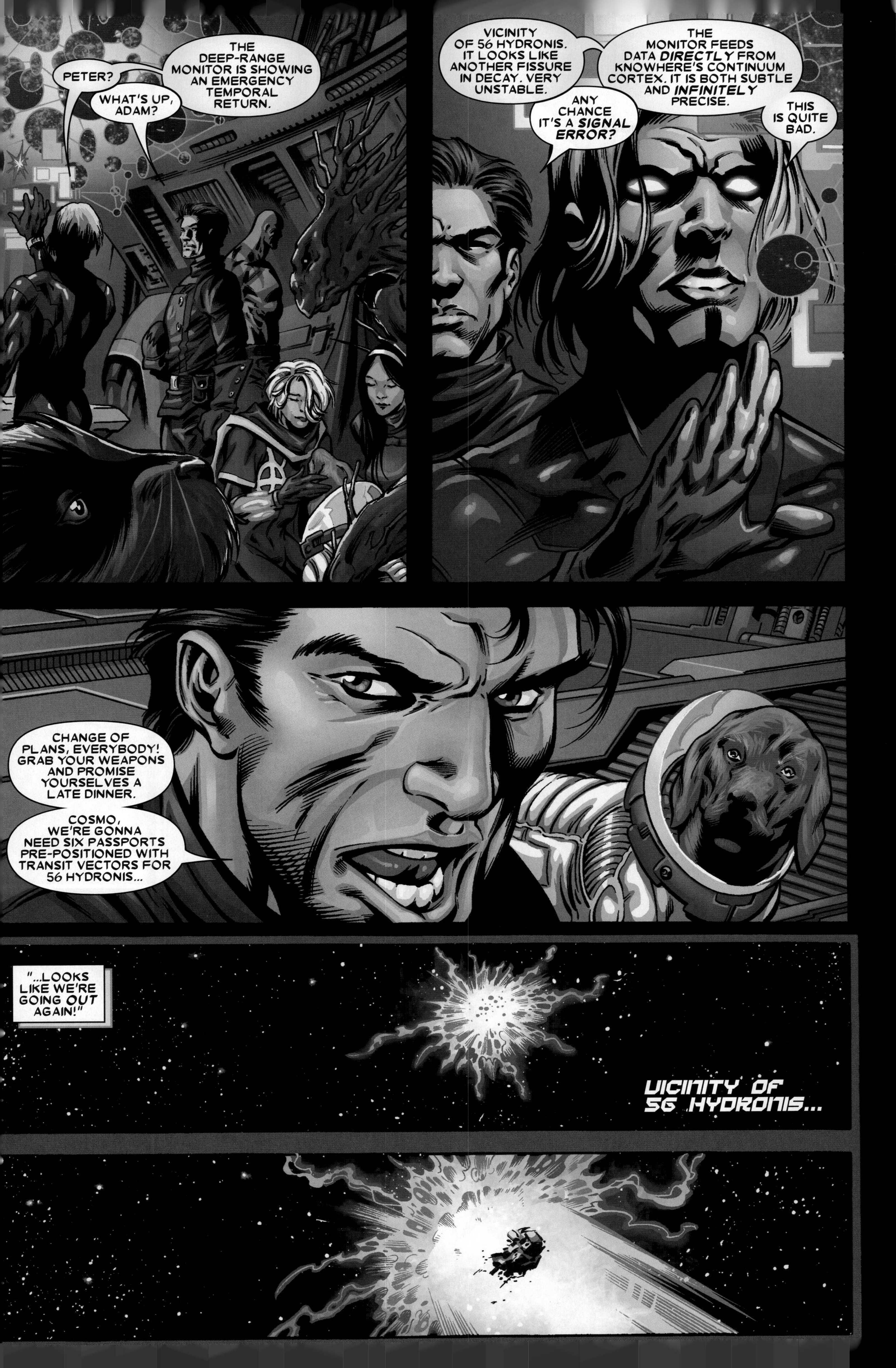
PETER?
WHAT'S UP, ADAM?
THE DEEP-RANGE MONITOR IS SHOWING AN EMERGENCY TEMPORAL RETURN.
VICINITY OF 56 HYDRONIS. IT LOOKS LIKE ANOTHER FISSURE IN DECAY. VERY UNSTABLE.
THE MONITOR FEEDS DATA DIRECTLY FROM KNOWHERE'S CONTINUUM CORTEX. IT IS BOTH SUBTLE AND INFINITELY PRECISE.
ANY CHANCE IT'S A SIGNAL ERROR?
THIS IS QUITE BAD.
CHANGE OF PLANS, EVERYBODY! GRAB YOUR WEAPONS AND PROMISE YOURSELVES A LATE DINNER.
COSMO, WE'RE GONNA NEED SIX PASSPORTS PRE-POSITIONED WITH TRANSIT VECTORS FOR 56 HYDRONIS...
"...LOOKS LIKE WE'RE GOING OUT AGAIN!"
VICINITY OF 56 HYDRONIS...

GUARDIANS OF THE GALAXY 1 (2008)

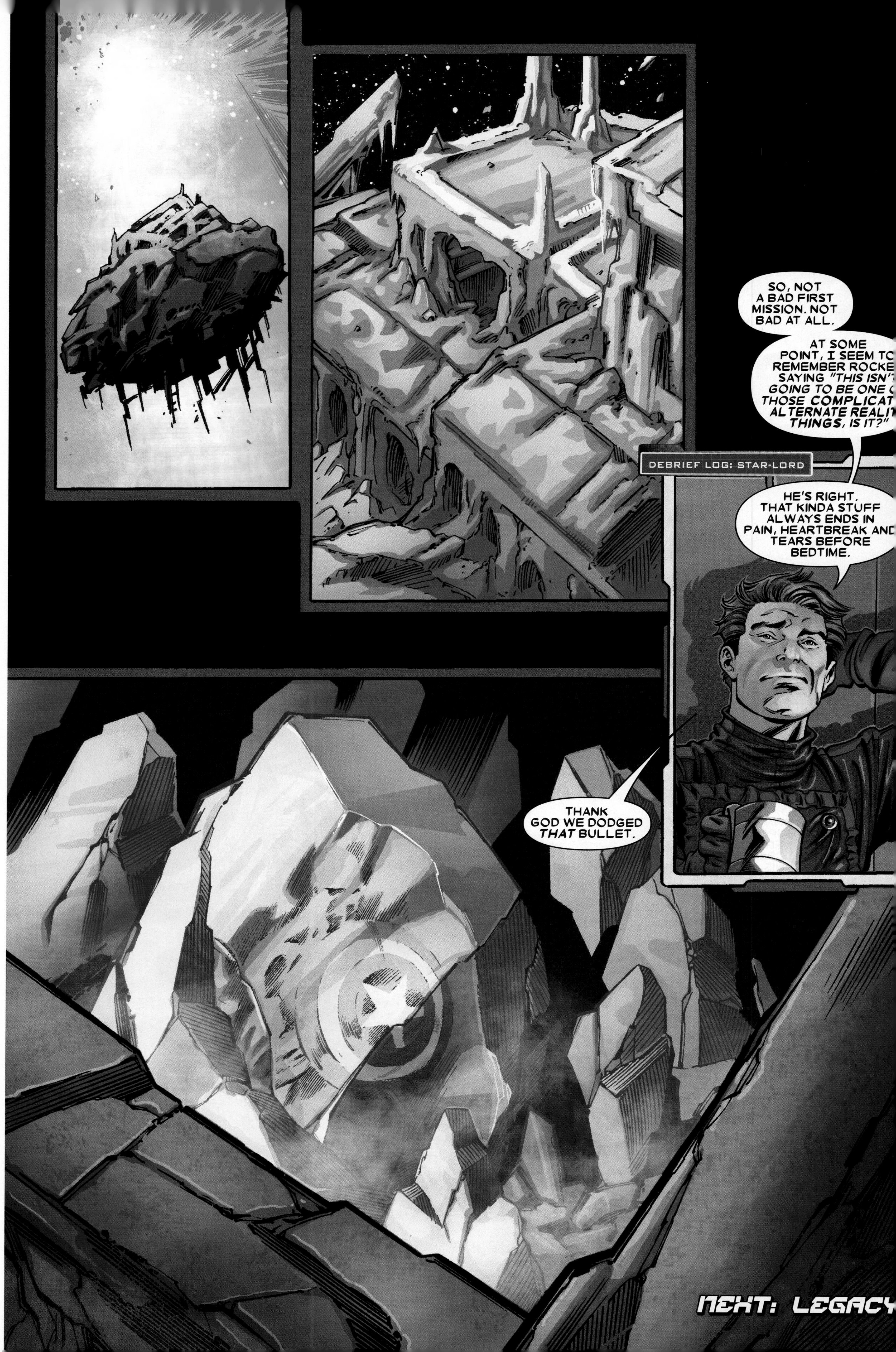
SO, NOT A BAD FIRST MISSION. NOT BAD AT ALL.
AT SOME POINT, I SEEM TO REMEMBER ROCKE SAYING "THIS ISN' GOING TO BE ONE O THOSE COMPLICAT ALTERNATE REALIT THINGS, IS IT?"
DEBRIEF LOG: STAR-LORD
HE'S RIGHT. THAT KINDA STUFF ALWAYS ENDS IN PAIN, HEARTBREAK AND TEARS BEFORE BEDTIME.
THANK GOD WE DODGED *THAT* BULLET.
NEXT: LEGACY

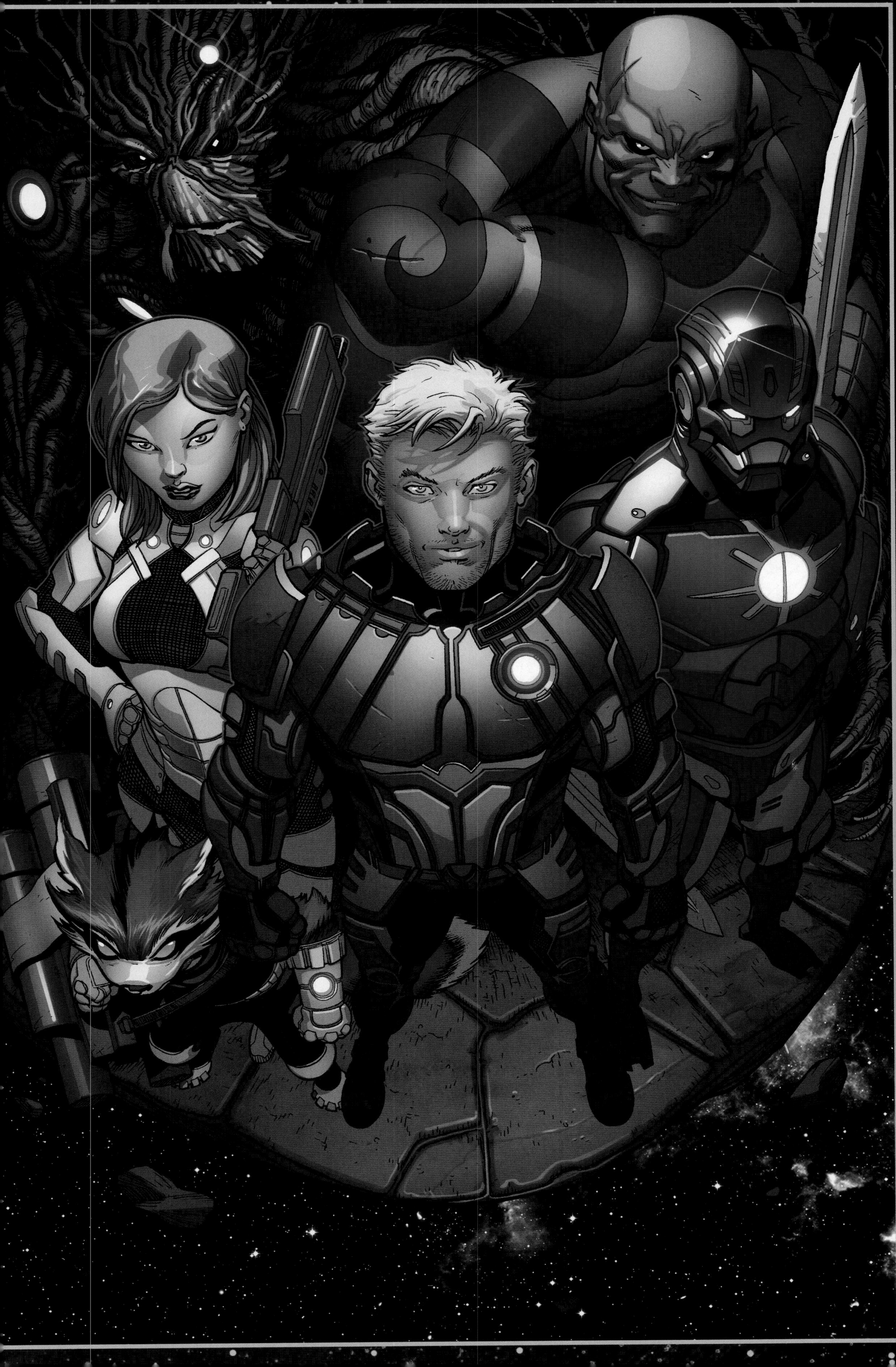

GUARDIANS OF THE GALAXY (2013) #0.1 VARIANT BY
ED McGUINNESS & MARTE GRACIA

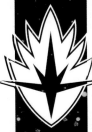

GUARDIANS OF THE GALAXY

0.1

(2013)

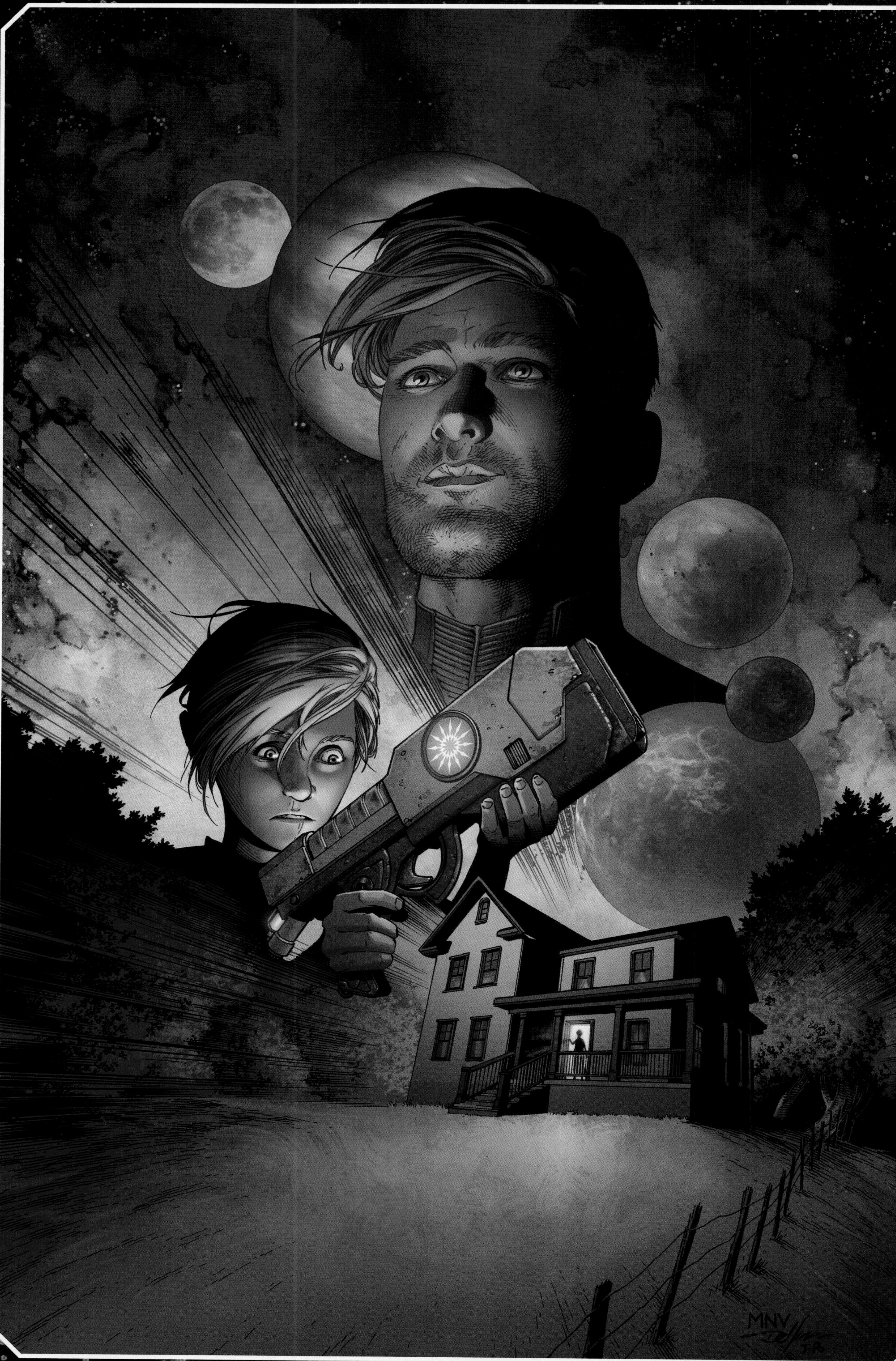
MNV

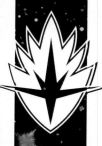

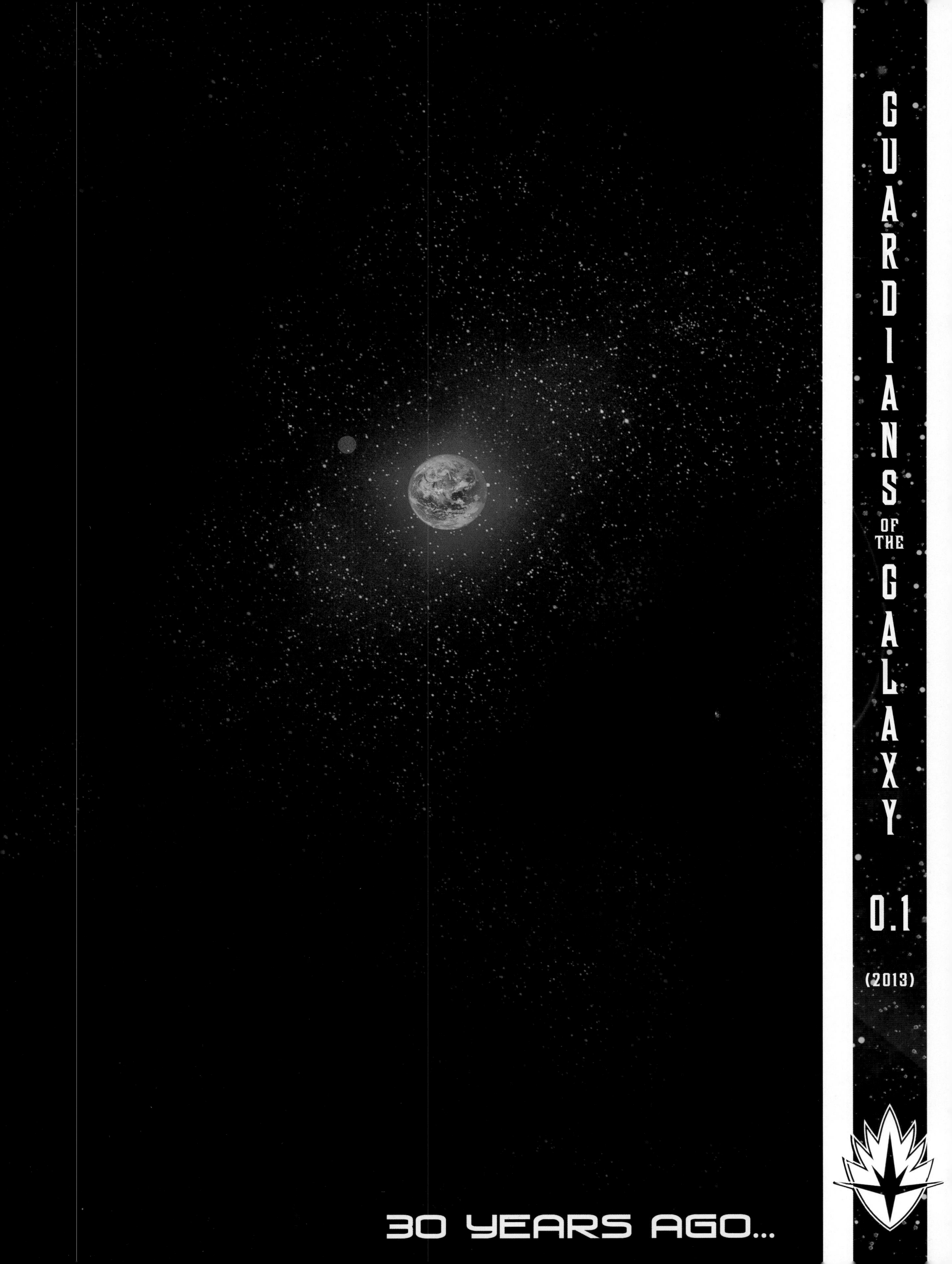
GUARDIANS OF THE GALAXY
0.1
(2013)
30 YEARS AGO...

WRITER **BRIAN MICHAEL B**

INKER **JOHN DELL** CO

PRODUCTION **IRENE Y. LEE** COVER BY S

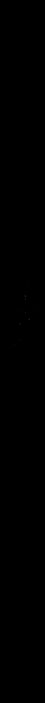

GUARDIANS OF THE GALAXY

0.1

(2013)

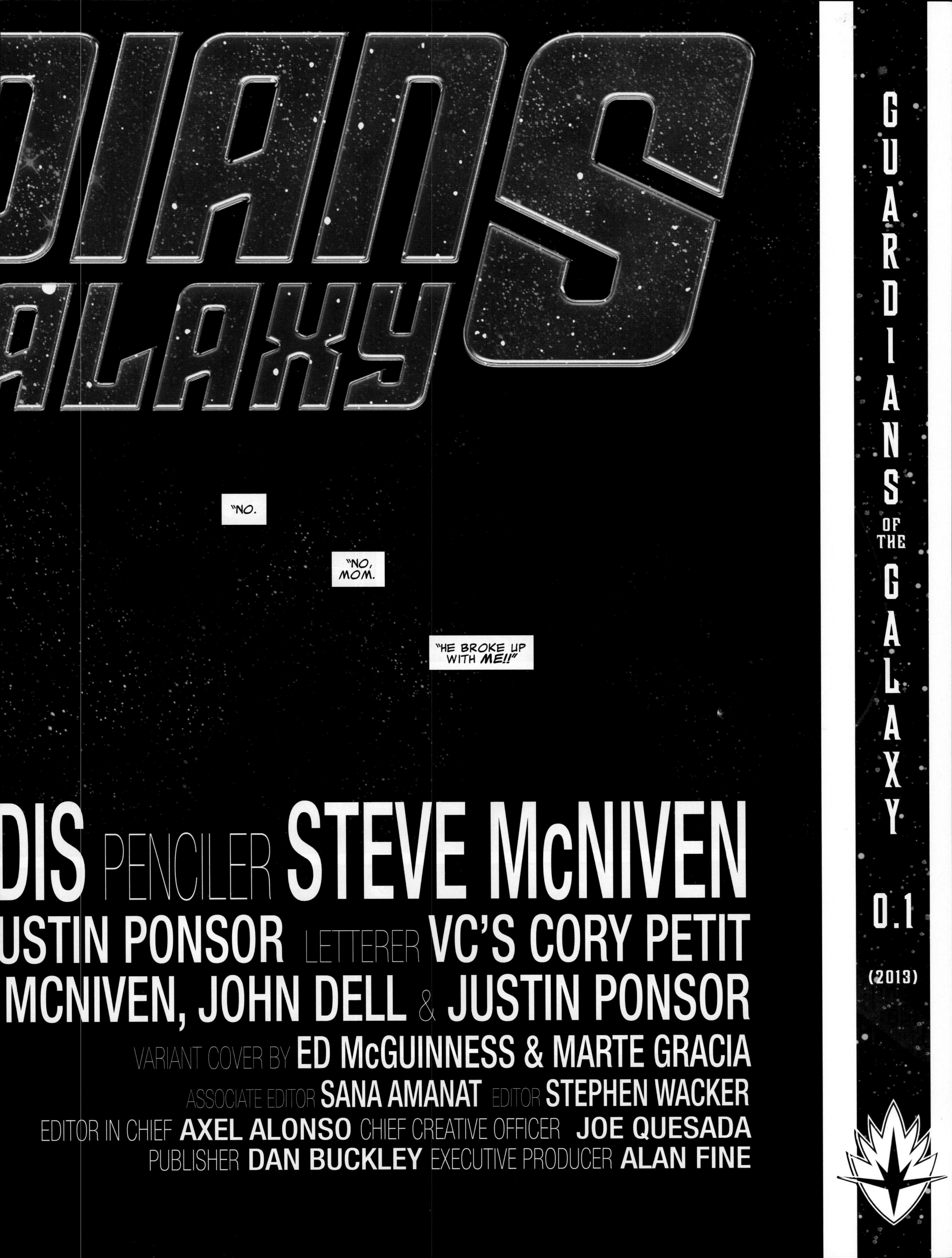
"NO.
"NO, MOM.
"HE BROKE UP WITH ME!!"
DIS PENCILER STEVE McNIVEN
USTIN PONSOR LETTERER VC'S CORY PETIT
MCNIVEN, JOHN DELL & JUSTIN PONSOR
VARIANT COVER BY ED McGUINNESS & MARTE GRACIA
ASSOCIATE EDITOR SANA AMANAT EDITOR STEPHEN WACKER
EDITOR IN CHIEF AXEL ALONSO CHIEF CREATIVE OFFICER JOE QUESADA
PUBLISHER DAN BUCKLEY EXECUTIVE PRODUCER ALAN FINE
GUARDIANS OF THE GALAXY
0.1
(2013)

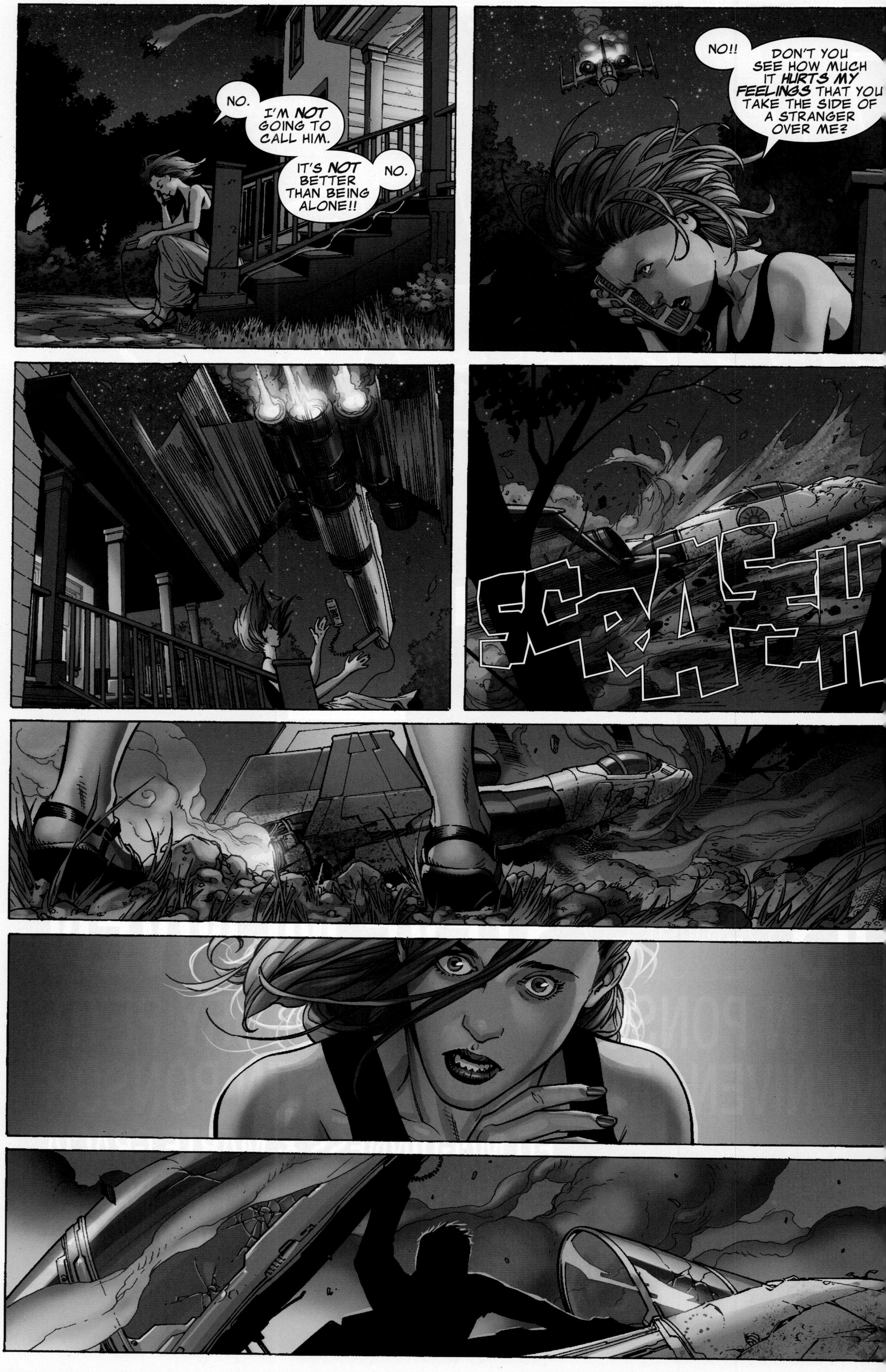
NO.
I'M NOT GOING TO CALL HIM.
IT'S NOT BETTER THAN BEING ALONE!!
NO.
NO!!
DON'T YOU SEE HOW MUCH IT HURTS MY FEELINGS THAT YOU TAKE THE SIDE OF A STRANGER OVER ME?

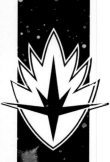

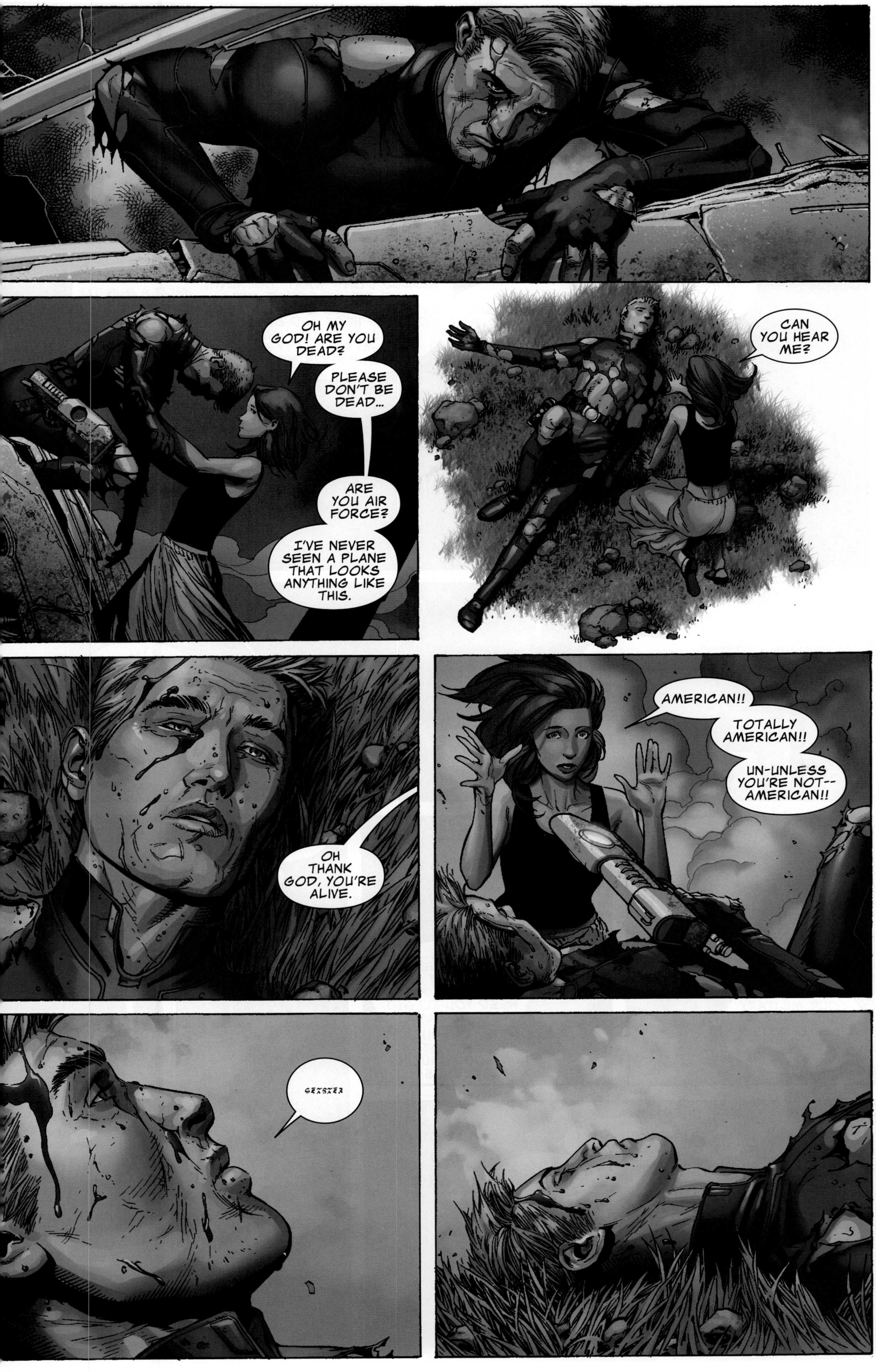
OH MY GOD! ARE YOU DEAD?
PLEASE DON'T BE DEAD...
ARE YOU AIR FORCE?
I'VE NEVER SEEN A PLANE THAT LOOKS ANYTHING LIKE THIS.
CAN YOU HEAR ME?
OH THANK GOD, YOU'RE ALIVE.
AMERICAN!!
TOTALLY AMERICAN!!
UN-UNLESS YOU'RE NOT-- AMERICAN!!

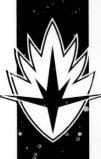

GUARDIANS OF THE GALAXY 0.1 (2013)

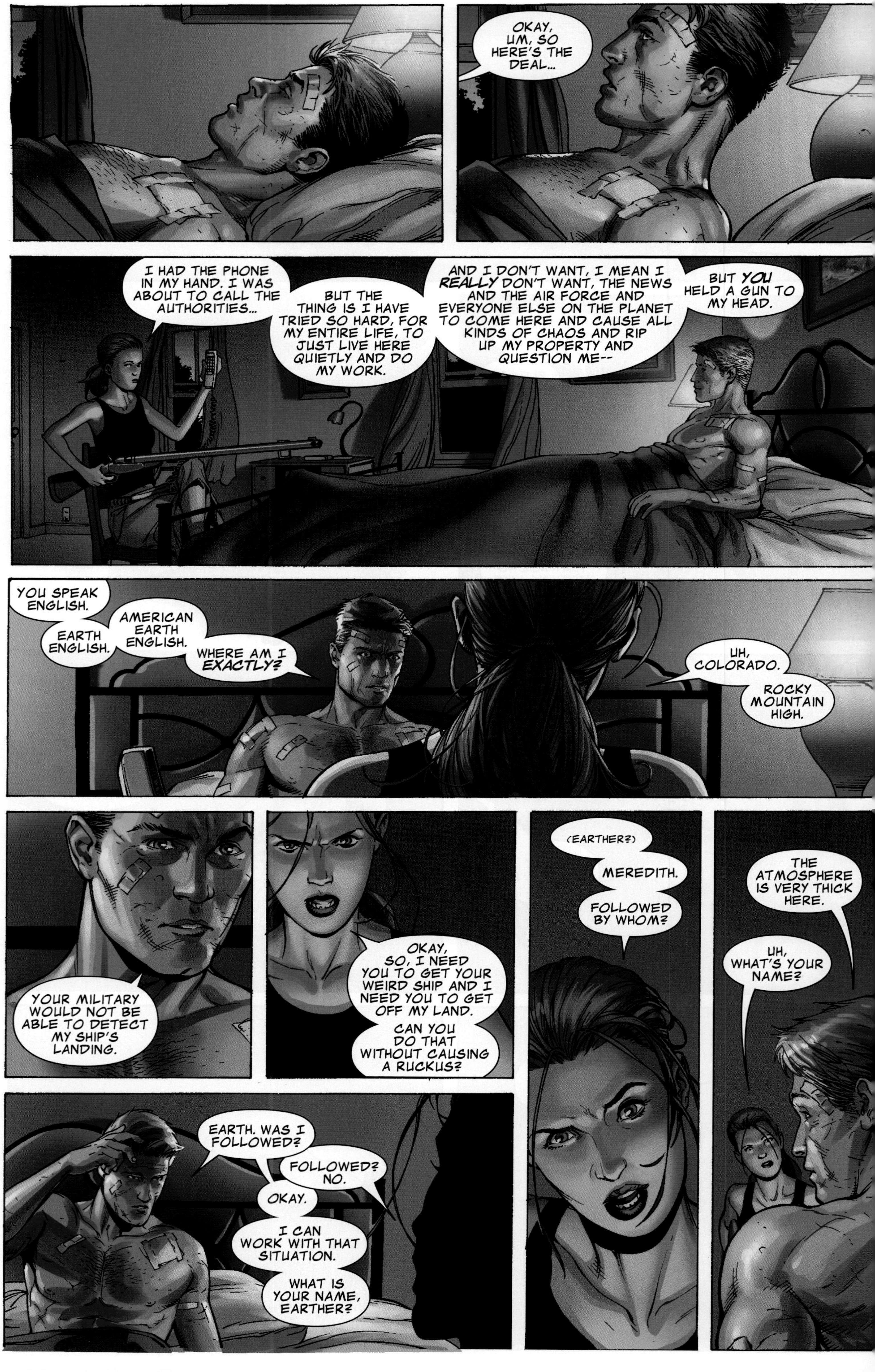

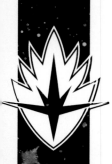

OKAY, UM, SO HERE'S THE DEAL...
I HAD THE PHONE IN MY HAND. I WAS ABOUT TO CALL THE AUTHORITIES...
BUT THE THING IS I HAVE TRIED SO HARD, FOR MY ENTIRE LIFE, TO JUST LIVE HERE QUIETLY AND DO MY WORK.
AND I DON'T WANT, I MEAN I REALLY DON'T WANT, THE NEWS AND THE AIR FORCE AND EVERYONE ELSE ON THE PLANET TO COME HERE AND CAUSE ALL KINDS OF CHAOS AND RIP UP MY PROPERTY AND QUESTION ME--
BUT YOU HELD A GUN TO MY HEAD.
YOU SPEAK ENGLISH.
EARTH ENGLISH.
AMERICAN EARTH ENGLISH.
WHERE AM I EXACTLY?
UH, COLORADO.
ROCKY MOUNTAIN HIGH.
YOUR MILITARY WOULD NOT BE ABLE TO DETECT MY SHIP'S LANDING.
OKAY, SO, I NEED YOU TO GET YOUR WEIRD SHIP AND I NEED YOU TO GET OFF MY LAND.
CAN YOU DO THAT WITHOUT CAUSING A RUCKUS?
EARTH. WAS I FOLLOWED?
FOLLOWED? NO.
OKAY.
I CAN WORK WITH THAT SITUATION.
WHAT IS YOUR NAME, EARTHER?
(EARTHER?)
MEREDITH.
FOLLOWED BY WHOM?
THE ATMOSPHERE IS VERY THICK HERE.
UH, WHAT'S YOUR NAME?

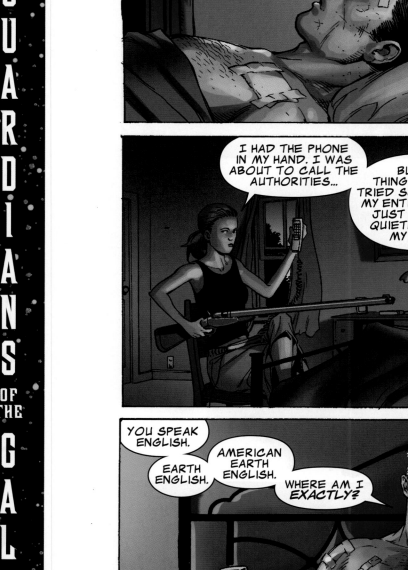

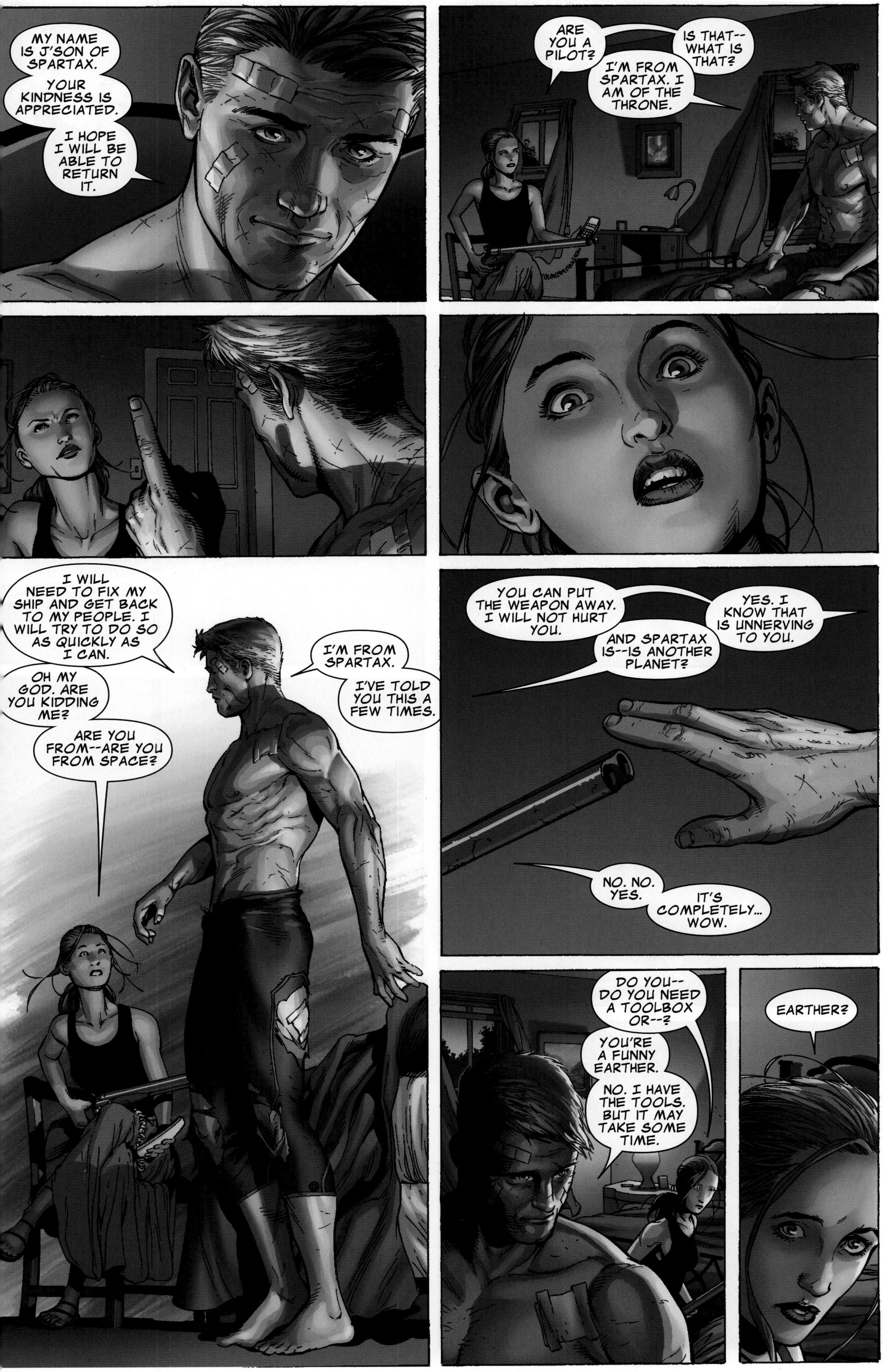

MY NAME IS J'SON OF SPARTAX.
YOUR KINDNESS IS APPRECIATED.
I HOPE I WILL BE ABLE TO RETURN IT.
ARE YOU A PILOT?
I'M FROM SPARTAX. I AM OF THE THRONE.
IS THAT-- WHAT IS THAT?
I WILL NEED TO FIX MY SHIP AND GET BACK TO MY PEOPLE. I WILL TRY TO DO SO AS QUICKLY AS I CAN.
OH MY GOD. ARE YOU KIDDING ME?
ARE YOU FROM--ARE YOU FROM SPACE?
I'M FROM SPARTAX.
I'VE TOLD YOU THIS A FEW TIMES.
YOU CAN PUT THE WEAPON AWAY. I WILL NOT HURT YOU.
AND SPARTAX IS--IS ANOTHER PLANET?
YES. I KNOW THAT IS UNNERVING TO YOU.
NO. NO. YES.
IT'S COMPLETELY... WOW.
DO YOU-- DO YOU NEED A TOOLBOX OR--?
YOU'RE A FUNNY EARTHER.
NO. I HAVE THE TOOLS. BUT IT MAY TAKE SOME TIME.
EARTHER?

GUARDIANS OF THE GALAXY

0.1

(2013)

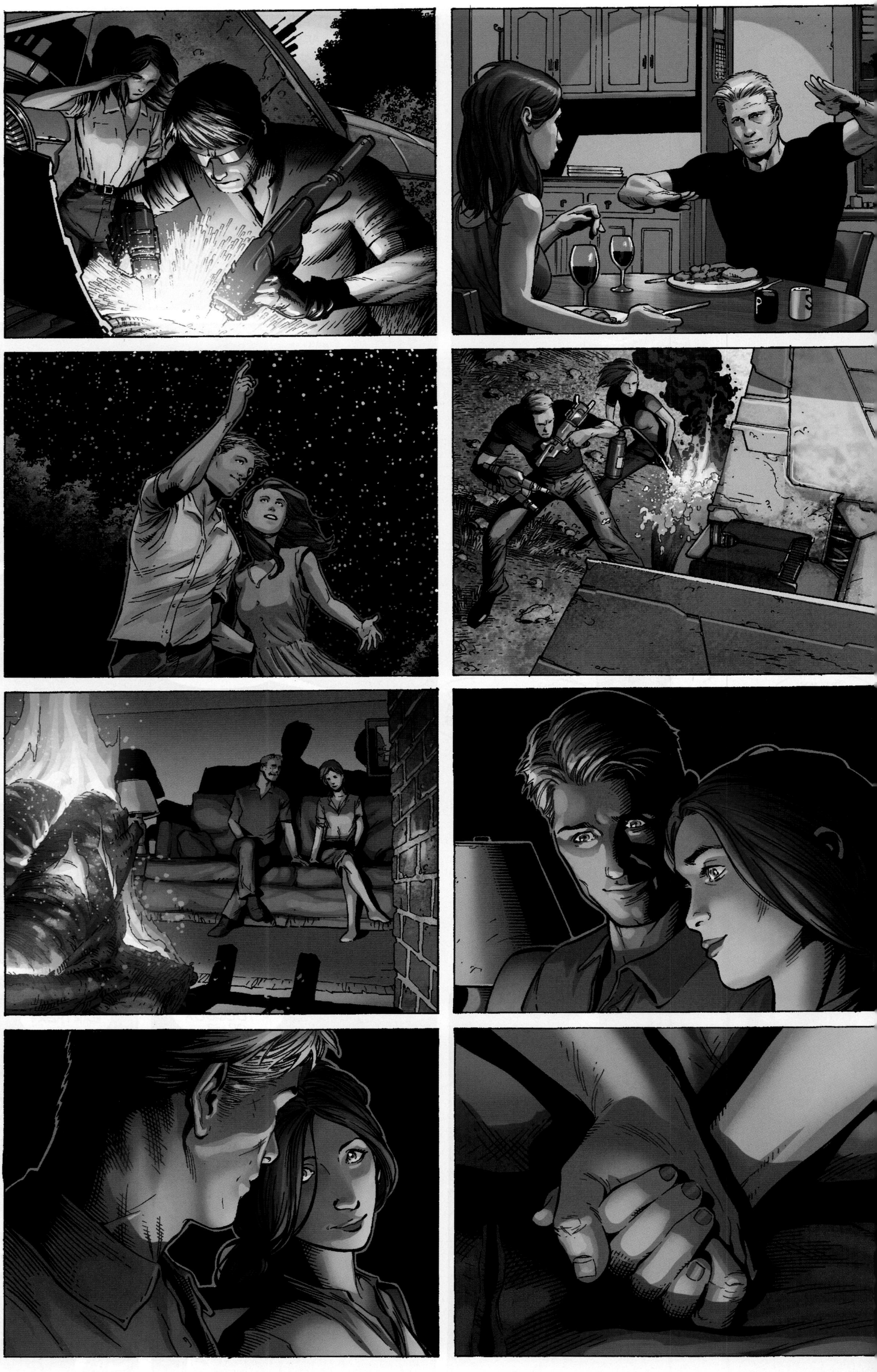
P
S

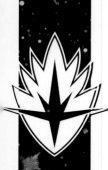

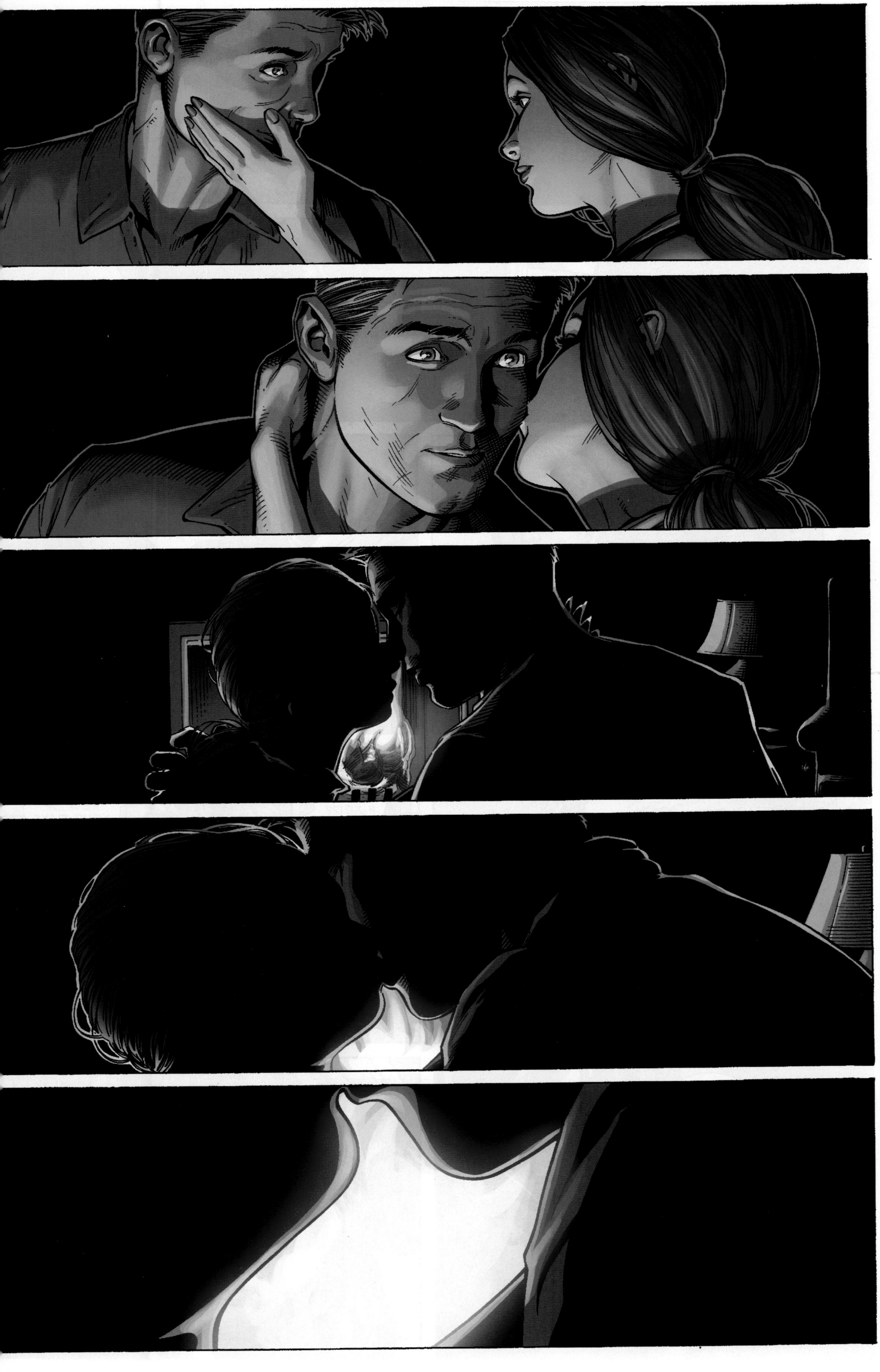

GUARDIANS OF THE GALAXY 0.1 (2013)

GUARDIANS OF THE GALAXY 0.1 (2013)

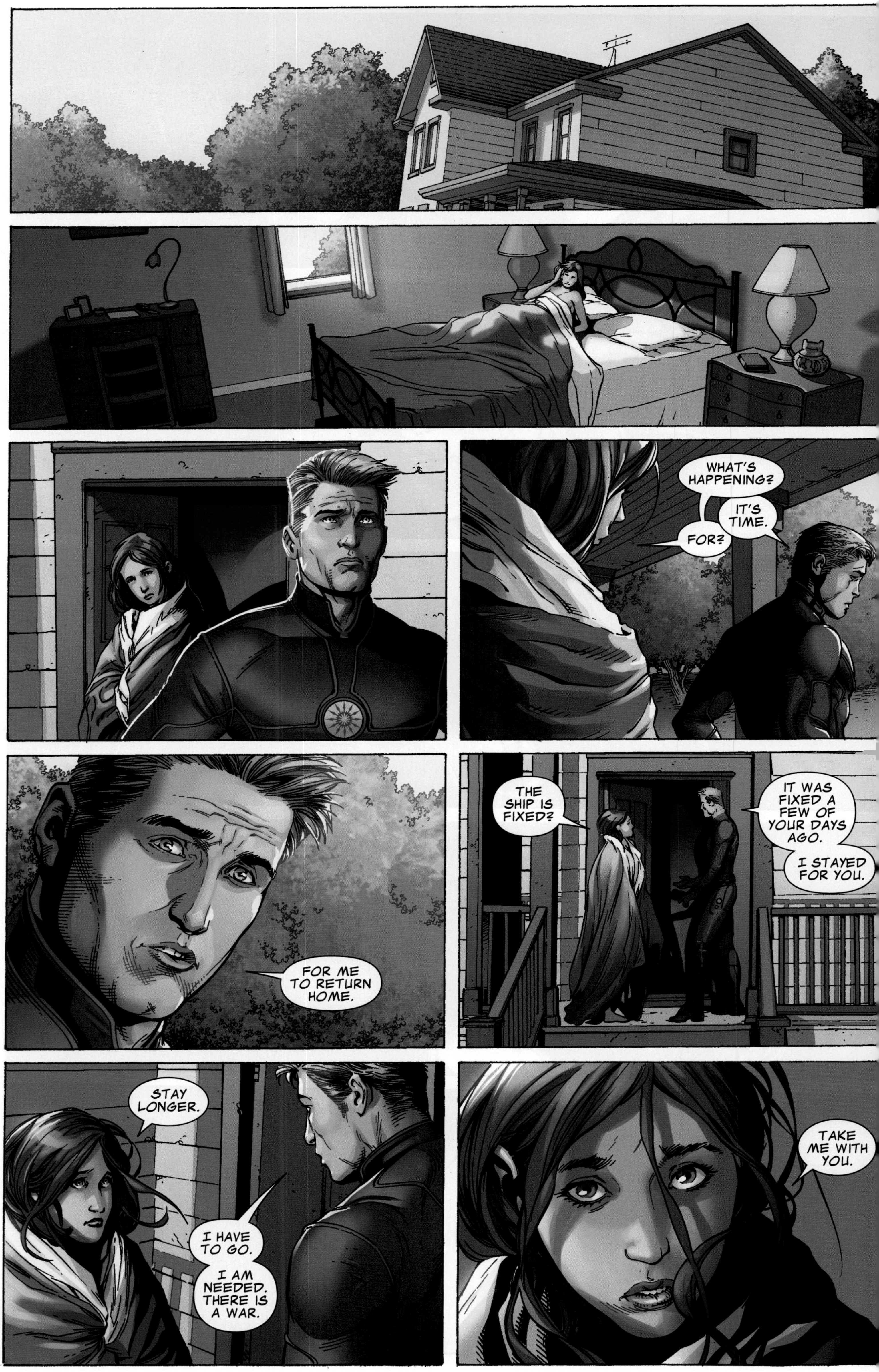
WHAT'S HAPPENING?
IT'S TIME.
FOR?
FOR ME TO RETURN HOME.
THE SHIP IS FIXED?
IT WAS FIXED A FEW OF YOUR DAYS AGO.
I STAYED FOR YOU.
STAY LONGER.
I HAVE TO GO.
I AM NEEDED. THERE IS A WAR.
TAKE ME WITH YOU.

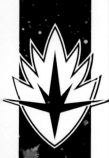

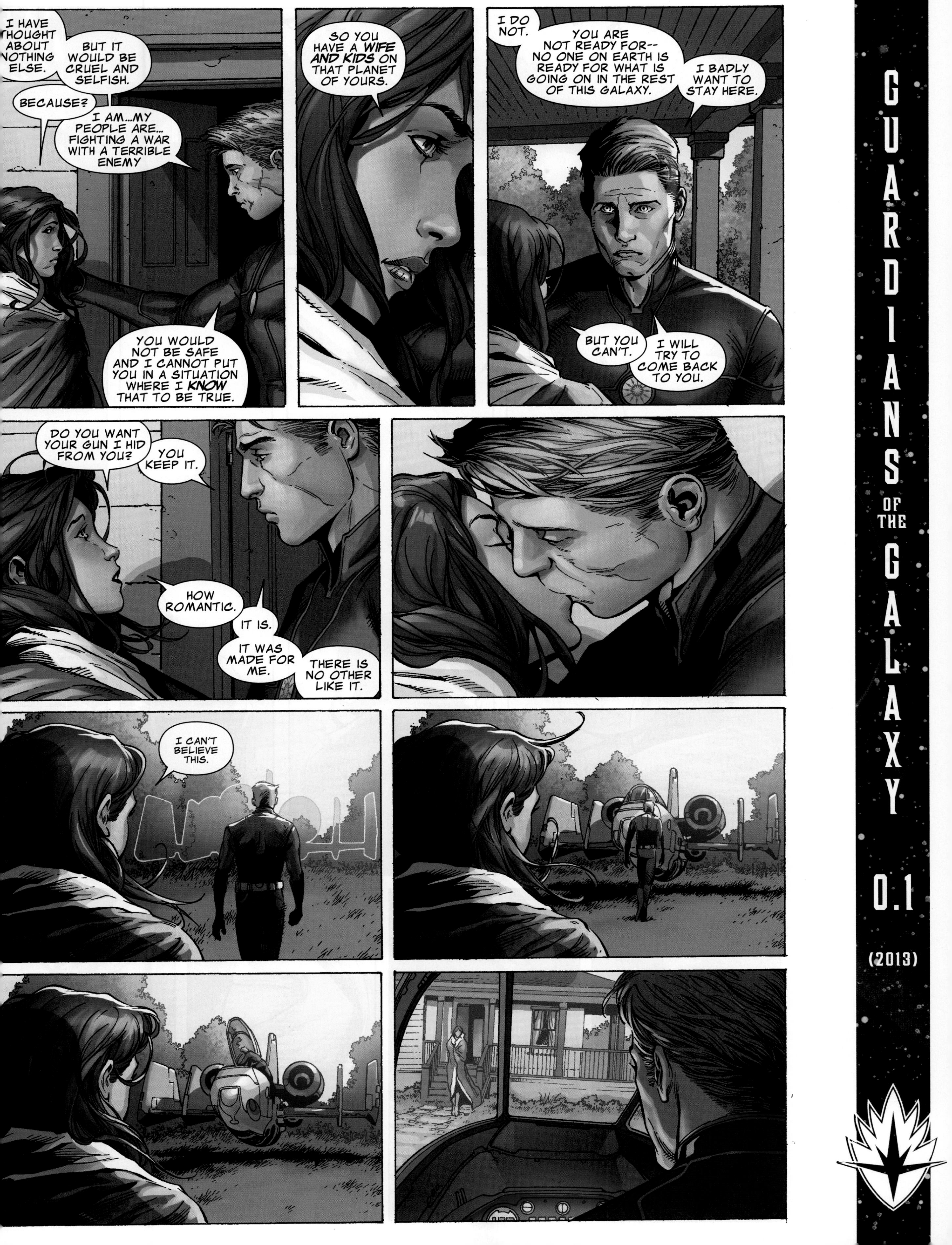

I HAVE THOUGHT ABOUT NOTHING ELSE.
BUT IT WOULD BE CRUEL AND SELFISH.
BECAUSE?
I AM...MY PEOPLE ARE... FIGHTING A WAR WITH A TERRIBLE ENEMY
YOU WOULD NOT BE SAFE AND I CANNOT PUT YOU IN A SITUATION WHERE I KNOW THAT TO BE TRUE.
SO YOU HAVE A WIFE AND KIDS ON THAT PLANET OF YOURS.
I DO NOT.
YOU ARE NOT READY FOR-- NO ONE ON EARTH IS READY FOR WHAT IS GOING ON IN THE REST OF THIS GALAXY.
I BADLY WANT TO STAY HERE.
BUT YOU CAN'T.
I WILL TRY TO COME BACK TO YOU.
DO YOU WANT YOUR GUN I HID FROM YOU?
YOU KEEP IT.
HOW ROMANTIC.
IT IS.
IT WAS MADE FOR ME.
THERE IS NO OTHER LIKE IT.
I CAN'T BELIEVE THIS.
GUARDIANS OF THE GALAXY
0.1
(2013)

GUARDIANS OF THE GALAXY 0.1 (2013)

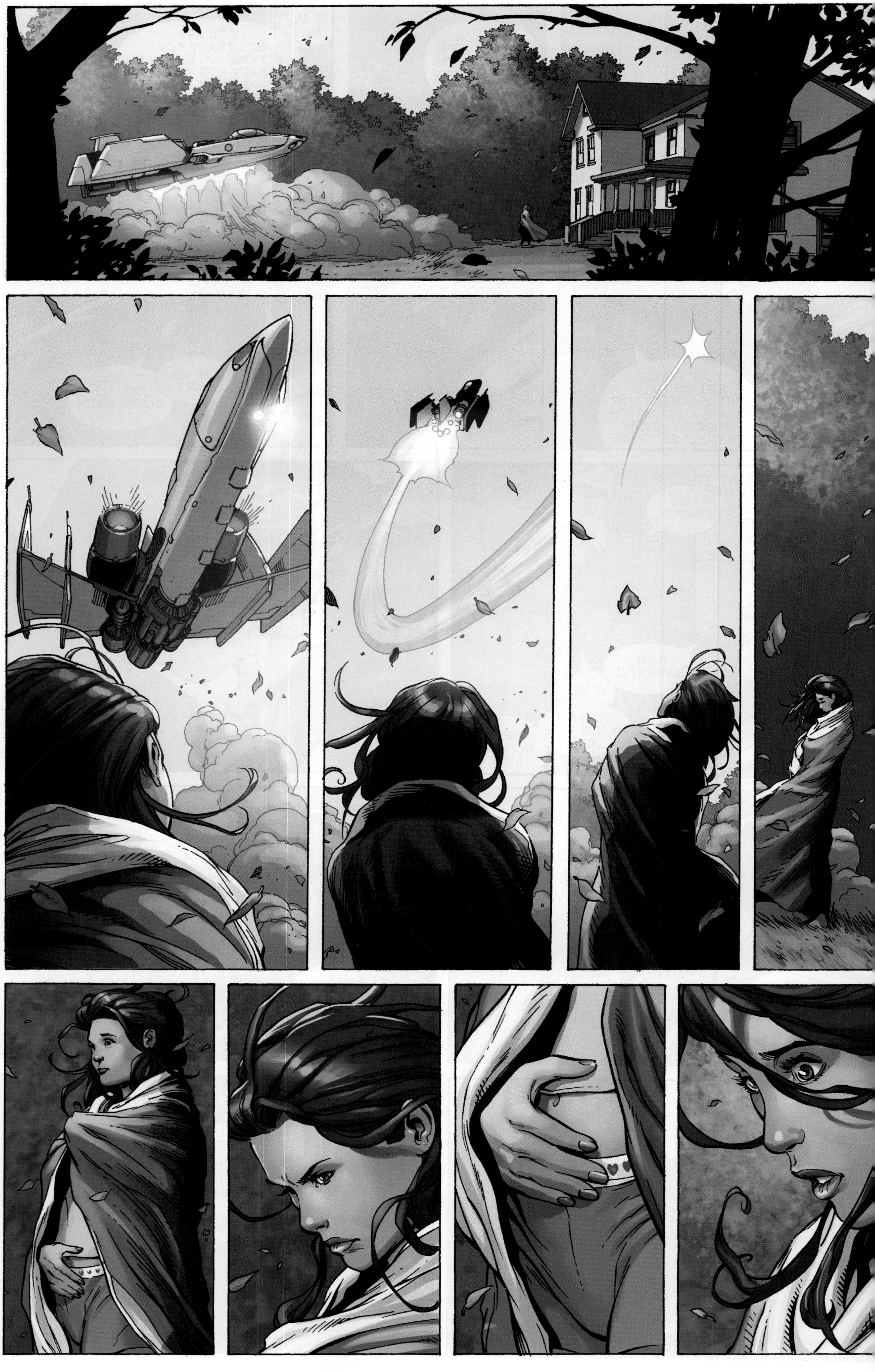

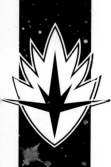

TWENTY YEARS AGO.

PETER QUILL!!

DID YOU DO YOUR MATH HOMEWORK?

I'M TAKIN' A BREAK.

WHAT DID I SAY ABOUT READING THAT CRAP?

IT'S NOT CRAP, MOM. I'M READING. THIS IS READING.

THAT IS NOT READING. YOU SHOULD READ IT. IT'LL BLOW YOUR MIND OUT THROUGH THE TOP OF YOUR HEAD AND THEN IT'LL--

GO FINISH YOUR HOMEWORK.

UGH!!

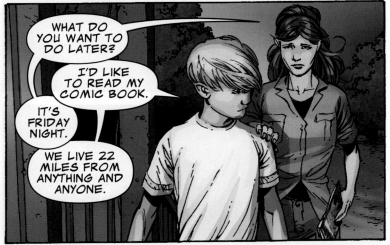

WHAT DO YOU WANT TO DO LATER?

I'D LIKE TO READ MY COMIC BOOK.

IT'S FRIDAY NIGHT.

WE LIVE 22 MILES FROM ANYTHING AND ANYONE.

WOW.

WHAT?

YOU LOOK JUST LIKE YOUR FATHER, ALL OF A SUDDEN.

GUARDIANS OF THE GALAXY 0.1 (2013)

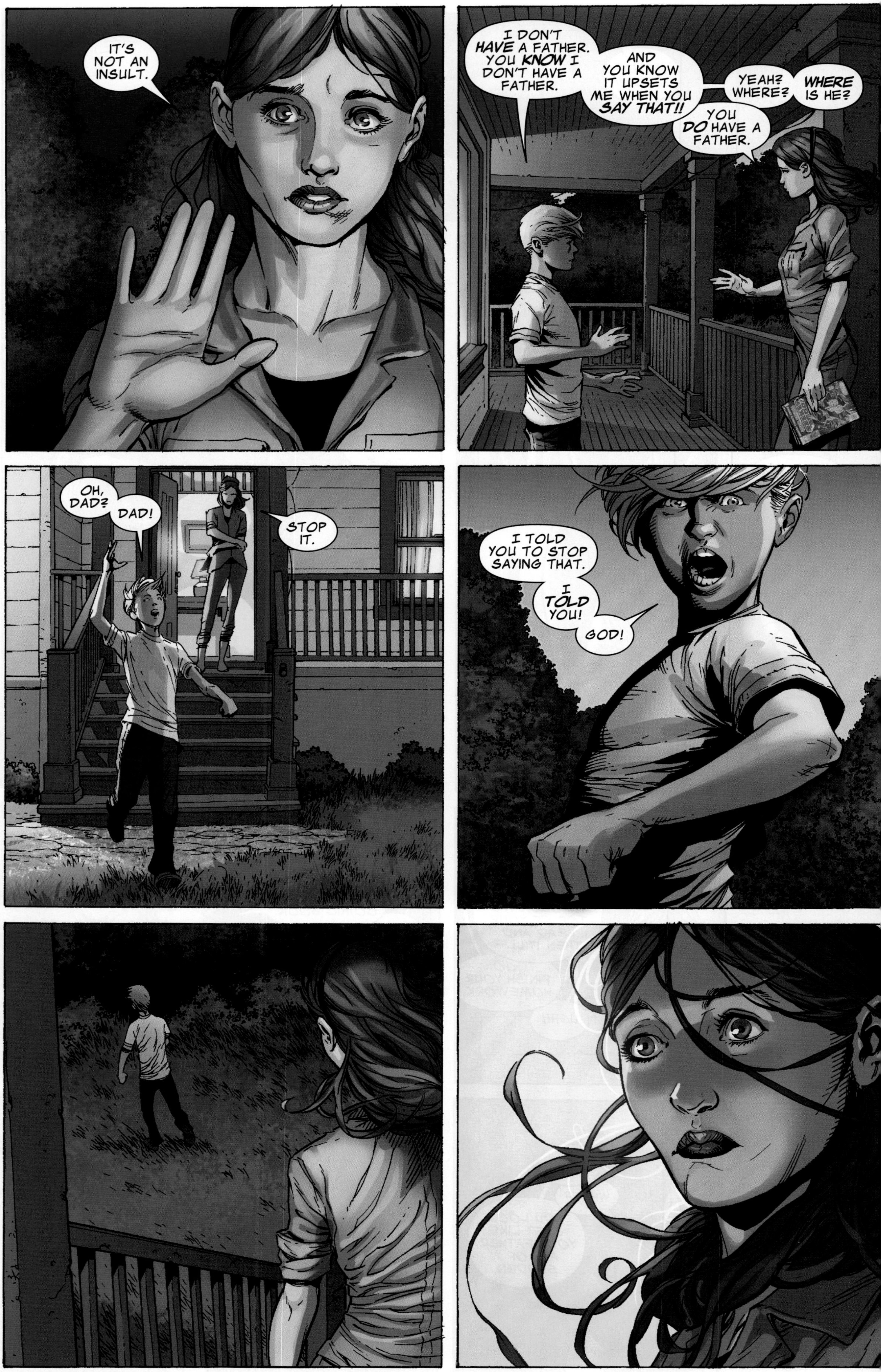

IT'S NOT AN INSULT.
I DON'T HAVE A FATHER. YOU KNOW I DON'T HAVE A FATHER.
AND YOU KNOW IT UPSETS ME WHEN YOU SAY THAT!!
YOU DO HAVE A FATHER.
YEAH? WHERE?
WHERE IS HE?
OH, DAD?
DAD!
STOP IT.
I TOLD YOU TO STOP SAYING THAT.
I TOLD YOU!
GOD!

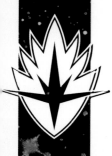

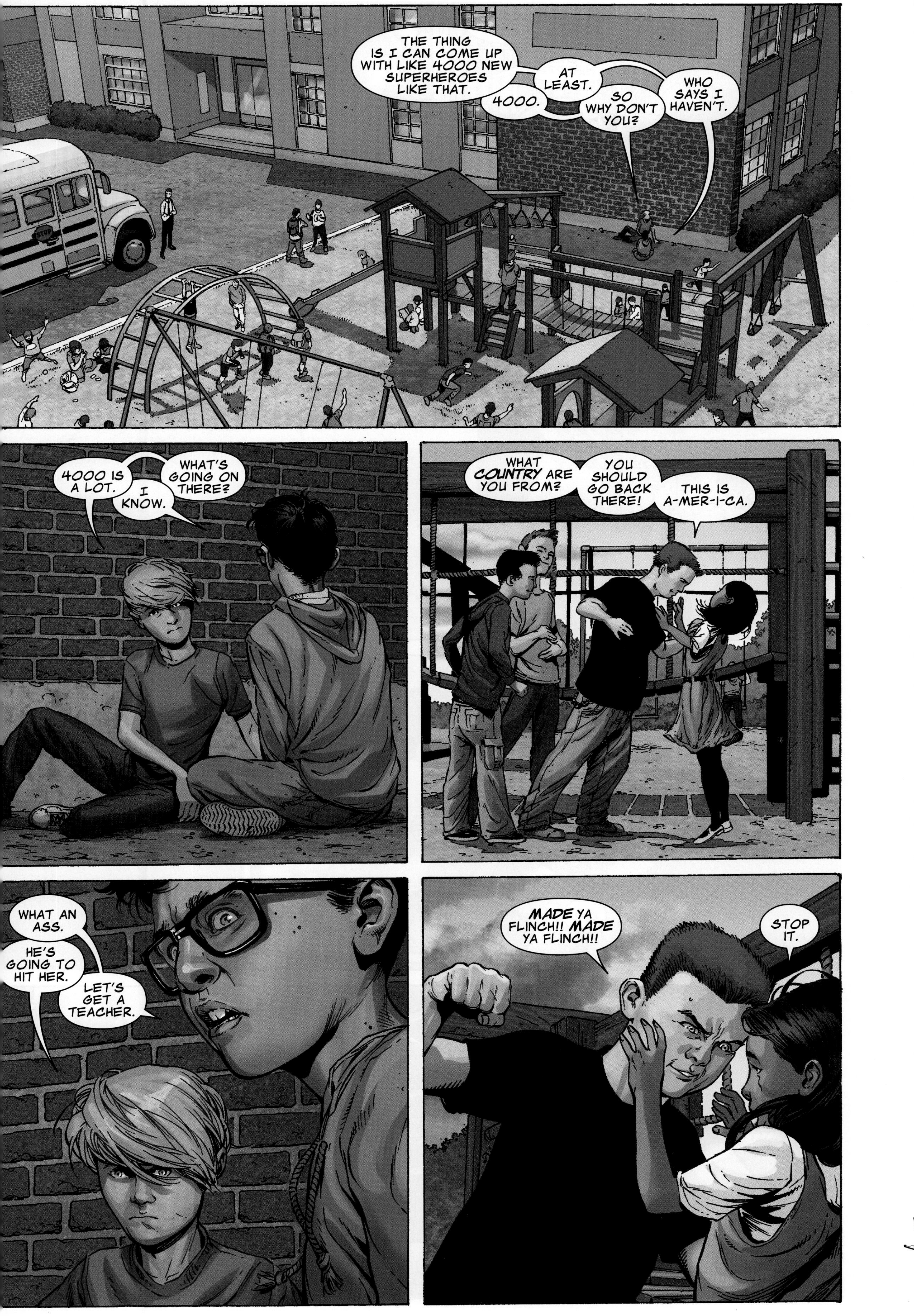

THE THING IS I CAN COME UP WITH LIKE 4000 NEW SUPERHEROES LIKE THAT.
4000.
AT LEAST.
SO WHY DON'T YOU?
WHO SAYS I HAVEN'T.
4000 IS A LOT.
I KNOW.
WHAT'S GOING ON THERE?
WHAT COUNTRY ARE YOU FROM?
YOU SHOULD GO BACK THERE!
THIS IS A-MER-I-CA.
WHAT AN ASS.
HE'S GOING TO HIT HER.
LET'S GET A TEACHER.
MADE YA FLINCH!! MADE YA FLINCH!!
STOP IT.

GUARDIANS OF THE GALAXY 0.1 (2013)

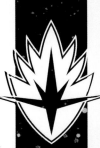

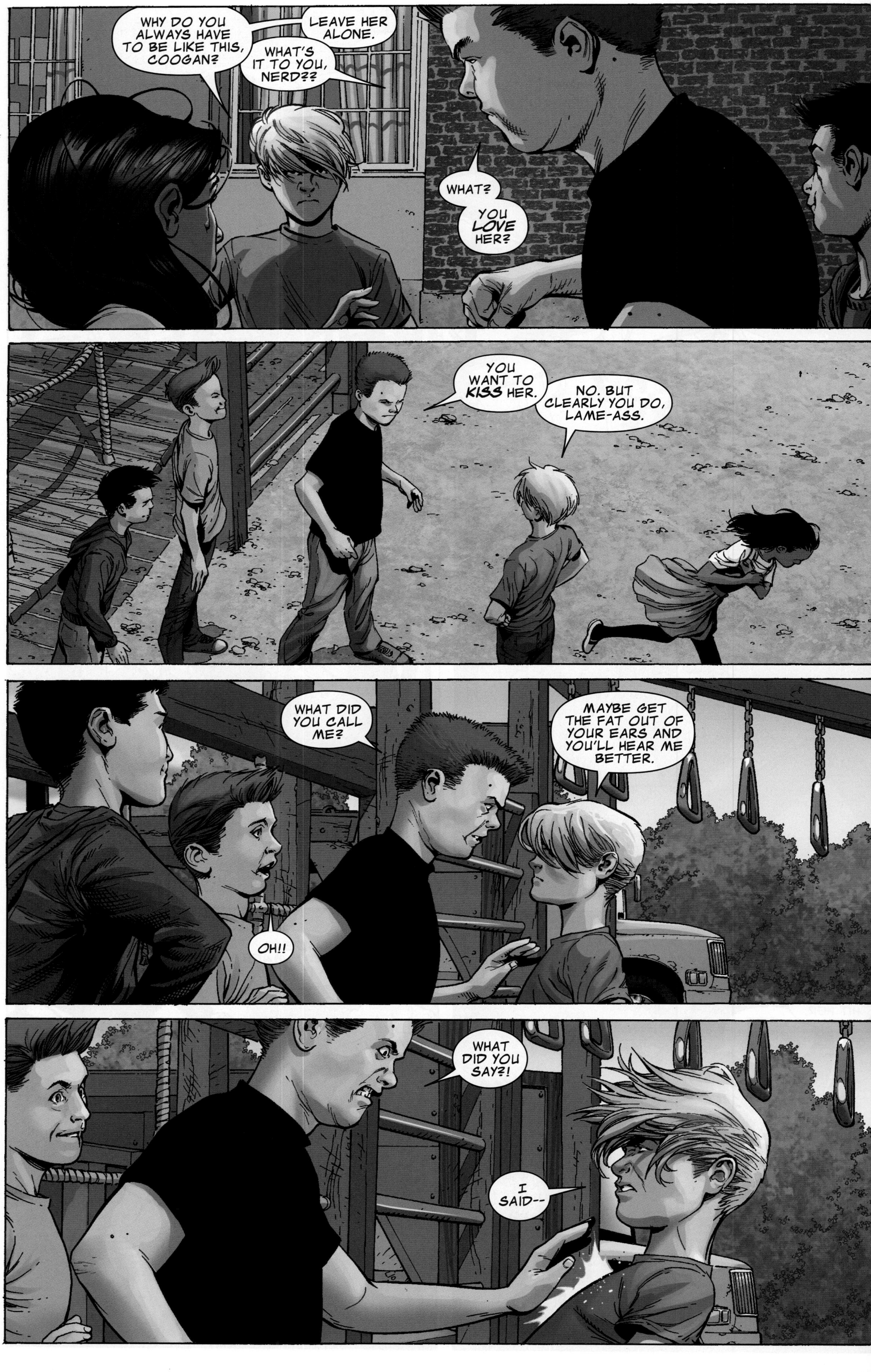

WHY DO YOU ALWAYS HAVE TO BE LIKE THIS, COOGAN?
LEAVE HER ALONE.
WHAT'S IT TO YOU, NERD??
WHAT?
YOU LOVE HER?
YOU WANT TO KISS HER.
NO. BUT CLEARLY YOU DO, LAME-ASS.
WHAT DID YOU CALL ME?
MAYBE GET THE FAT OUT OF YOUR EARS AND YOU'LL HEAR ME BETTER.
OH!!
WHAT DID YOU SAY?!
I SAID--

GUARDIANS OF THE GALAXY 0.1 (2013)

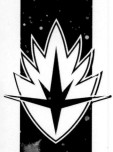

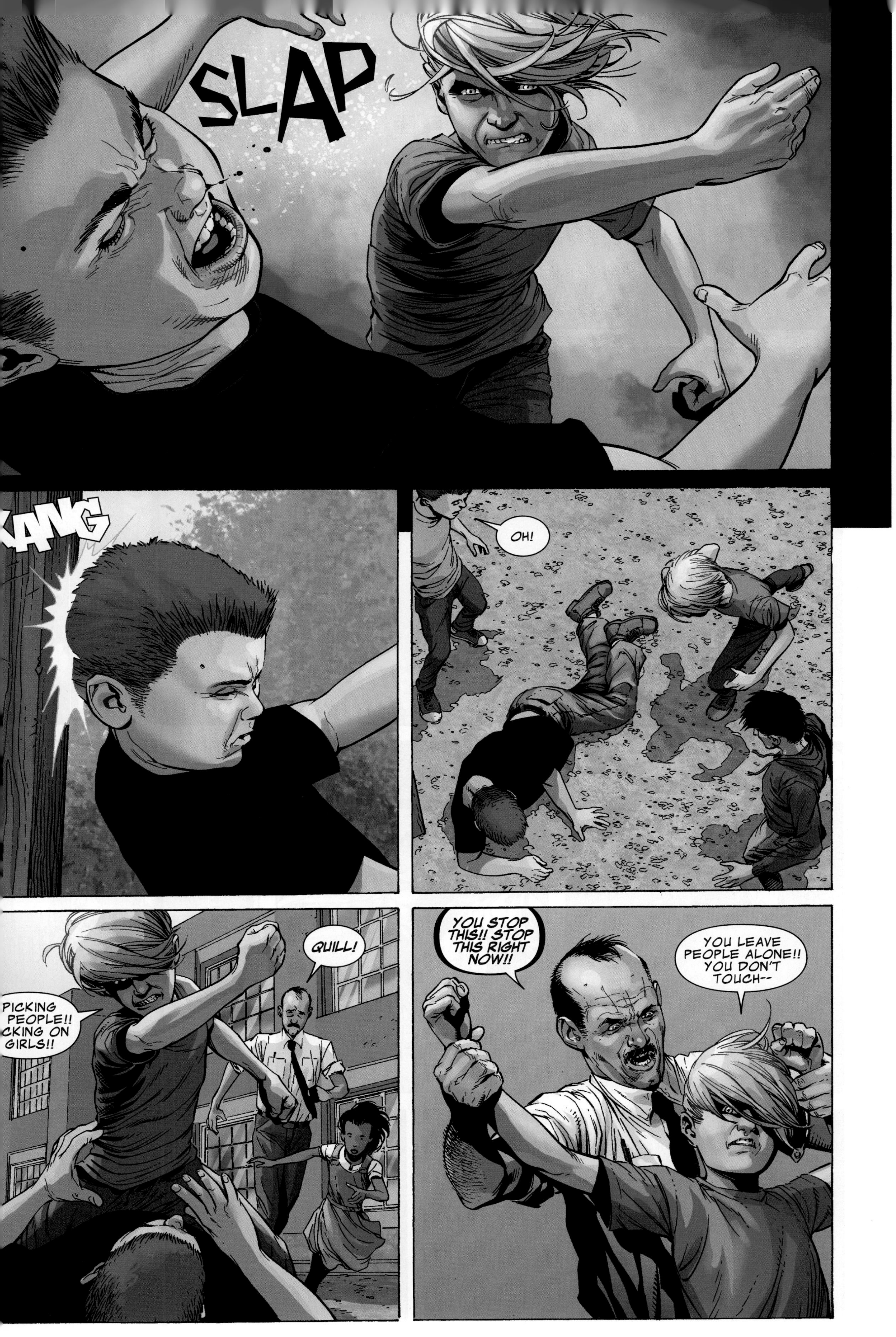
SLAP
KANG
OH!
PICKING PEOPLE!! ...CKING ON GIRLS!!
QUILL!
YOU STOP THIS!! STOP THIS RIGHT NOW!!
YOU LEAVE PEOPLE ALONE!! YOU DON'T TOUCH--

GUARDIANS OF THE GALAXY 0.1 (2013)

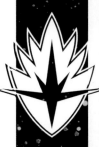

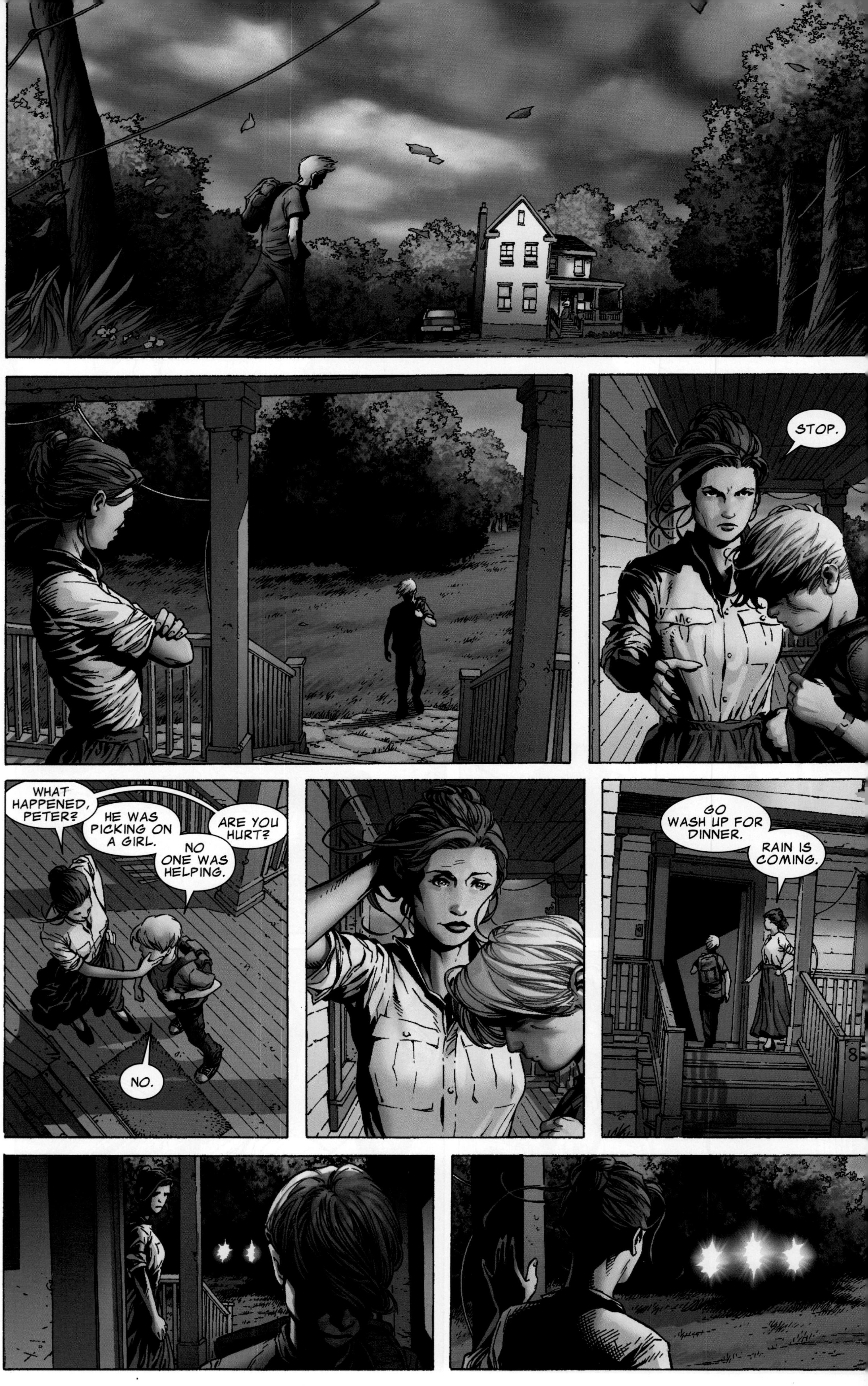

STOP.
WHAT HAPPENED, PETER?
HE WAS PICKING ON A GIRL.
NO ONE WAS HELPING.
ARE YOU HURT?
NO.
GO WASH UP FOR DINNER.
RAIN IS COMING.

GUARDIANS OF THE GALAXY 0.1 (2013)

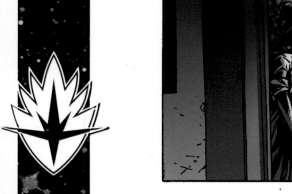

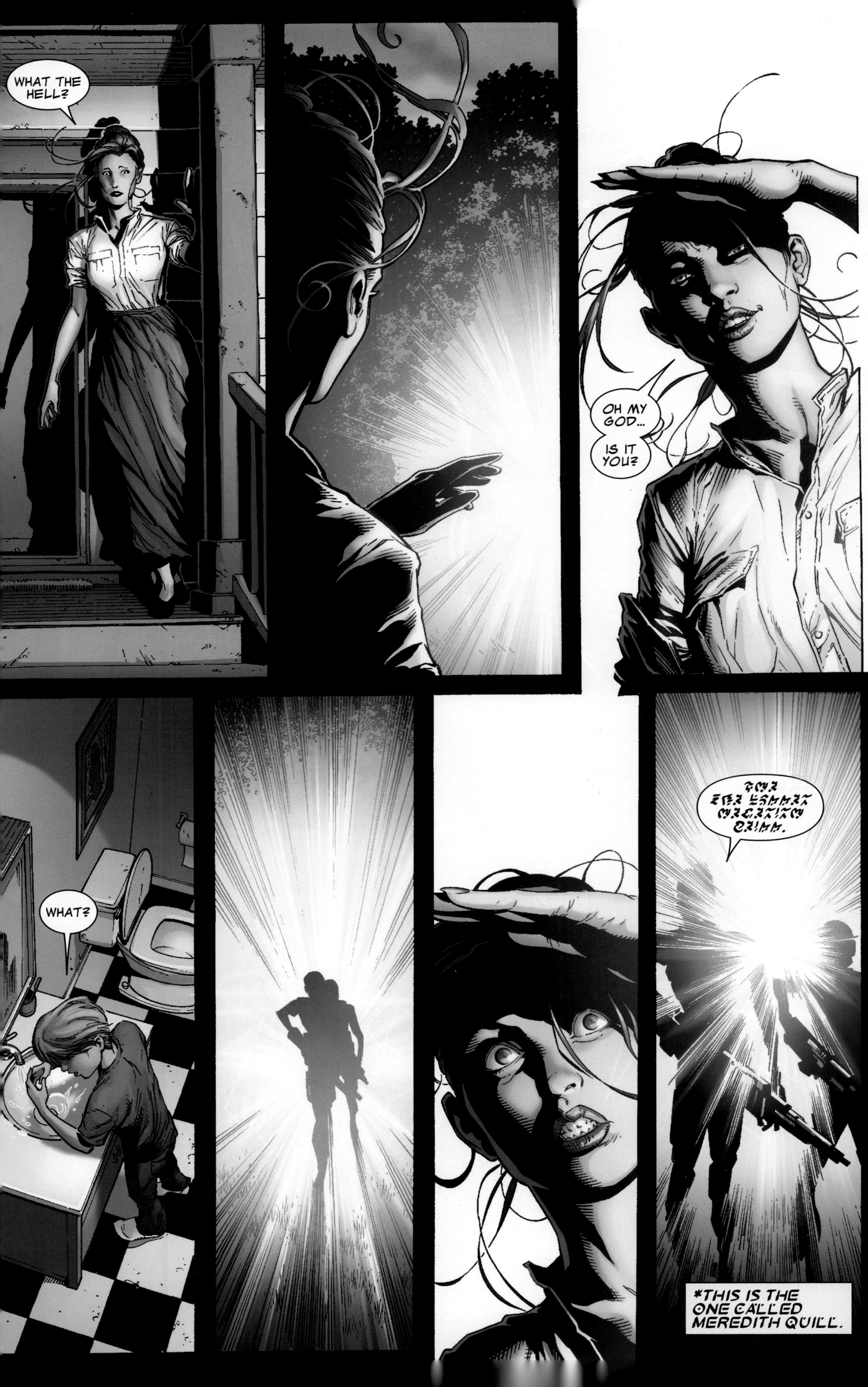
WHAT THE HELL?
OH MY GOD... IS IT YOU?
WHAT?
*THIS IS THE ONE CALLED MEREDITH QUILL.

GUARDIANS OF THE GALAXY 0.1 (2013)

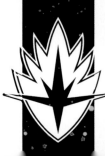

GUARDIANS OF THE GALAXY 0.1 (2013)

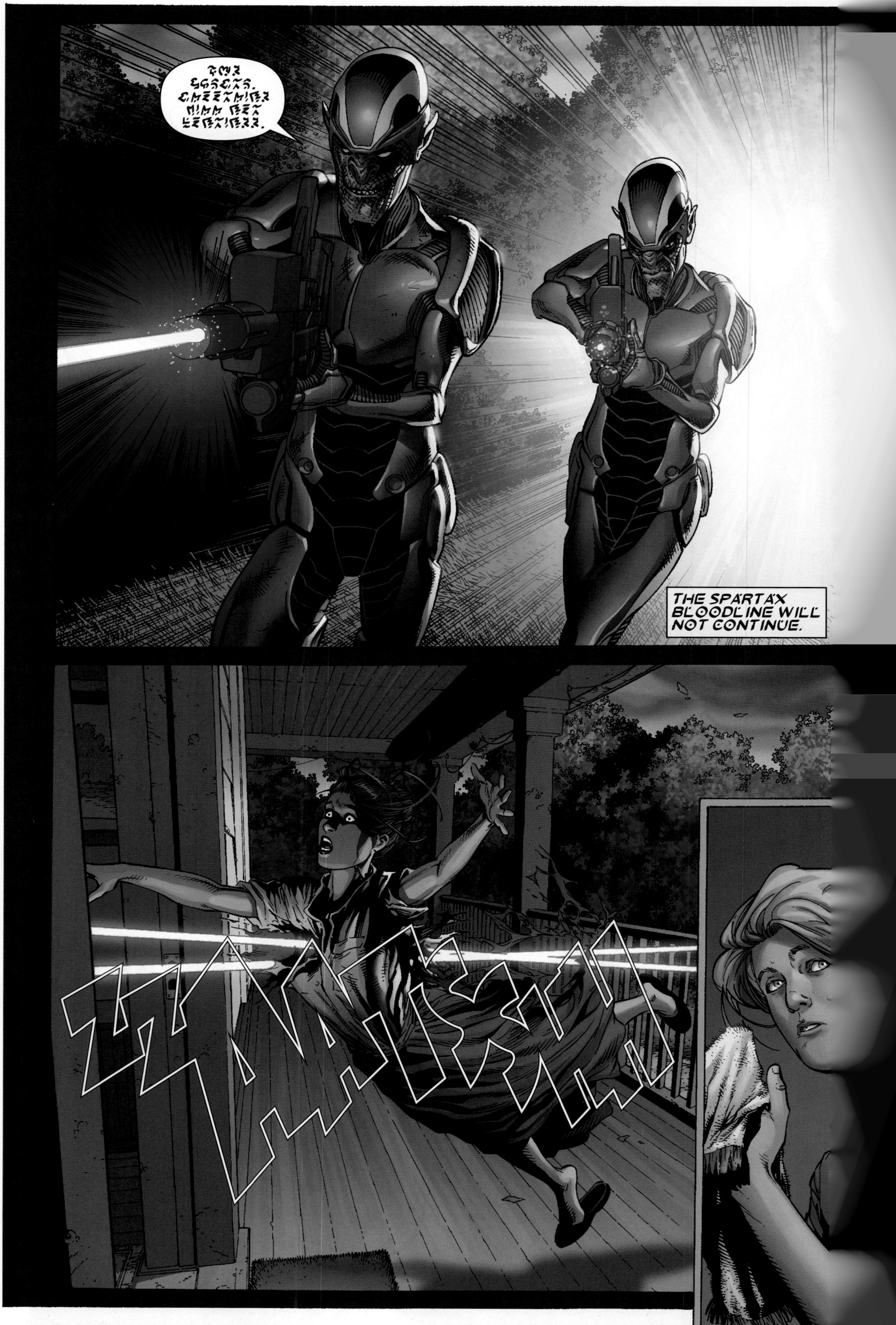

THE SPARTAX BLOODLINE WILL NOT CONTINUE.

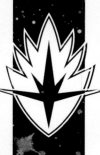

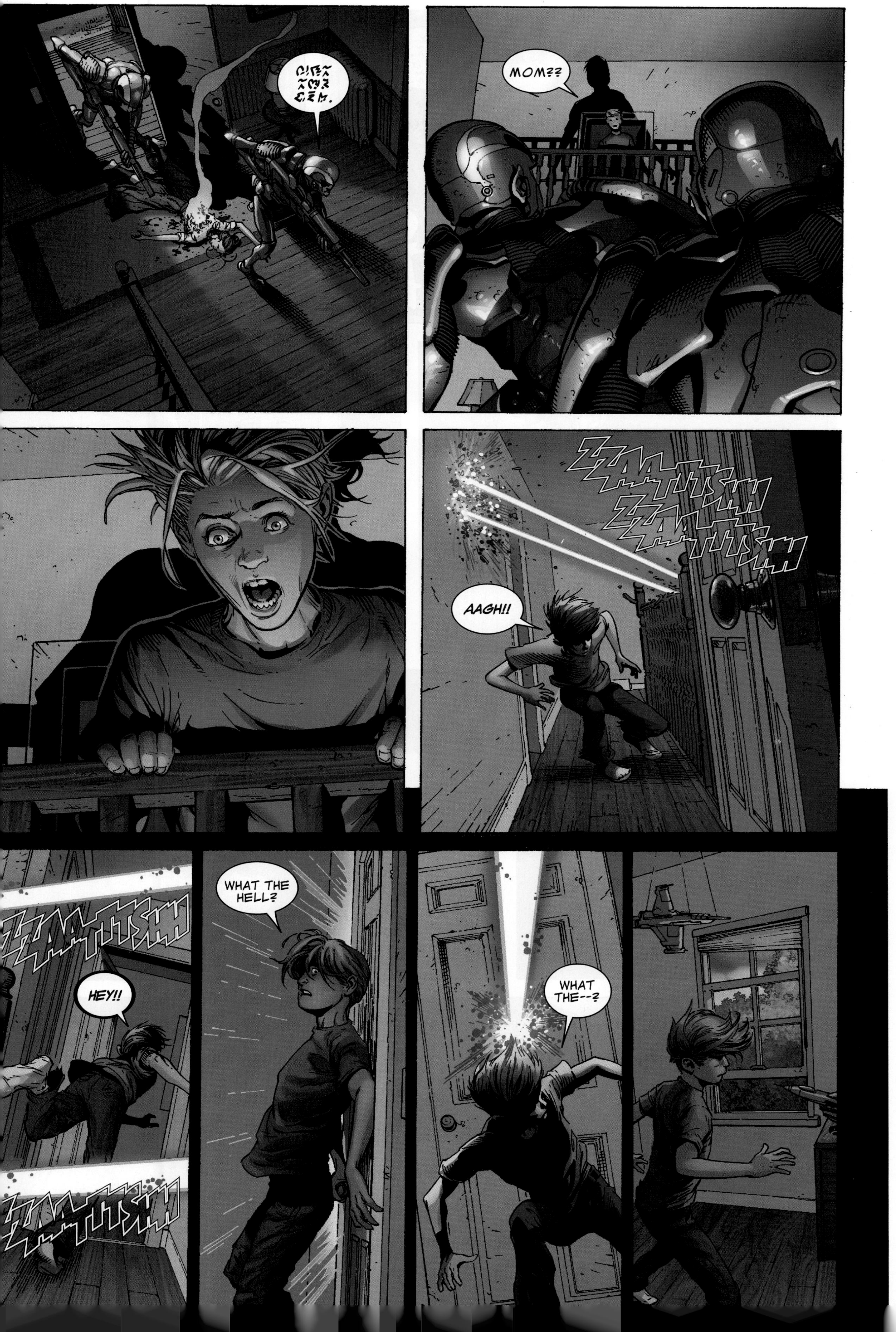
MOM??
AAGH!!
ZZAATTTSHH
ZZAATTTSHH
ZZAATTTSHH
HEY!!
ZZAATTTSHH
WHAT THE HELL?
WHAT THE--?

GUARDIANS OF THE GALAXY 0.1 (2013)

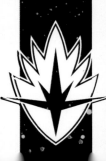

GUARDIANS OF THE GALAXY 0.1 (2013)

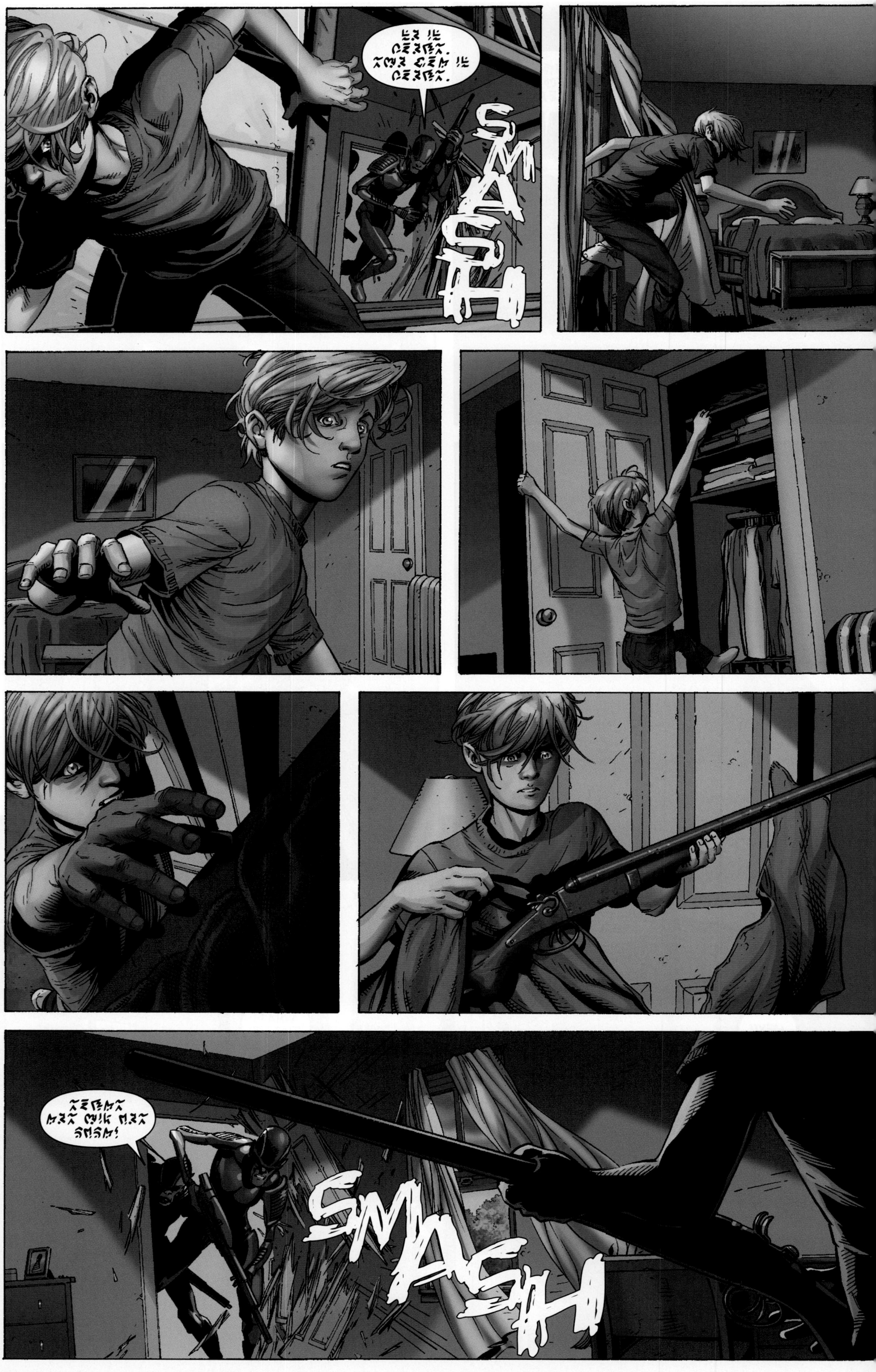
SMASH
SMASH

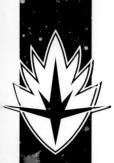

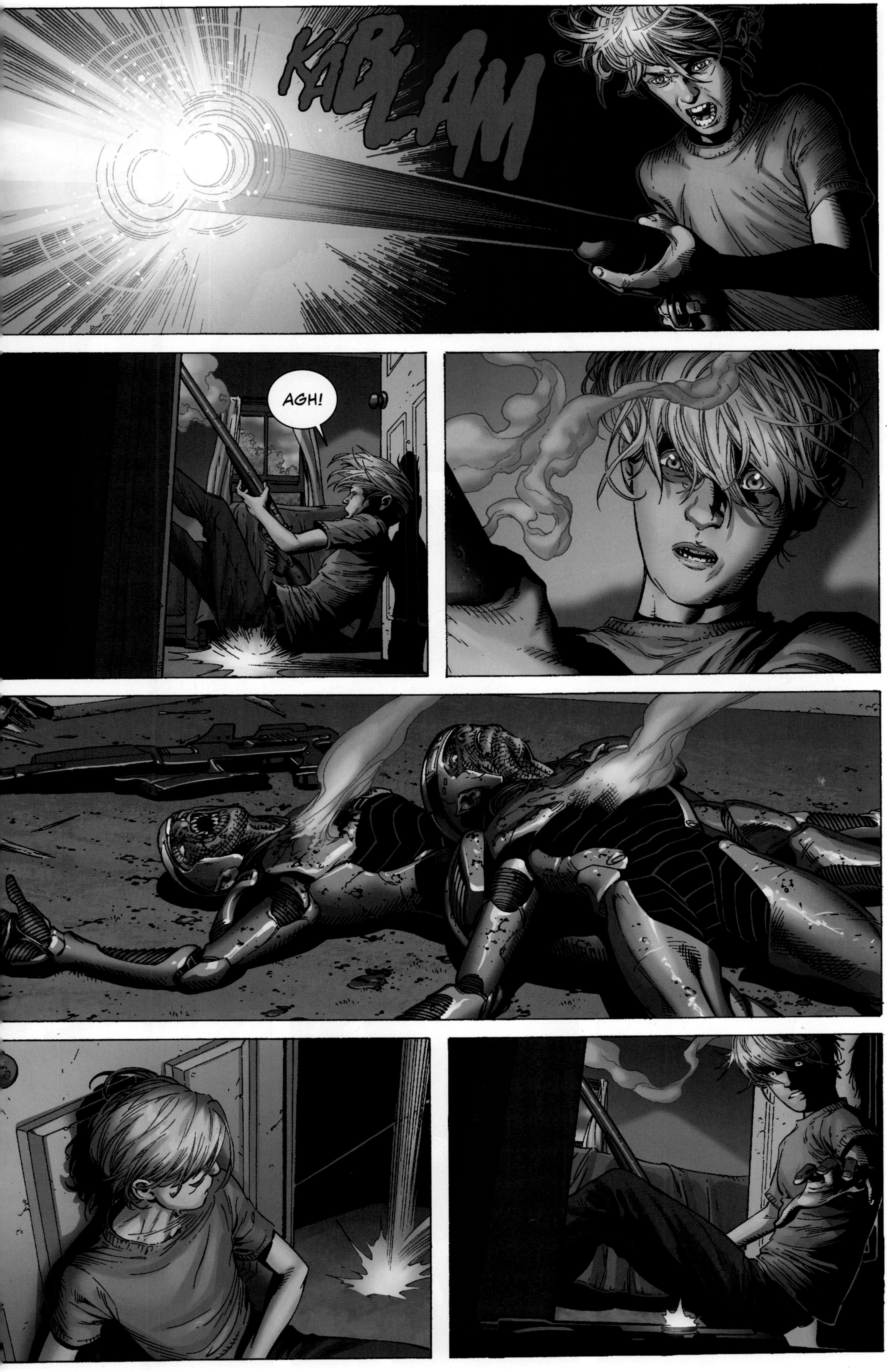
KABLAM
AGH!

GUARDIANS OF THE GALAXY 0.1 (2013)

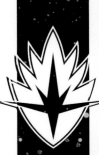

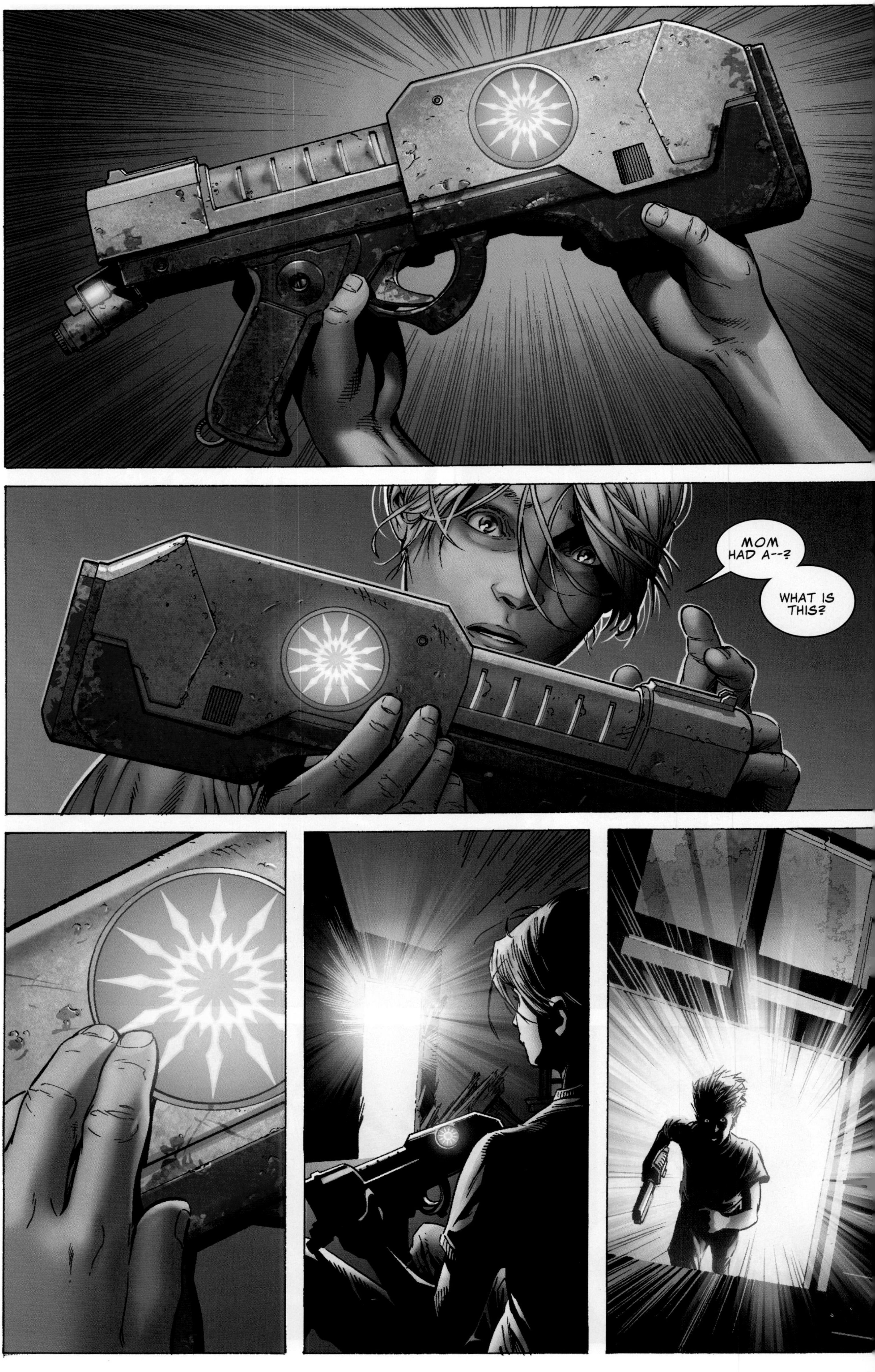

MOM HAD A--?
WHAT IS THIS?

GUARDIANS OF THE GALAXY 0.1 (2013)

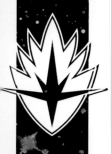

MOM!!

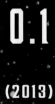

GUARDIANS OF THE GALAXY 0.1 (2013)

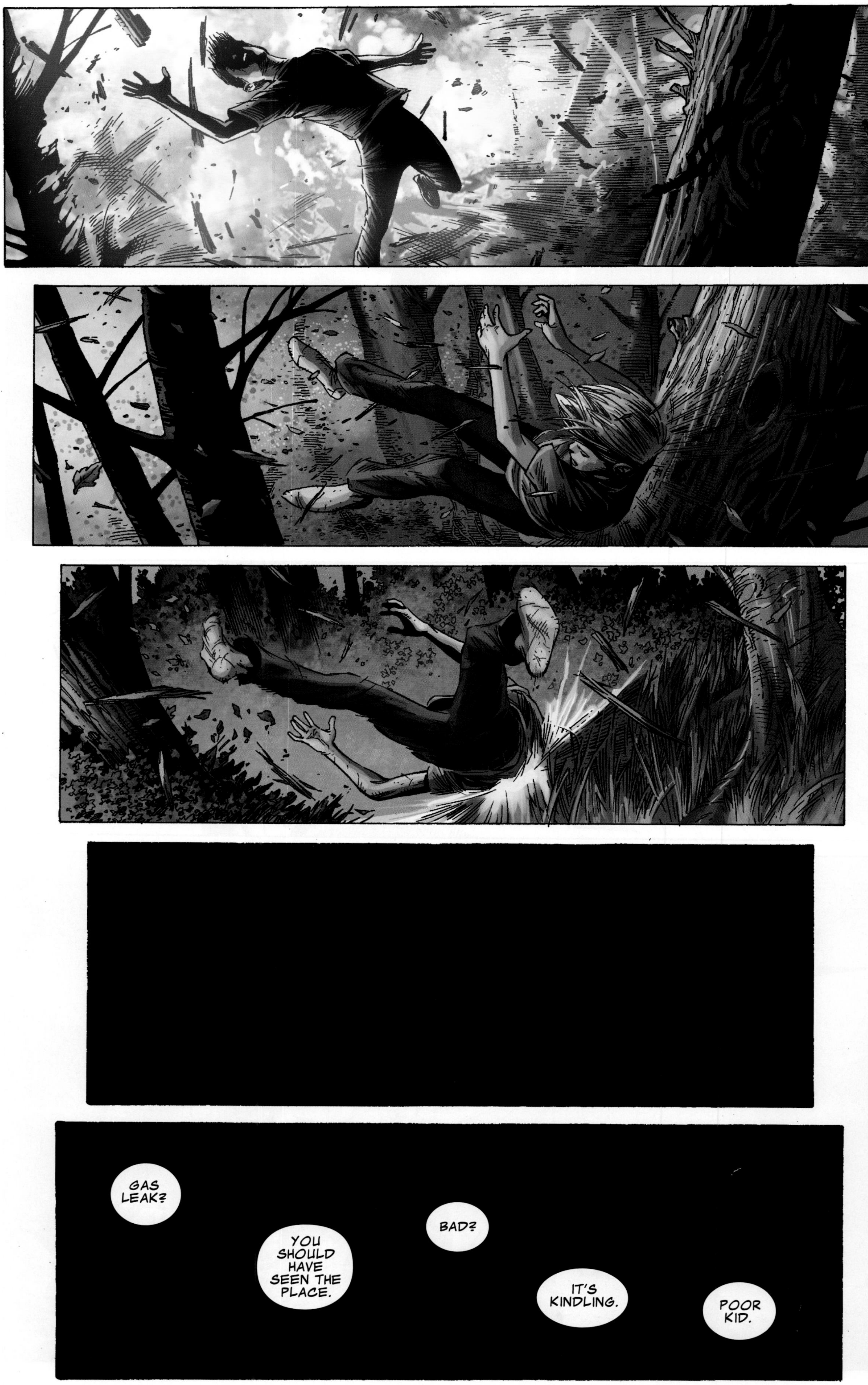
GAS LEAK?
YOU SHOULD HAVE SEEN THE PLACE.
BAD?
IT'S KINDLING.
POOR KID.

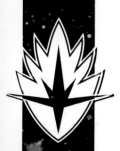

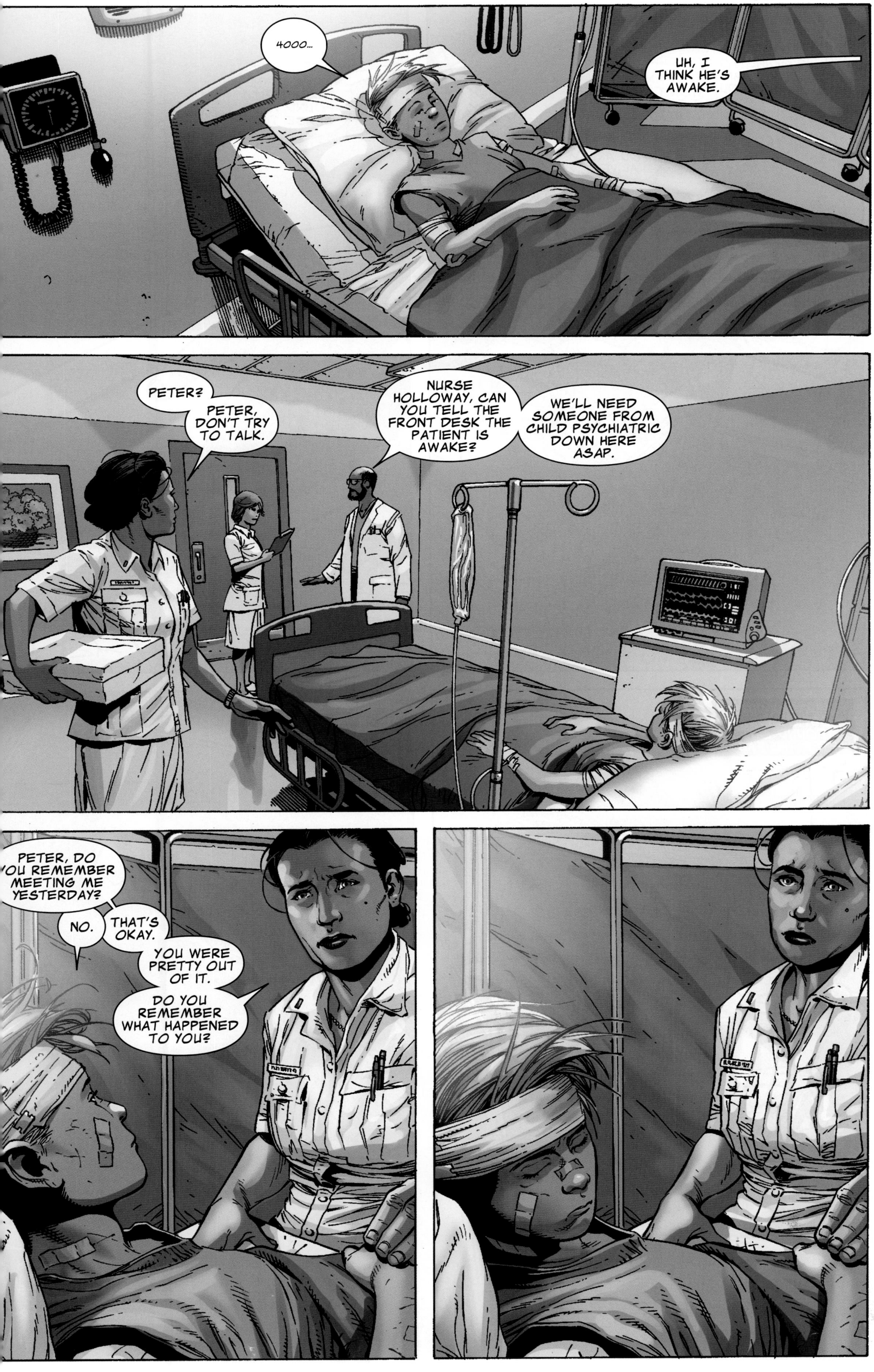
4000...
UH, I THINK HE'S AWAKE.
PETER?
PETER, DON'T TRY TO TALK.
NURSE HOLLOWAY, CAN YOU TELL THE FRONT DESK THE PATIENT IS AWAKE?
WE'LL NEED SOMEONE FROM CHILD PSYCHIATRIC DOWN HERE ASAP.
PETER, DO YOU REMEMBER MEETING ME YESTERDAY?
NO.
THAT'S OKAY.
YOU WERE PRETTY OUT OF IT.
DO YOU REMEMBER WHAT HAPPENED TO YOU?

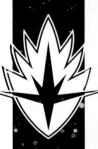

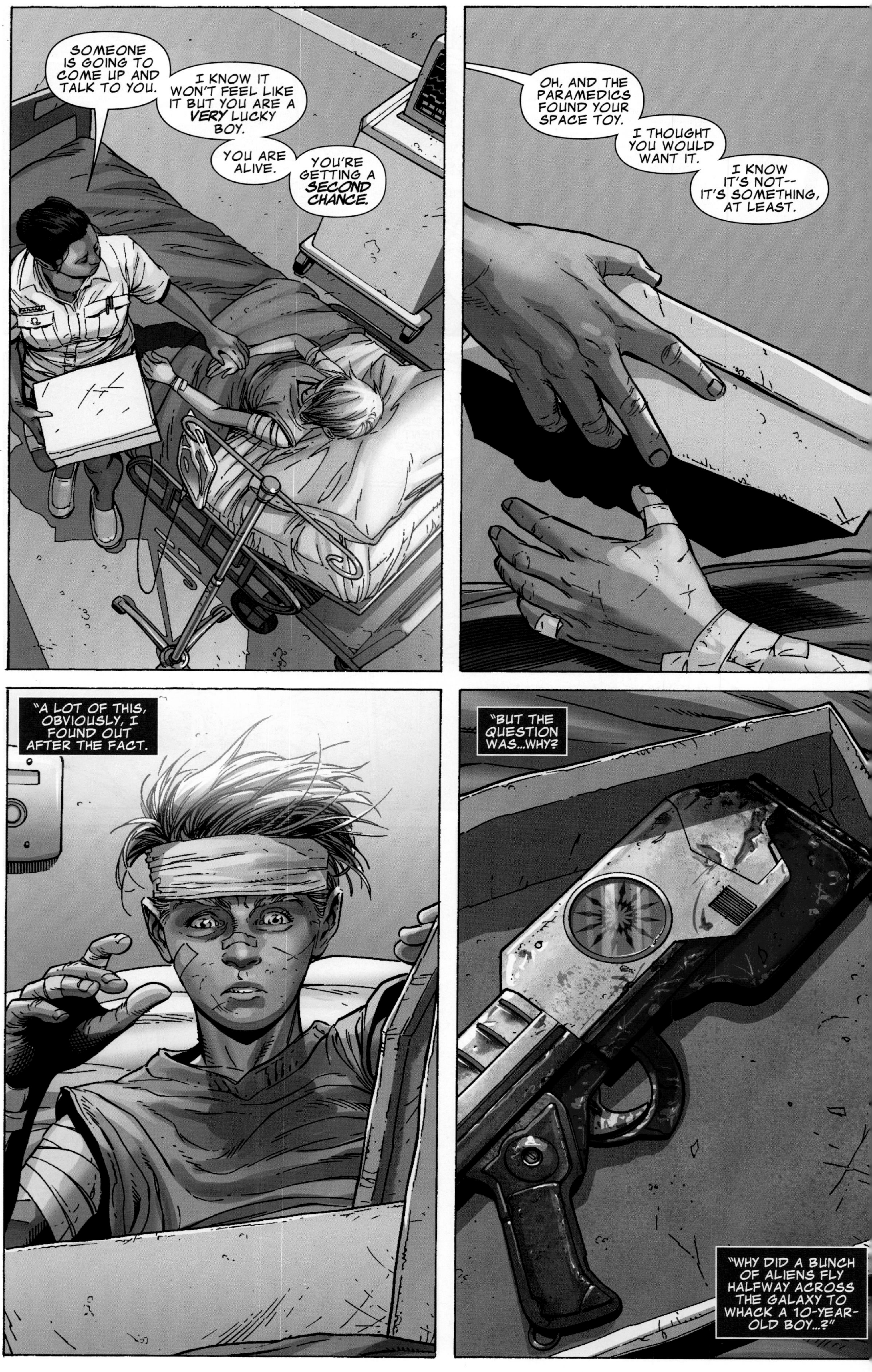
SOMEONE IS GOING TO COME UP AND TALK TO YOU.
I KNOW IT WON'T FEEL LIKE IT BUT YOU ARE A VERY LUCKY BOY.
YOU ARE ALIVE.
YOU'RE GETTING A SECOND CHANCE.
OH, AND THE PARAMEDICS FOUND YOUR SPACE TOY.
I THOUGHT YOU WOULD WANT IT.
I KNOW IT'S NOT-- IT'S SOMETHING, AT LEAST.
"A LOT OF THIS, OBVIOUSLY, I FOUND OUT AFTER THE FACT.
"BUT THE QUESTION WAS...WHY?
"WHY DID A BUNCH OF ALIENS FLY HALFWAY ACROSS THE GALAXY TO WHACK A 10-YEAR-OLD BOY...?"

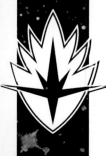

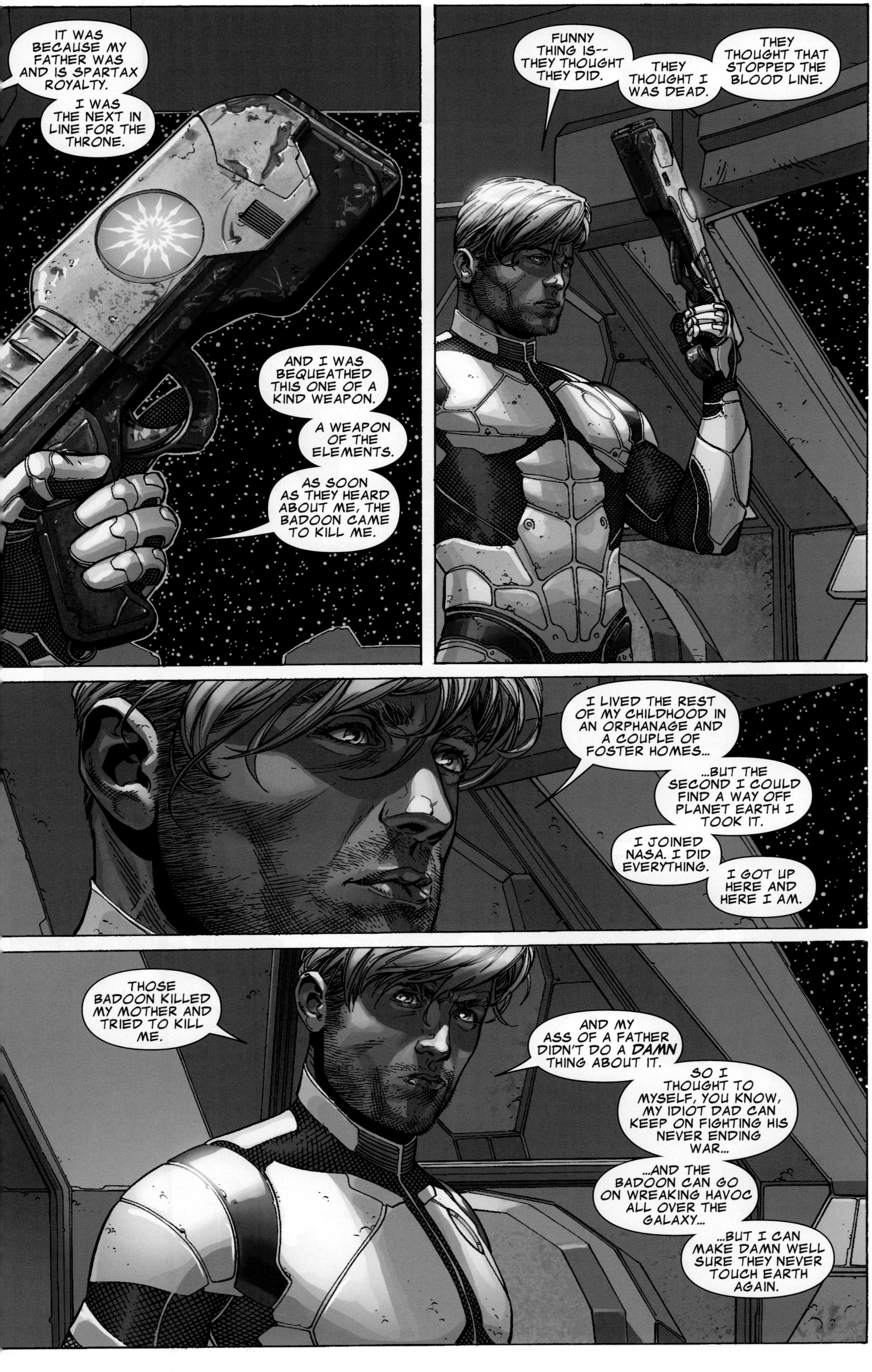
IT WAS BECAUSE MY FATHER WAS AND IS SPARTAX ROYALTY.
I WAS THE NEXT IN LINE FOR THE THRONE.
AND I WAS BEQUEATHED THIS ONE OF A KIND WEAPON.
A WEAPON OF THE ELEMENTS.
AS SOON AS THEY HEARD ABOUT ME, THE BADOON CAME TO KILL ME.
FUNNY THING IS-- THEY THOUGHT THEY DID.
THEY THOUGHT I WAS DEAD.
THEY THOUGHT THAT STOPPED THE BLOOD LINE.
I LIVED THE REST OF MY CHILDHOOD IN AN ORPHANAGE AND A COUPLE OF FOSTER HOMES...
...BUT THE SECOND I COULD FIND A WAY OFF PLANET EARTH I TOOK IT.
I JOINED NASA. I DID EVERYTHING.
I GOT UP HERE AND HERE I AM.
THOSE BADOON KILLED MY MOTHER AND TRIED TO KILL ME.
AND MY ASS OF A FATHER DIDN'T DO A *DAMN* THING ABOUT IT.
SO I THOUGHT TO MYSELF, YOU KNOW, MY IDIOT DAD CAN KEEP ON FIGHTING HIS NEVER ENDING WAR...
...AND THE BADOON CAN GO ON WREAKING HAVOC ALL OVER THE GALAXY...
...BUT I CAN MAKE DAMN WELL SURE THEY NEVER TOUCH EARTH AGAIN.

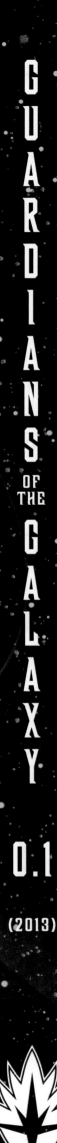

GUARDIANS OF THE GALAXY 0.1 (2013)

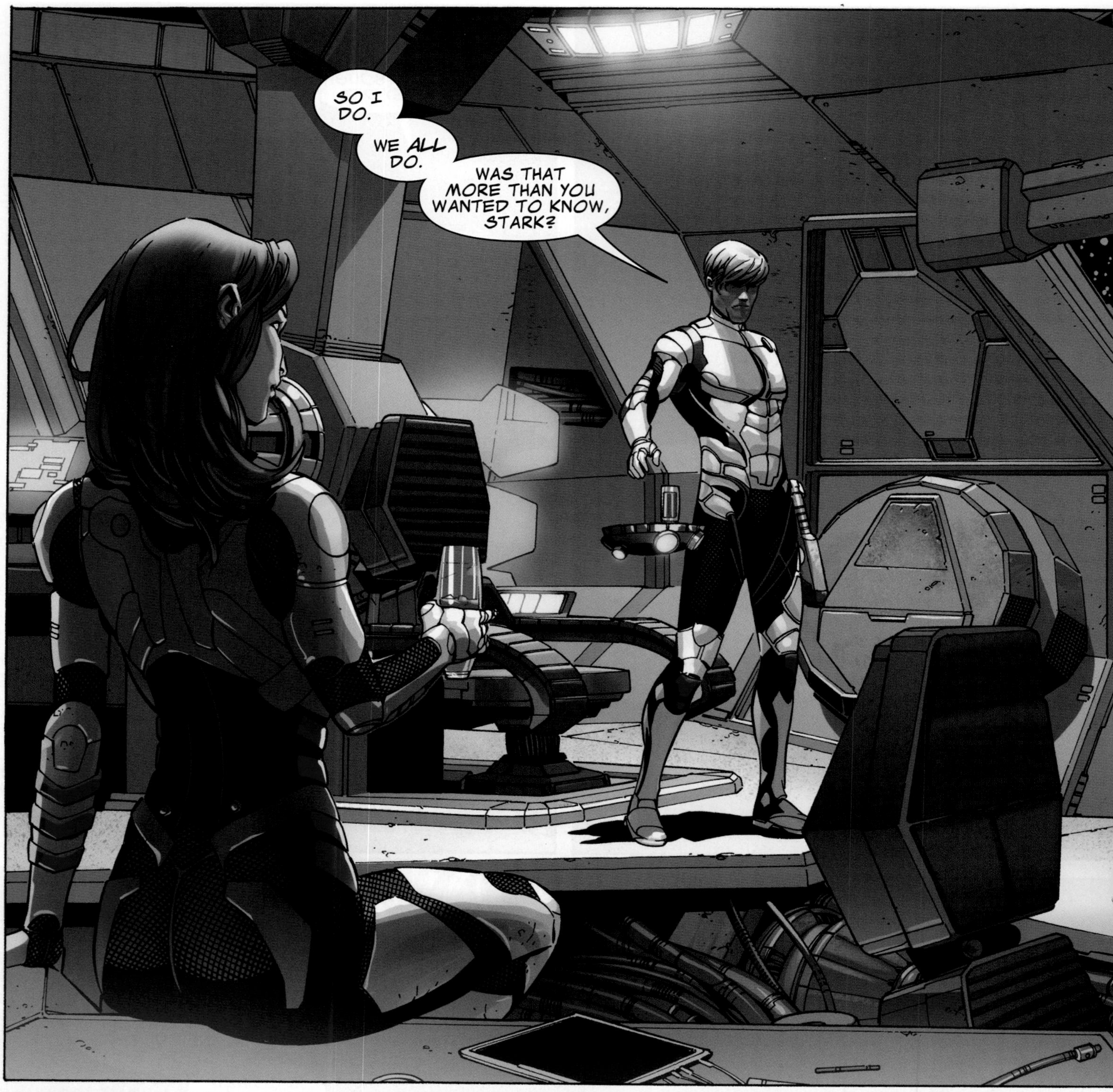
SO I DO.
WE ALL DO.
WAS THAT MORE THAN YOU WANTED TO KNOW, STARK?

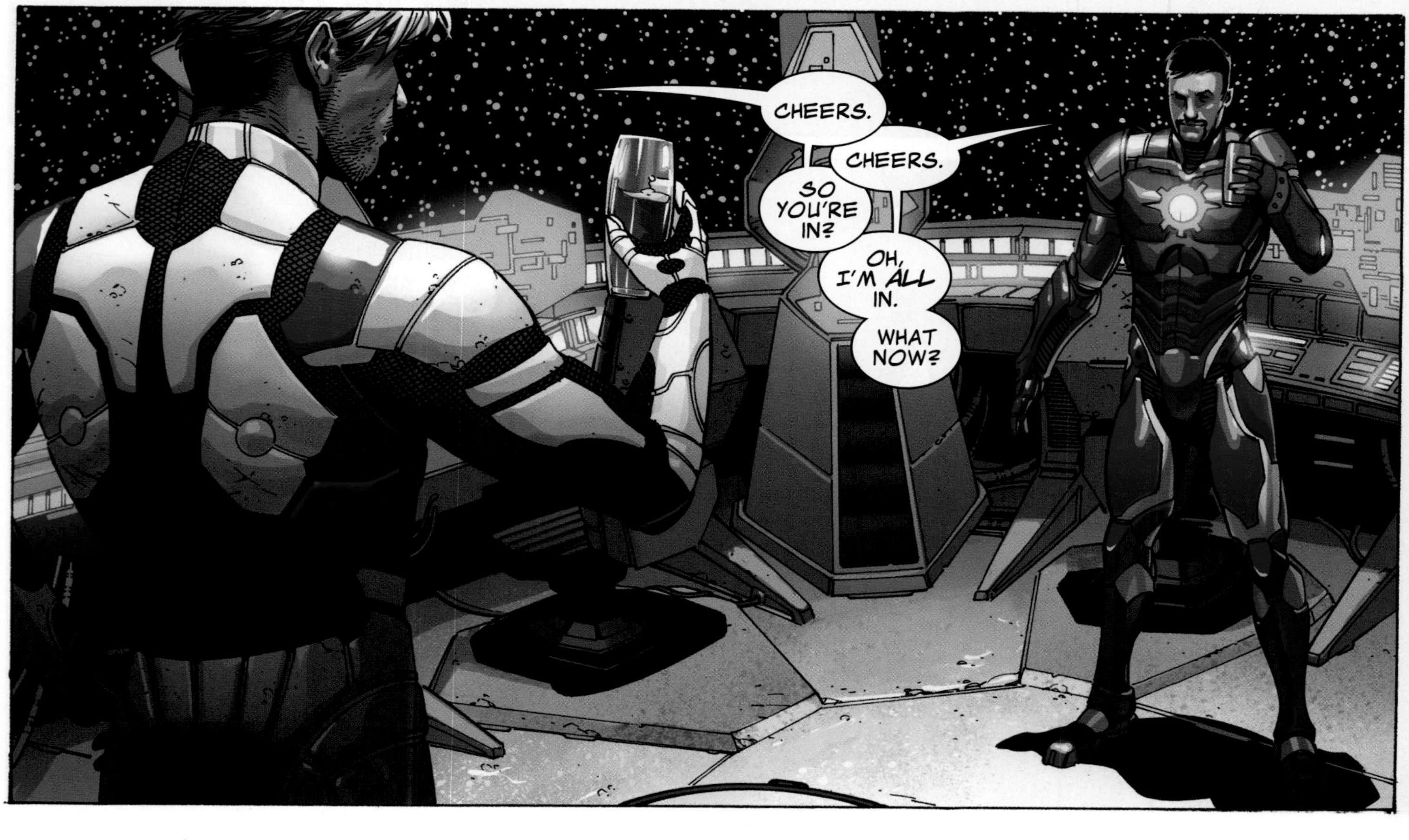
CHEERS.
CHEERS.
SO YOU'RE IN?
OH, I'M ALL IN.
WHAT NOW?

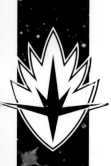

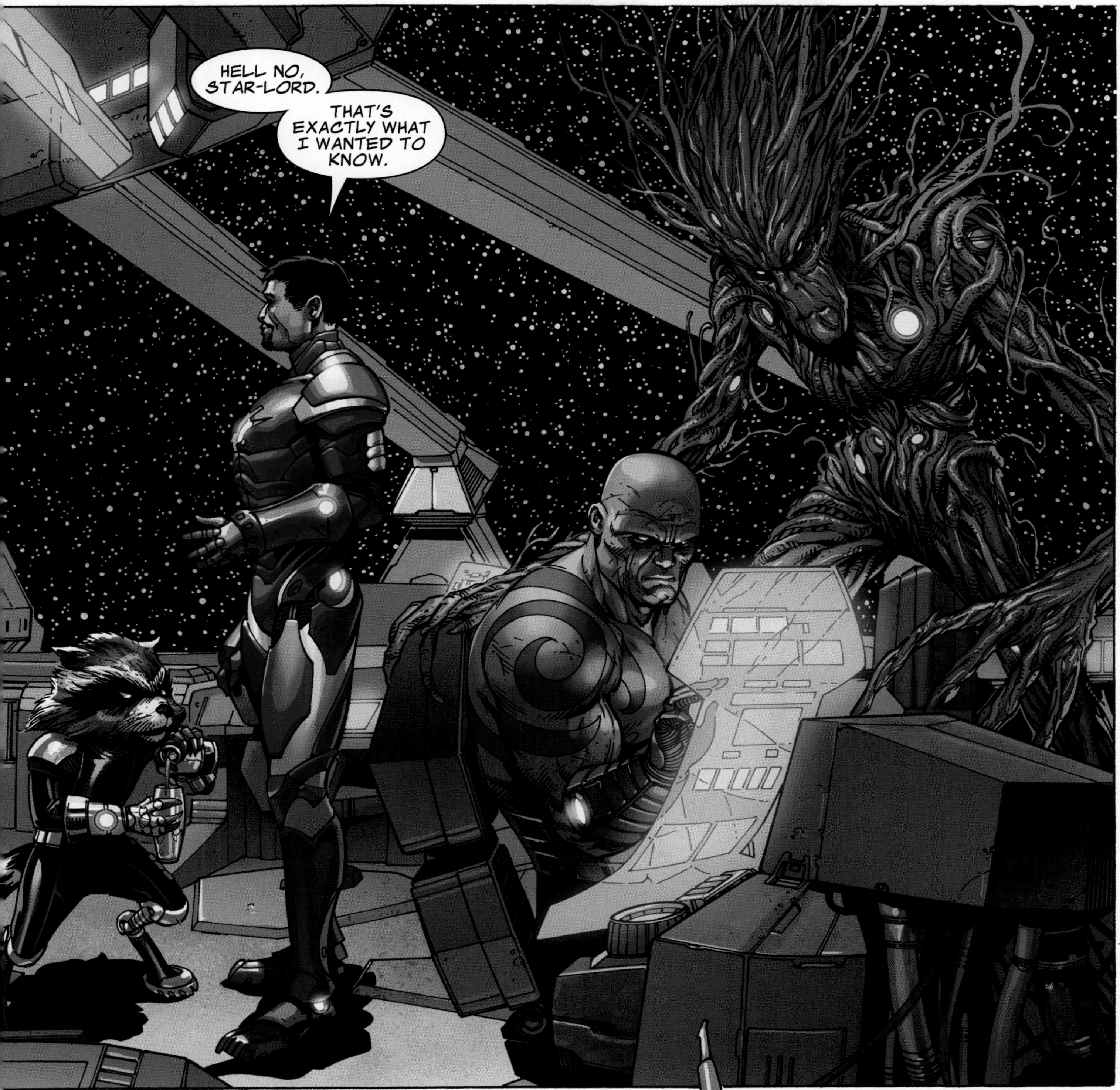
HELL NO, STAR-LORD.
THAT'S EXACTLY WHAT I WANTED TO KNOW.

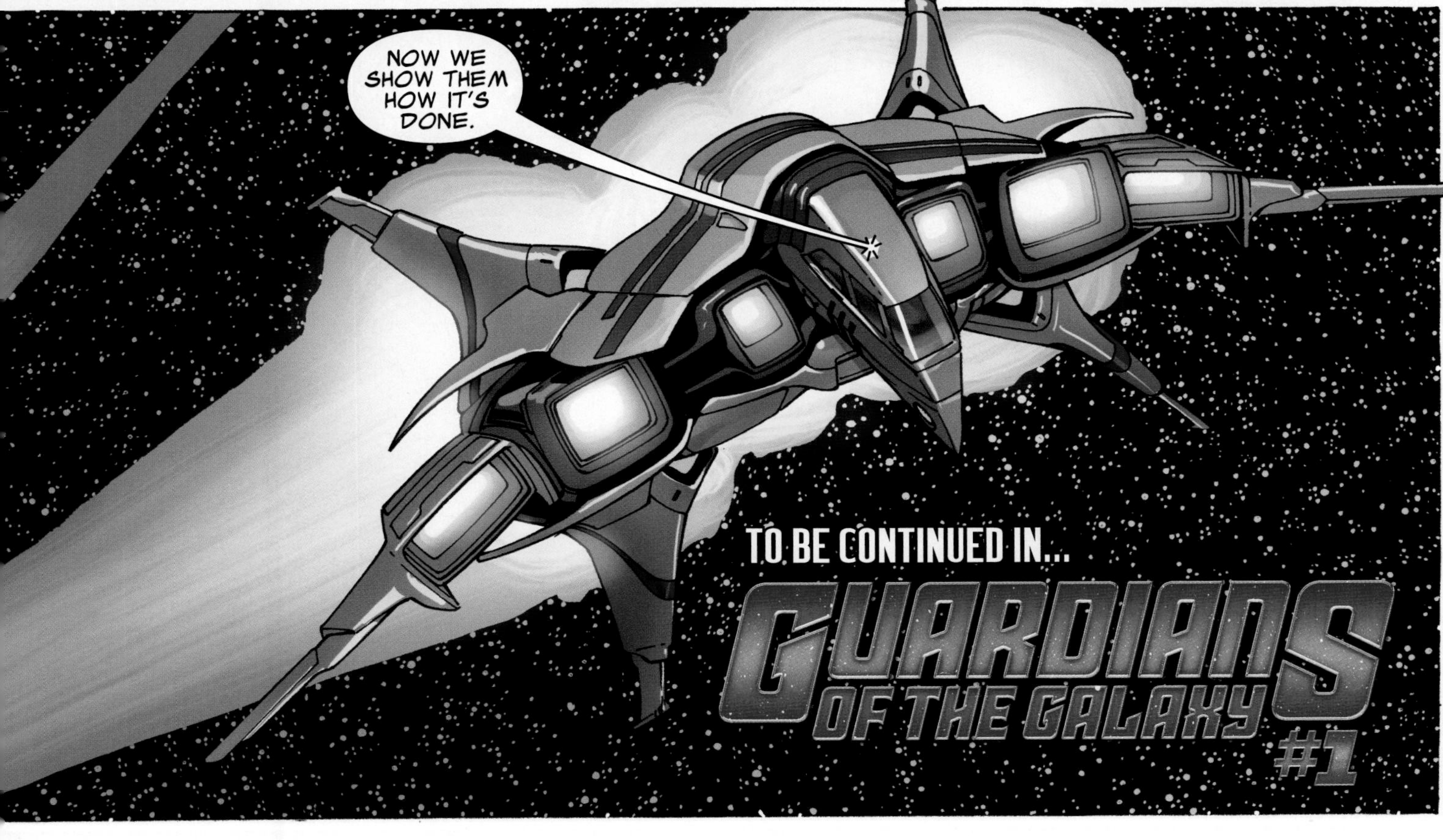
NOW WE SHOW THEM HOW IT'S DONE.
TO BE CONTINUED IN...
GUARDIANS OF THE GALAXY #1

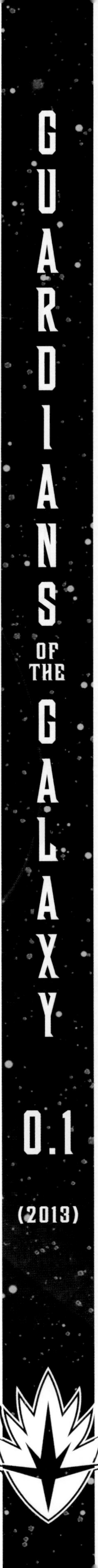
GUARDIANS OF THE GALAXY
0.1
(2013)

GUARDIANS OF THE GALAXY 1

(2013)

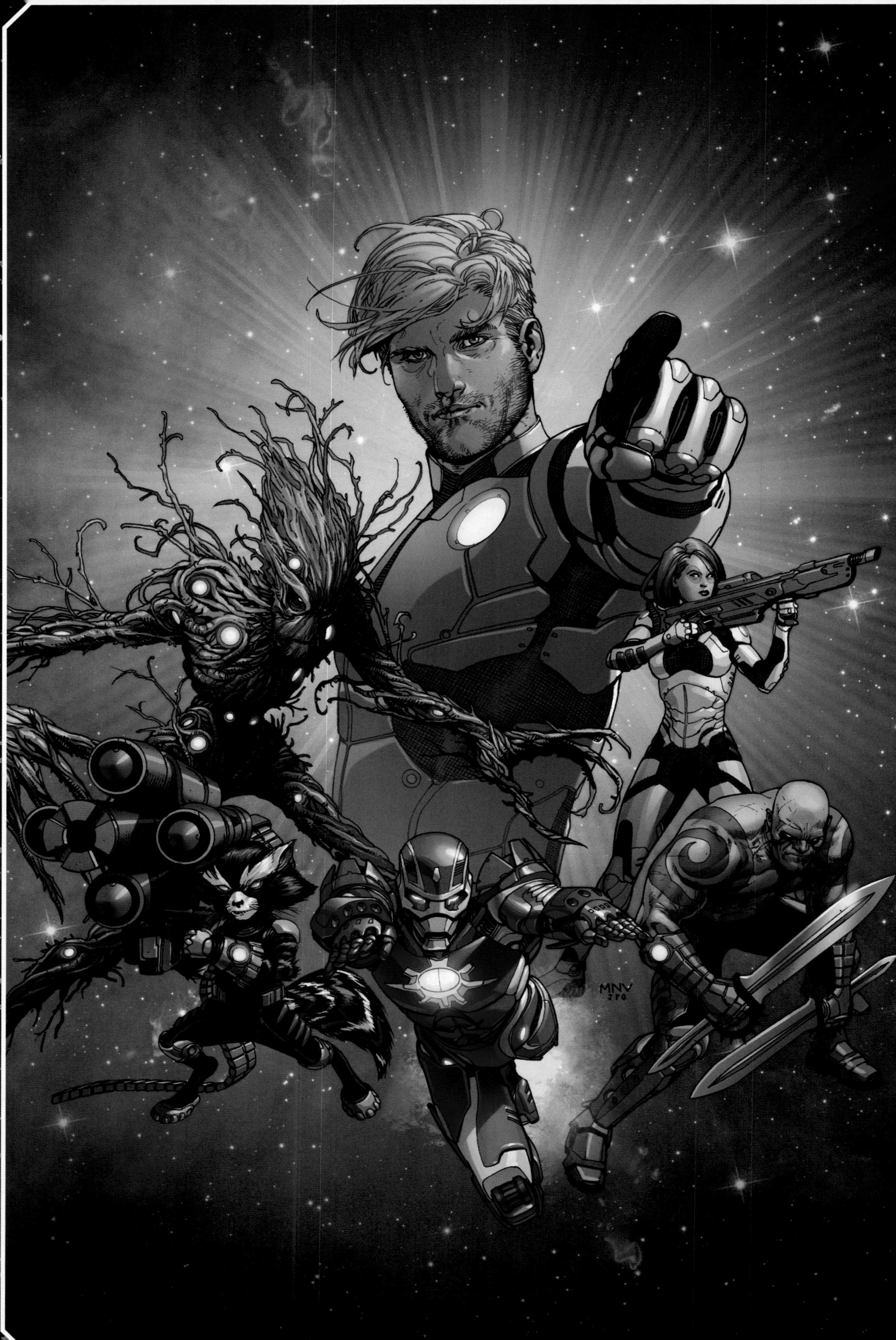
MNV

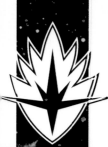

GUARDIANS OF THE GALAXY

WRITER **BRIAN MICHAEL BENDIS**   PENCILER **STEVE McNIVEN**

INKER **JOHN DELL** COLORS **JUSTIN PONSOR** LETTERER **VC'S CORY PETIT**

PRODUCTION **MANNY MEDEROS** COVER BY **STEVE McNIVEN, JOHN DELL** & **JUSTIN PONSOR**

ASSISTANT EDITOR **ELLIE PYLE**   ASSOCIATE EDITOR **SANA AMANAT**   EDITOR **STEPHEN WACKER**

EDITOR IN CHIEF **AXEL ALONSO** CHIEF CREATIVE OFFICER **JOE QUESADA**
PUBLISHER **DAN BUCKLEY** EXECUTIVE PRODUCER **ALAN FINE**

GUARDIANS OF THE GALAXY 1 (2013)

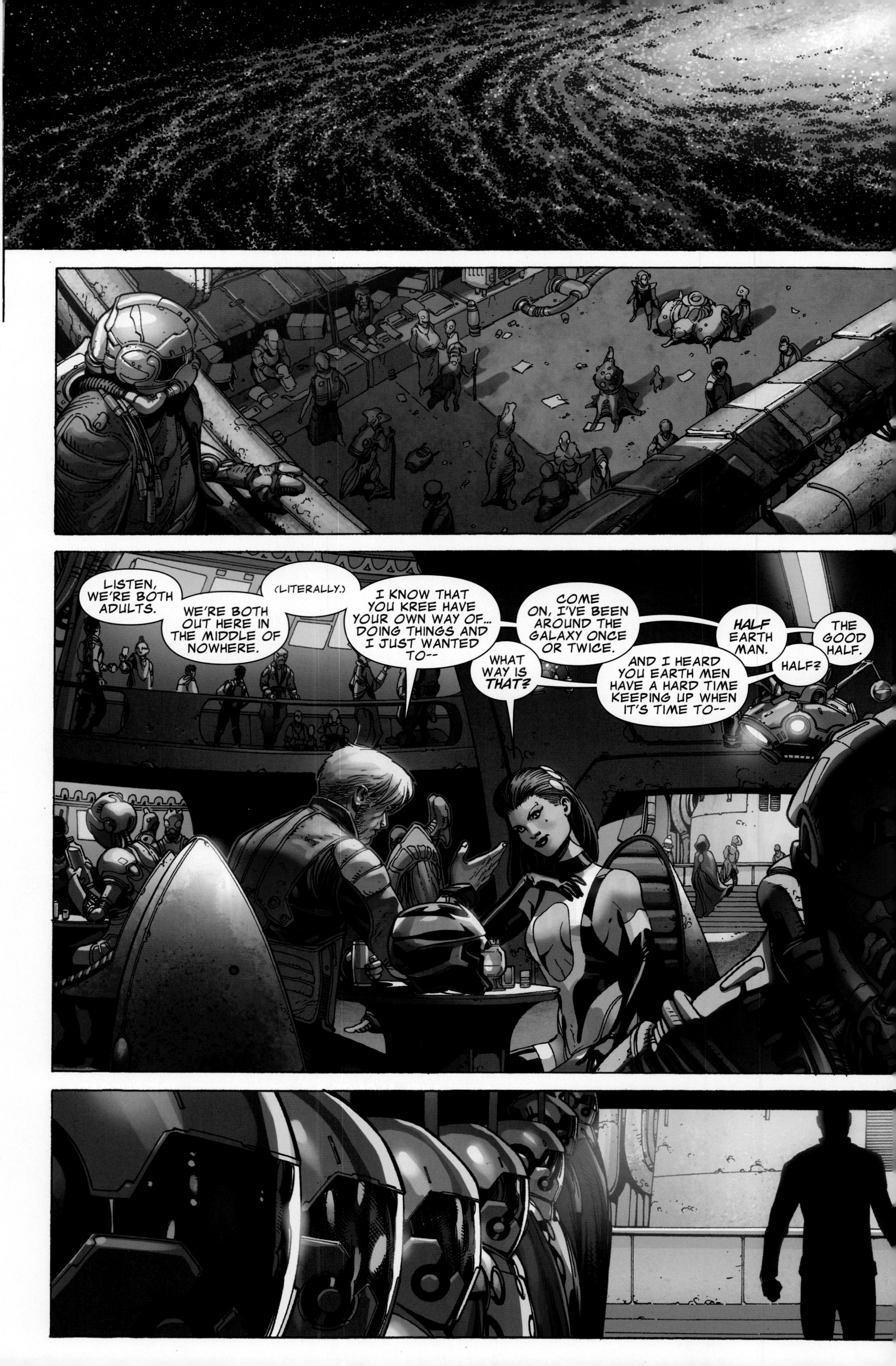
LISTEN, WE'RE BOTH ADULTS.
WE'RE BOTH OUT HERE IN THE MIDDLE OF NOWHERE.
(LITERALLY.)
I KNOW THAT YOU KREE HAVE YOUR OWN WAY OF... DOING THINGS AND I JUST WANTED TO--
WHAT WAY IS *THAT?*
COME ON, I'VE BEEN AROUND THE GALAXY ONCE OR TWICE.
AND I HEARD YOU EARTH MEN HAVE A HARD TIME KEEPING UP WHEN IT'S TIME TO--
HALF EARTH MAN.
HALF?
THE GOOD HALF.

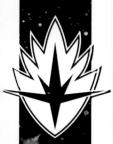

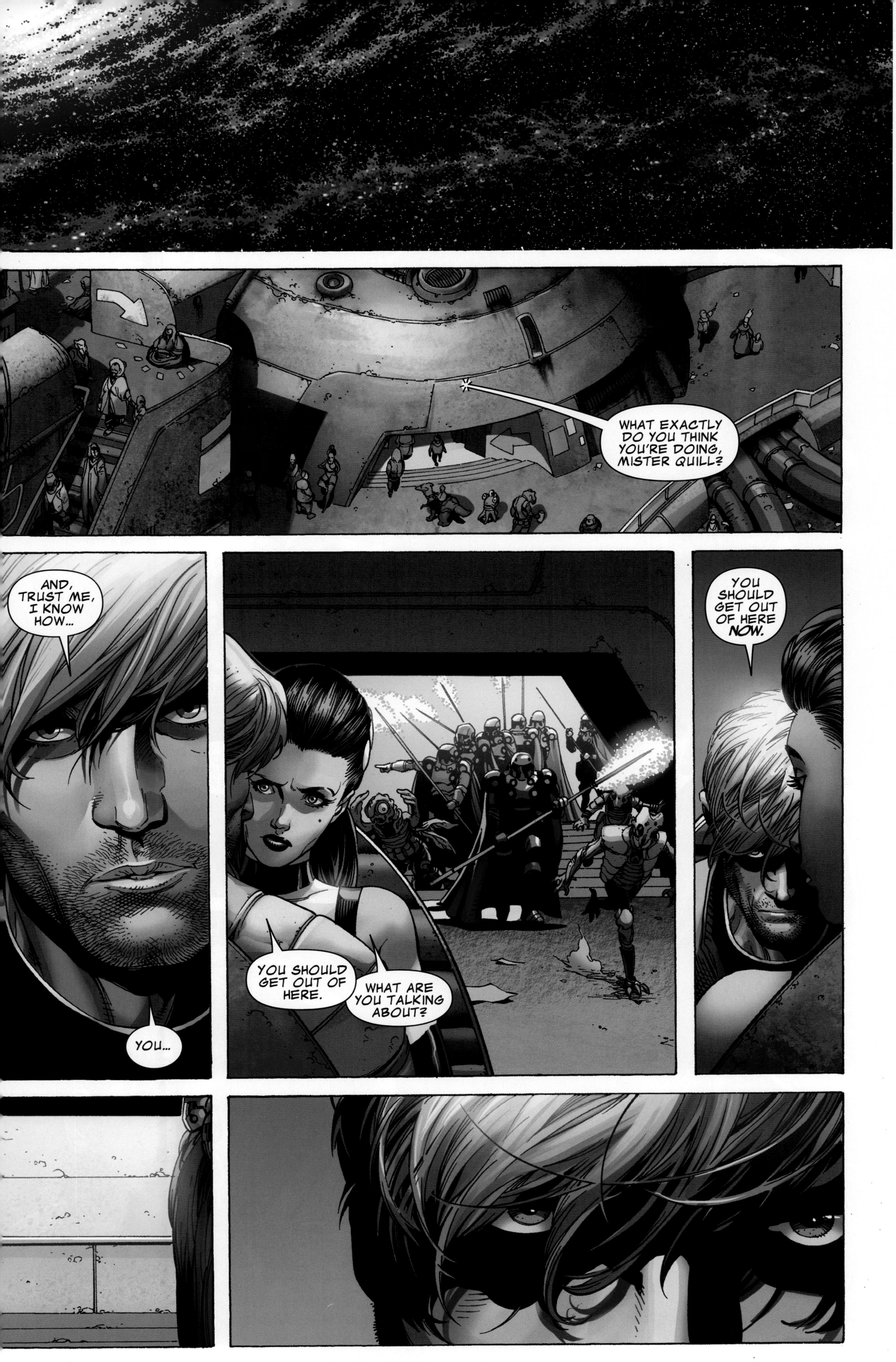
WHAT EXACTLY DO YOU THINK YOU'RE DOING, MISTER QUILL?
AND, TRUST ME, I KNOW HOW...
YOU...
YOU SHOULD GET OUT OF HERE.
WHAT ARE YOU TALKING ABOUT?
YOU SHOULD GET OUT OF HERE NOW.

GUARDIANS OF THE GALAXY 1 (2013)

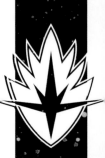

GUARDIANS OF THE GALAXY 1 (2013)

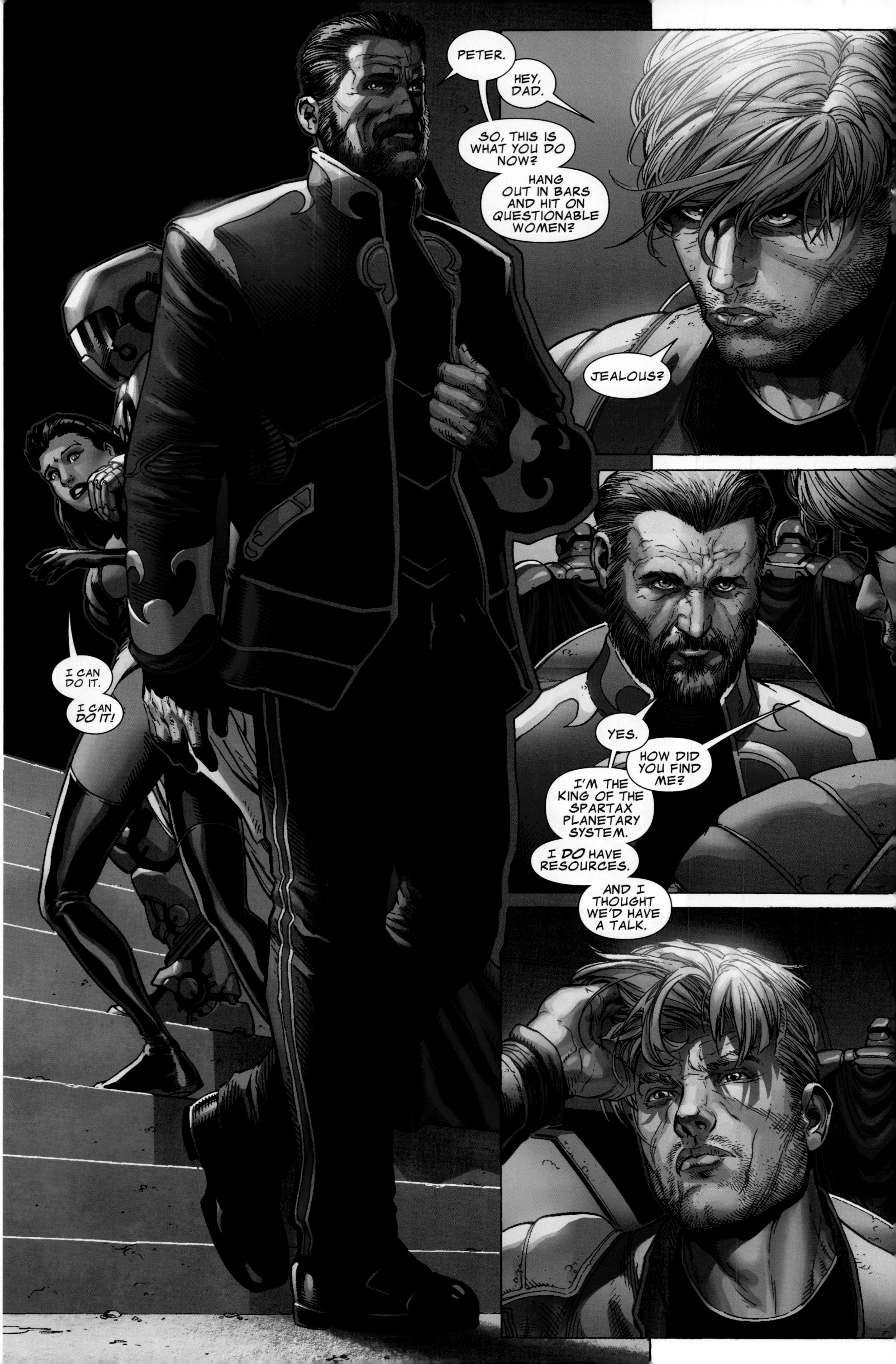
PETER.
HEY, DAD.
SO, THIS IS WHAT YOU DO NOW?
HANG OUT IN BARS AND HIT ON QUESTIONABLE WOMEN?
JEALOUS?
I CAN DO IT.
I CAN *DO IT!*
YES.
HOW DID YOU FIND ME?
I'M THE KING OF THE SPARTAX PLANETARY SYSTEM.
I *DO* HAVE RESOURCES.
AND I THOUGHT WE'D HAVE A TALK.

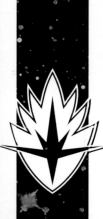

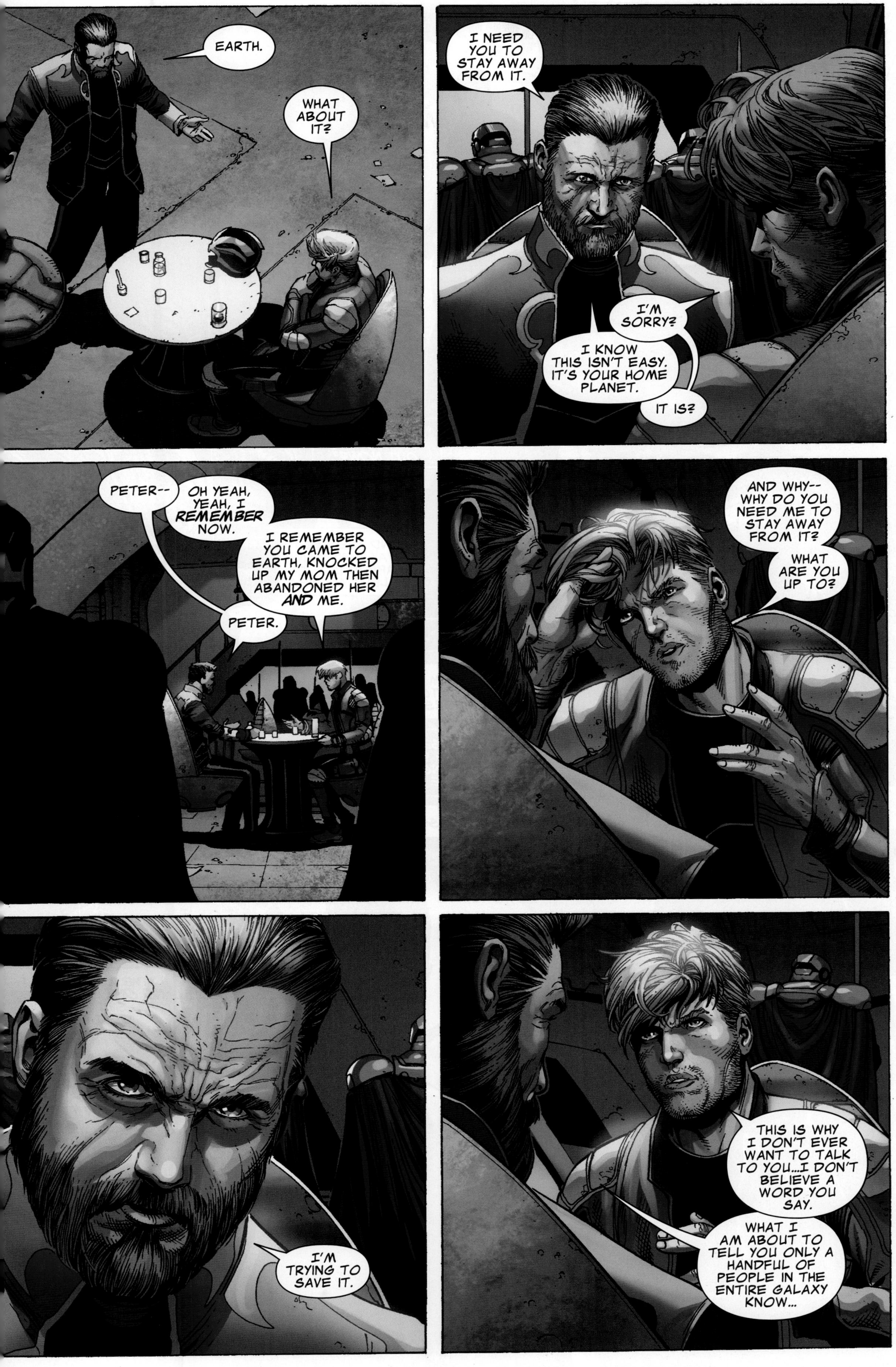
EARTH.
WHAT ABOUT IT?
I NEED YOU TO STAY AWAY FROM IT.
I'M SORRY?
I KNOW THIS ISN'T EASY. IT'S YOUR HOME PLANET.
IT IS?
PETER--
OH YEAH, YEAH, I REMEMBER NOW.
I REMEMBER YOU CAME TO EARTH, KNOCKED UP MY MOM THEN ABANDONED HER AND ME.
PETER.
AND WHY-- WHY DO YOU NEED ME TO STAY AWAY FROM IT?
WHAT ARE YOU UP TO?
I'M TRYING TO SAVE IT.
THIS IS WHY I DON'T EVER WANT TO TALK TO YOU...I DON'T BELIEVE A WORD YOU SAY.
WHAT I AM ABOUT TO TELL YOU ONLY A HANDFUL OF PEOPLE IN THE ENTIRE GALAXY KNOW...

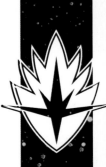

GUARDIANS OF THE GALAXY 1 (2013)

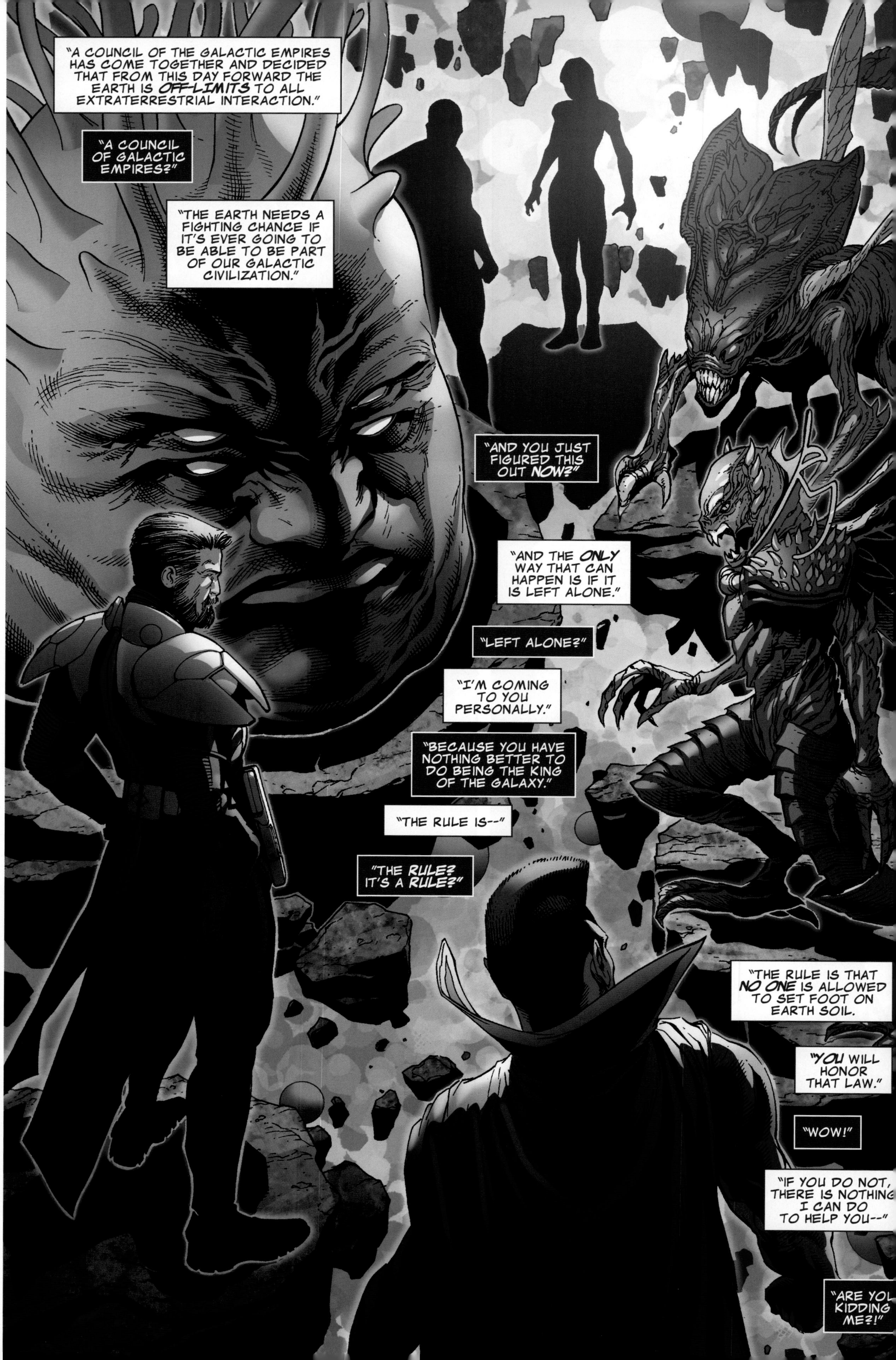
"A COUNCIL OF THE GALACTIC EMPIRES HAS COME TOGETHER AND DECIDED THAT FROM THIS DAY FORWARD THE EARTH IS OFF-LIMITS TO ALL EXTRATERRESTRIAL INTERACTION."
"A COUNCIL OF GALACTIC EMPIRES?"
"THE EARTH NEEDS A FIGHTING CHANCE IF IT'S EVER GOING TO BE ABLE TO BE PART OF OUR GALACTIC CIVILIZATION."
"AND YOU JUST FIGURED THIS OUT NOW?"
"AND THE ONLY WAY THAT CAN HAPPEN IS IF IT IS LEFT ALONE."
"LEFT ALONE?"
"I'M COMING TO YOU PERSONALLY."
"BECAUSE YOU HAVE NOTHING BETTER TO DO BEING THE KING OF THE GALAXY."
"THE RULE IS--"
"THE RULE? IT'S A RULE?"
"THE RULE IS THAT NO ONE IS ALLOWED TO SET FOOT ON EARTH SOIL.
"YOU WILL HONOR THAT LAW."
"WOW!"
"IF YOU DO NOT, THERE IS NOTHING I CAN DO TO HELP YOU--"
"ARE YOU KIDDING ME?!"

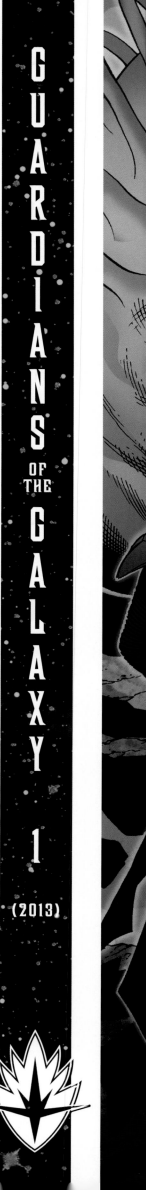

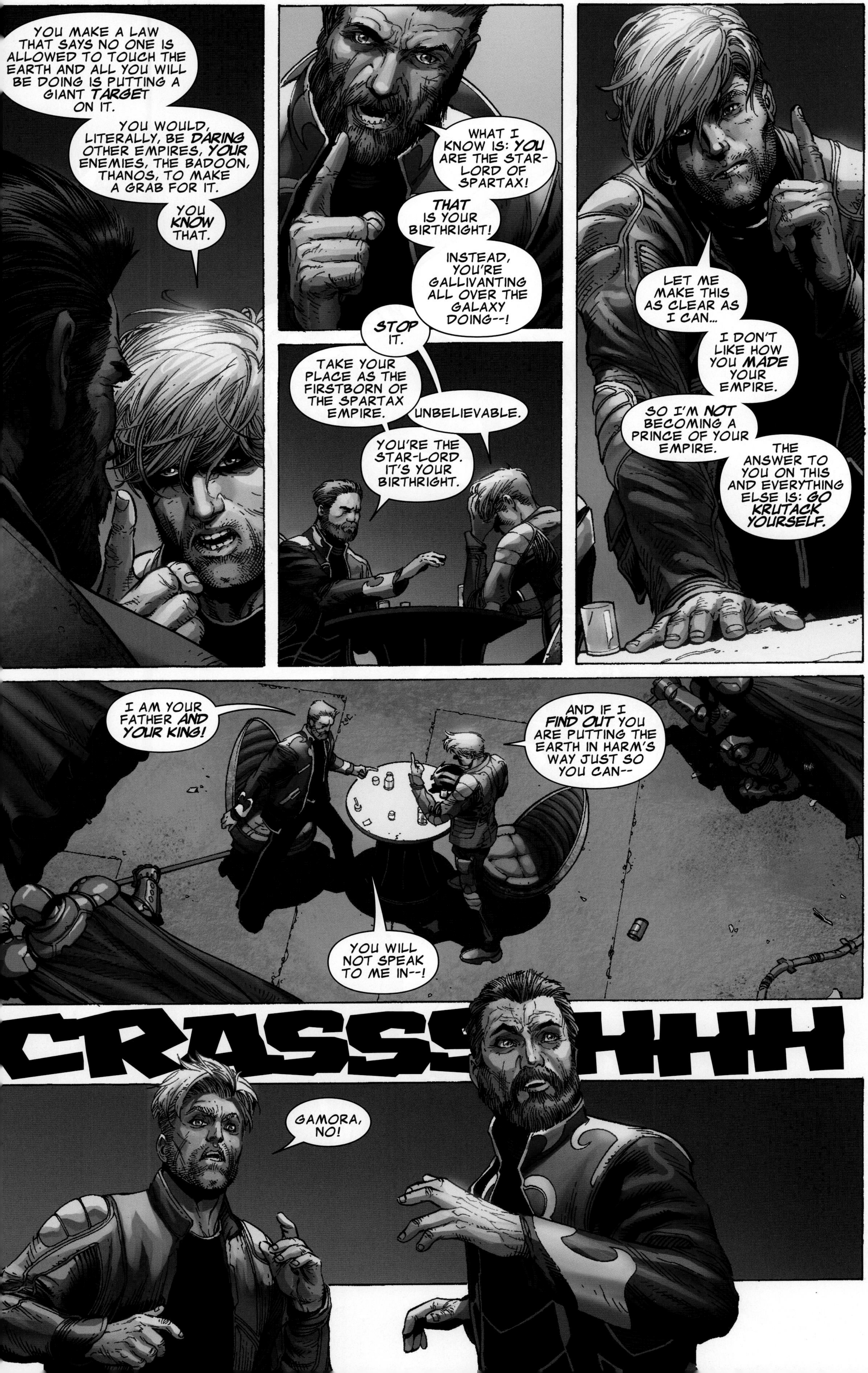

YOU MAKE A LAW THAT SAYS NO ONE IS ALLOWED TO TOUCH THE EARTH AND ALL YOU WILL BE DOING IS PUTTING A GIANT TARGET ON IT.
YOU WOULD, LITERALLY, BE DARING OTHER EMPIRES, YOUR ENEMIES, THE BADOON, THANOS, TO MAKE A GRAB FOR IT.
YOU KNOW THAT.
WHAT I KNOW IS: YOU ARE THE STAR-LORD OF SPARTAX!
THAT IS YOUR BIRTHRIGHT!
INSTEAD, YOU'RE GALLIVANTING ALL OVER THE GALAXY DOING--!
STOP IT.
TAKE YOUR PLACE AS THE FIRSTBORN OF THE SPARTAX EMPIRE.
UNBELIEVABLE.
YOU'RE THE STAR-LORD. IT'S YOUR BIRTHRIGHT.
LET ME MAKE THIS AS CLEAR AS I CAN...
I DON'T LIKE HOW YOU MADE YOUR EMPIRE.
SO I'M NOT BECOMING A PRINCE OF YOUR EMPIRE.
THE ANSWER TO YOU ON THIS AND EVERYTHING ELSE IS: GO KRUTACK YOURSELF.
I AM YOUR FATHER AND YOUR KING!
AND IF I FIND OUT YOU ARE PUTTING THE EARTH IN HARM'S WAY JUST SO YOU CAN--
YOU WILL NOT SPEAK TO ME IN--!
CRASSSHHHH
GAMORA, NO!

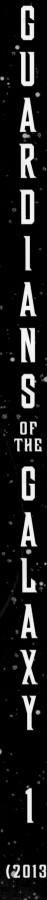

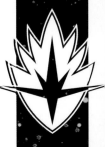

GUARDIANS OF THE GALAXY 1

(2013)

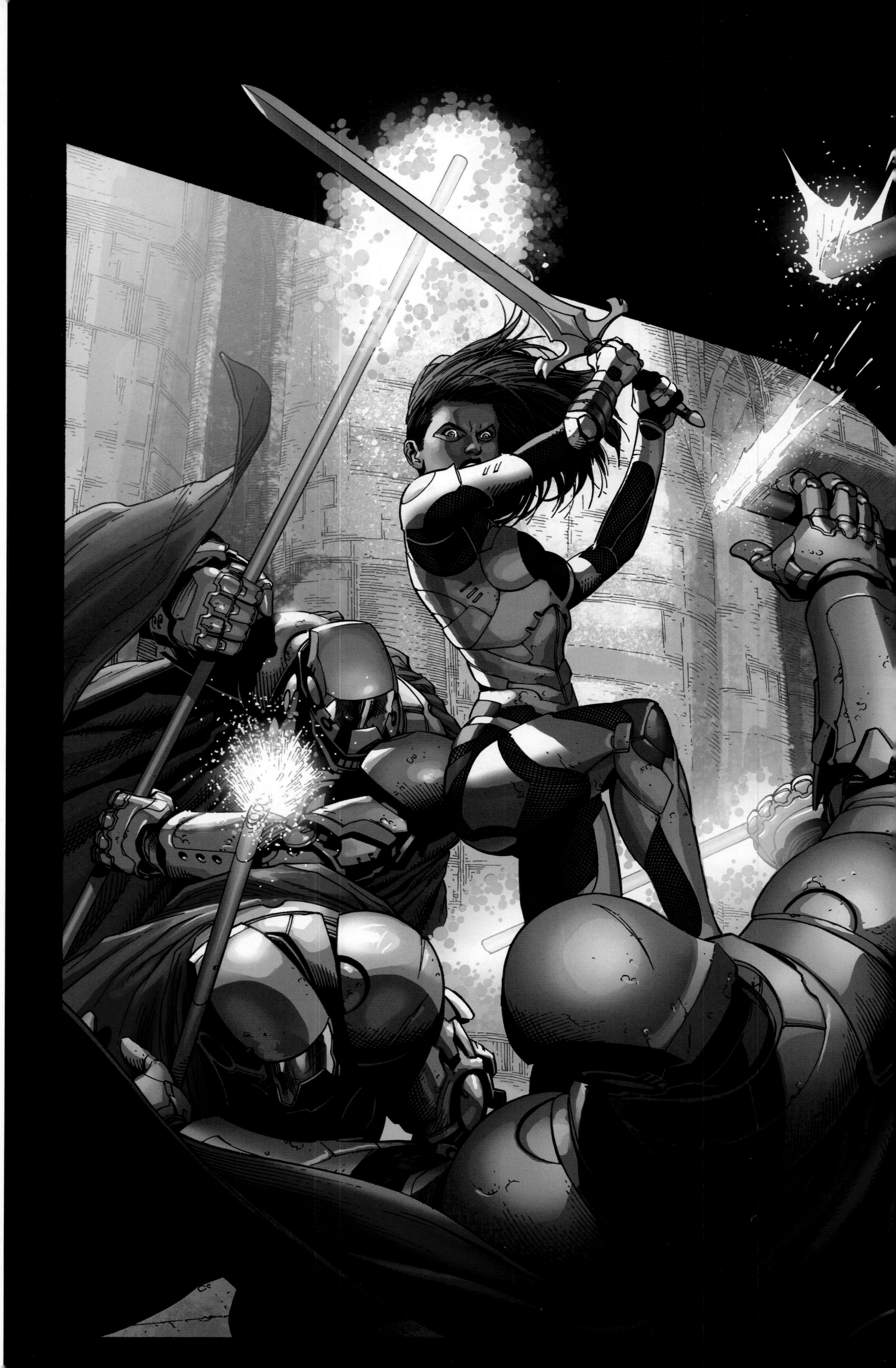

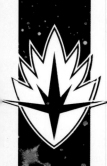

GUARDIANS OF THE GALAXY 1 (2013)

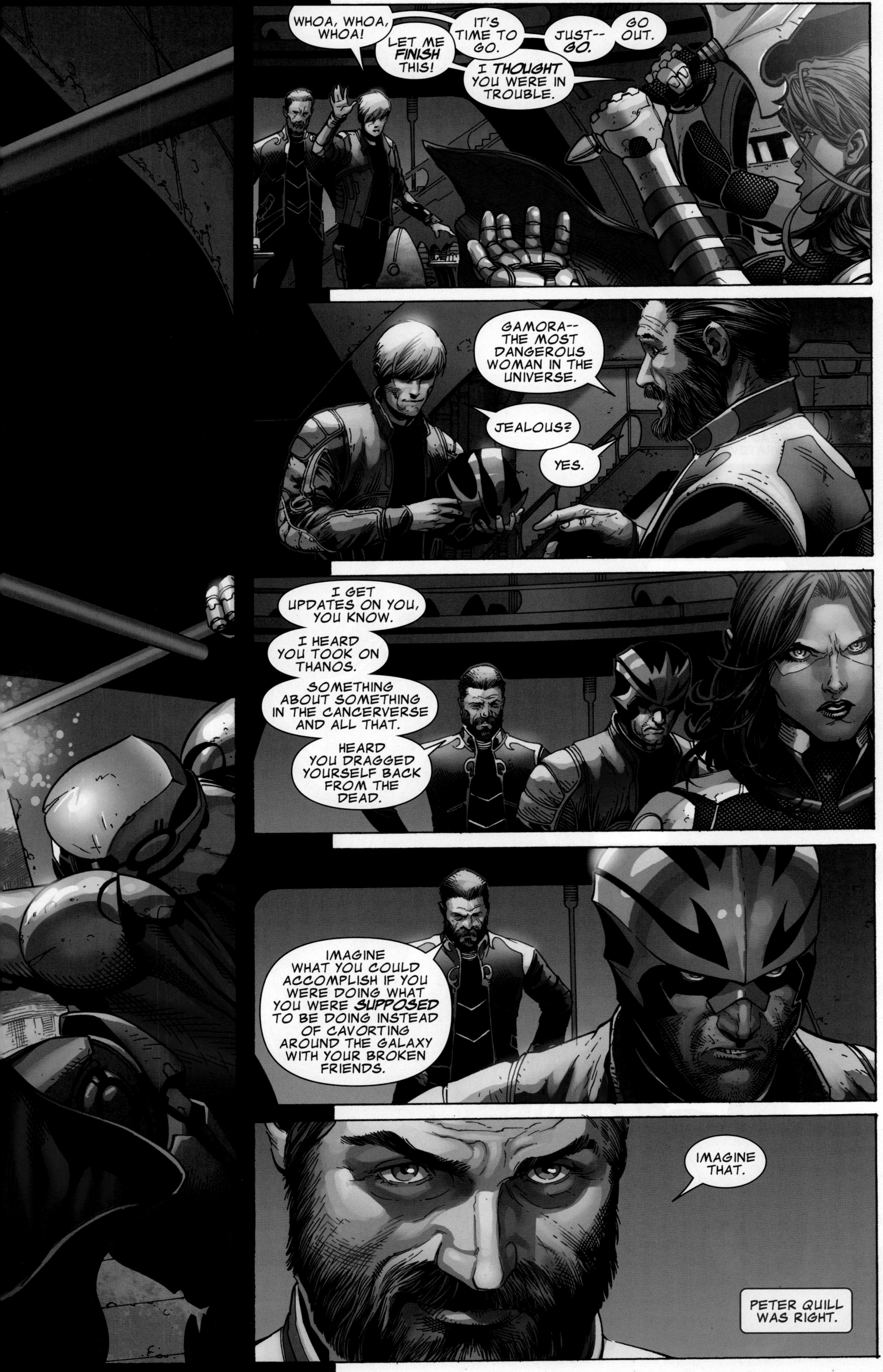
WHOA, WHOA, WHOA!
LET ME FINISH THIS!
IT'S TIME TO GO.
JUST-- GO.
GO OUT.
I THOUGHT YOU WERE IN TROUBLE.
GAMORA-- THE MOST DANGEROUS WOMAN IN THE UNIVERSE.
JEALOUS?
YES.
I GET UPDATES ON YOU, YOU KNOW.
I HEARD YOU TOOK ON THANOS.
SOMETHING ABOUT SOMETHING IN THE CANCERVERSE AND ALL THAT.
HEARD YOU DRAGGED YOURSELF BACK FROM THE DEAD.
IMAGINE WHAT YOU COULD ACCOMPLISH IF YOU WERE DOING WHAT YOU WERE SUPPOSED TO BE DOING INSTEAD OF CAVORTING AROUND THE GALAXY WITH YOUR BROKEN FRIENDS.
IMAGINE THAT.
PETER QUILL WAS RIGHT.

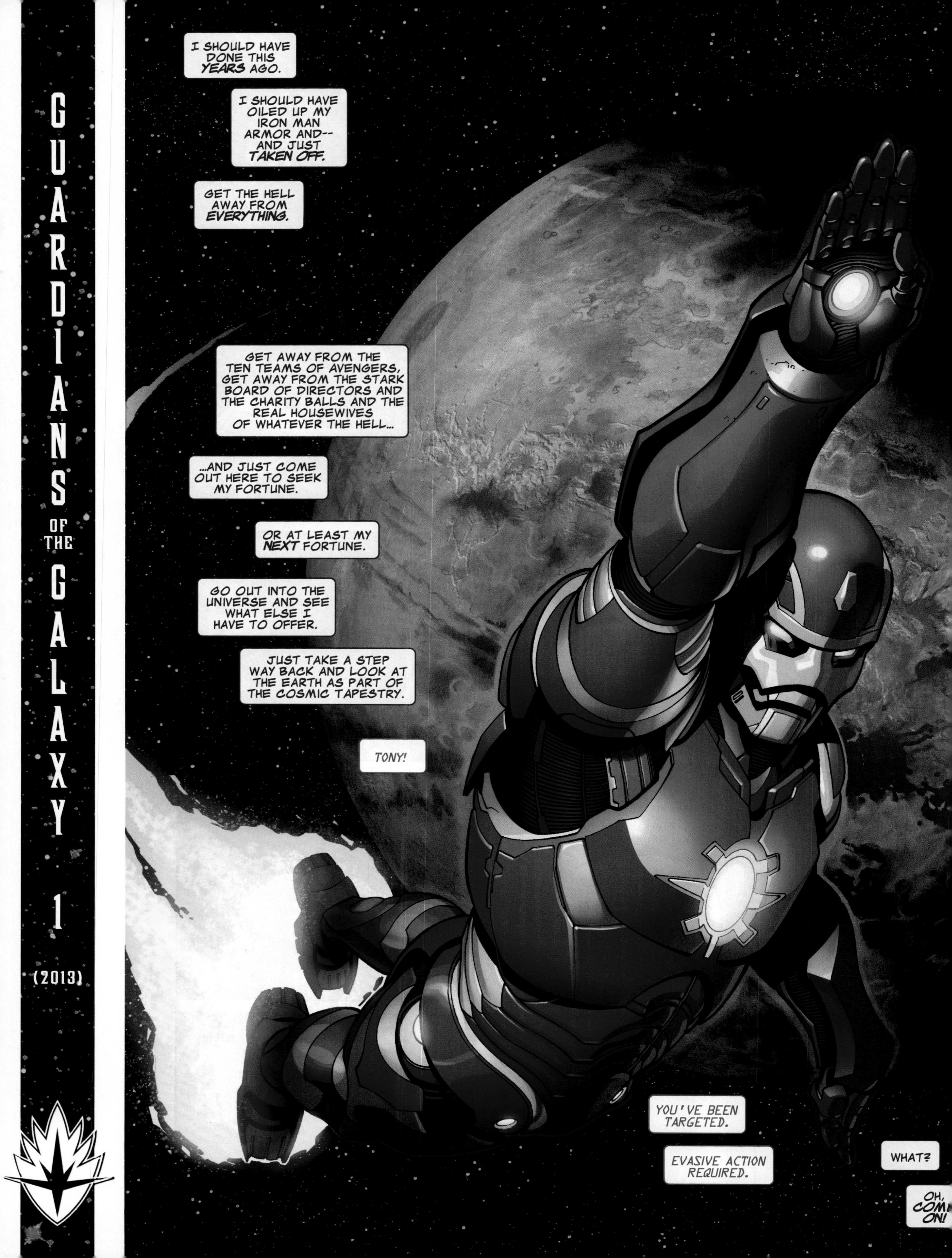

GUARDIANS OF THE GALAXY 1 (2013)
I SHOULD HAVE DONE THIS YEARS AGO.
I SHOULD HAVE OILED UP MY IRON MAN ARMOR AND-- AND JUST TAKEN OFF.
GET THE HELL AWAY FROM EVERYTHING.
GET AWAY FROM THE TEN TEAMS OF AVENGERS, GET AWAY FROM THE STARK BOARD OF DIRECTORS AND THE CHARITY BALLS AND THE REAL HOUSEWIVES OF WHATEVER THE HELL...
...AND JUST COME OUT HERE TO SEEK MY FORTUNE.
OR AT LEAST MY NEXT FORTUNE.
GO OUT INTO THE UNIVERSE AND SEE WHAT ELSE I HAVE TO OFFER.
JUST TAKE A STEP WAY BACK AND LOOK AT THE EARTH AS PART OF THE COSMIC TAPESTRY.
TONY!
YOU'VE BEEN TARGETED.
EVASIVE ACTION REQUIRED.
WHAT?
OH, COME ON!

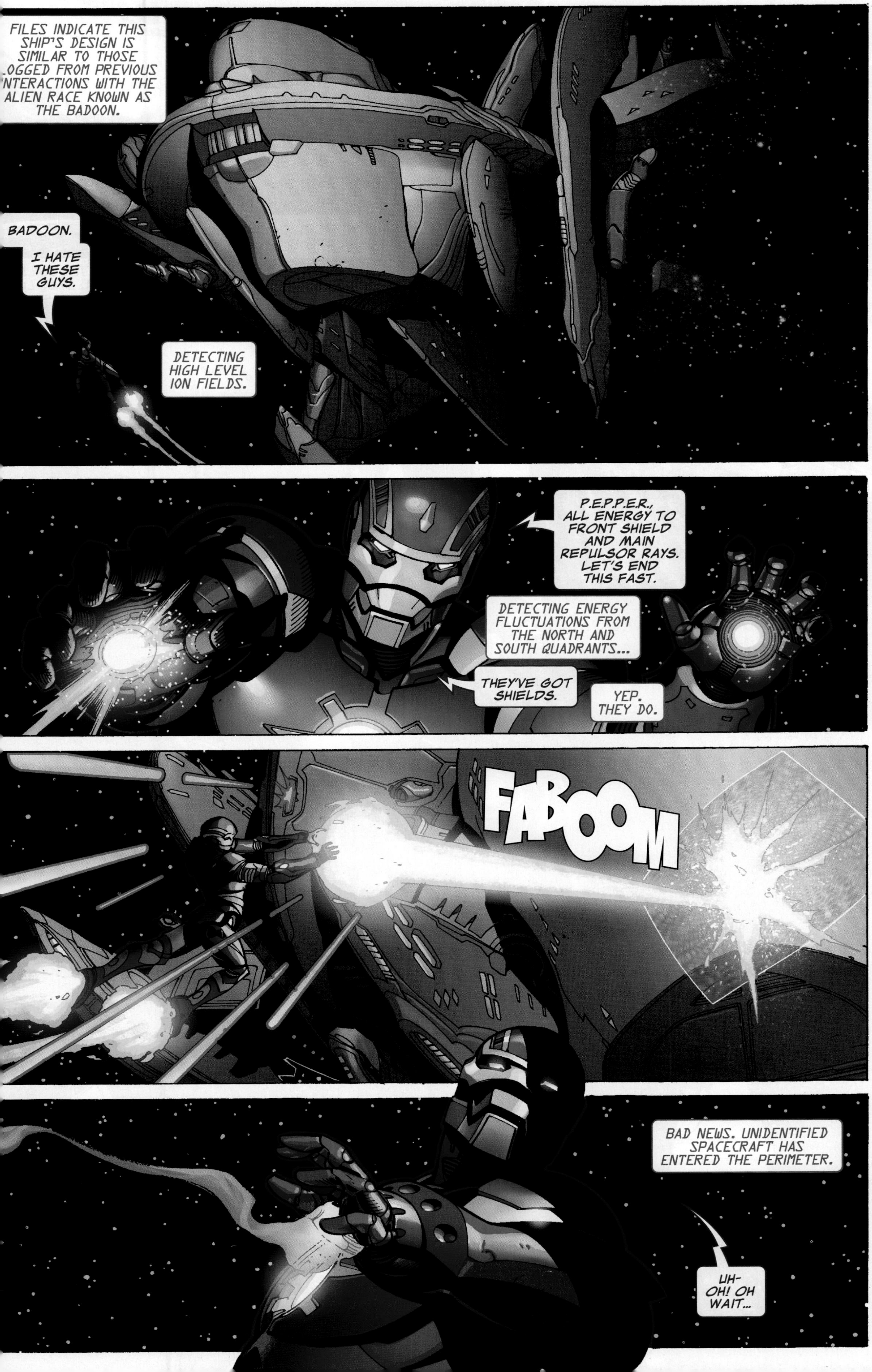
FILES INDICATE THIS SHIP'S DESIGN IS SIMILAR TO THOSE LOGGED FROM PREVIOUS INTERACTIONS WITH THE ALIEN RACE KNOWN AS THE BADOON.
BADOON.
I HATE THESE GUYS.
DETECTING HIGH LEVEL ION FIELDS.
P.E.P.P.E.R., ALL ENERGY TO FRONT SHIELD AND MAIN REPULSOR RAYS. LET'S END THIS FAST.
DETECTING ENERGY FLUCTUATIONS FROM THE NORTH AND SOUTH QUADRANTS...
THEY'VE GOT SHIELDS.
YEP. THEY DO.
FABOOM
BAD NEWS. UNIDENTIFIED SPACECRAFT HAS ENTERED THE PERIMETER.
UH-OH! OH WAIT...

GUARDIANS OF THE GALAXY 1 (2013)

GUARDIANS OF THE GALAXY 1 (2013)

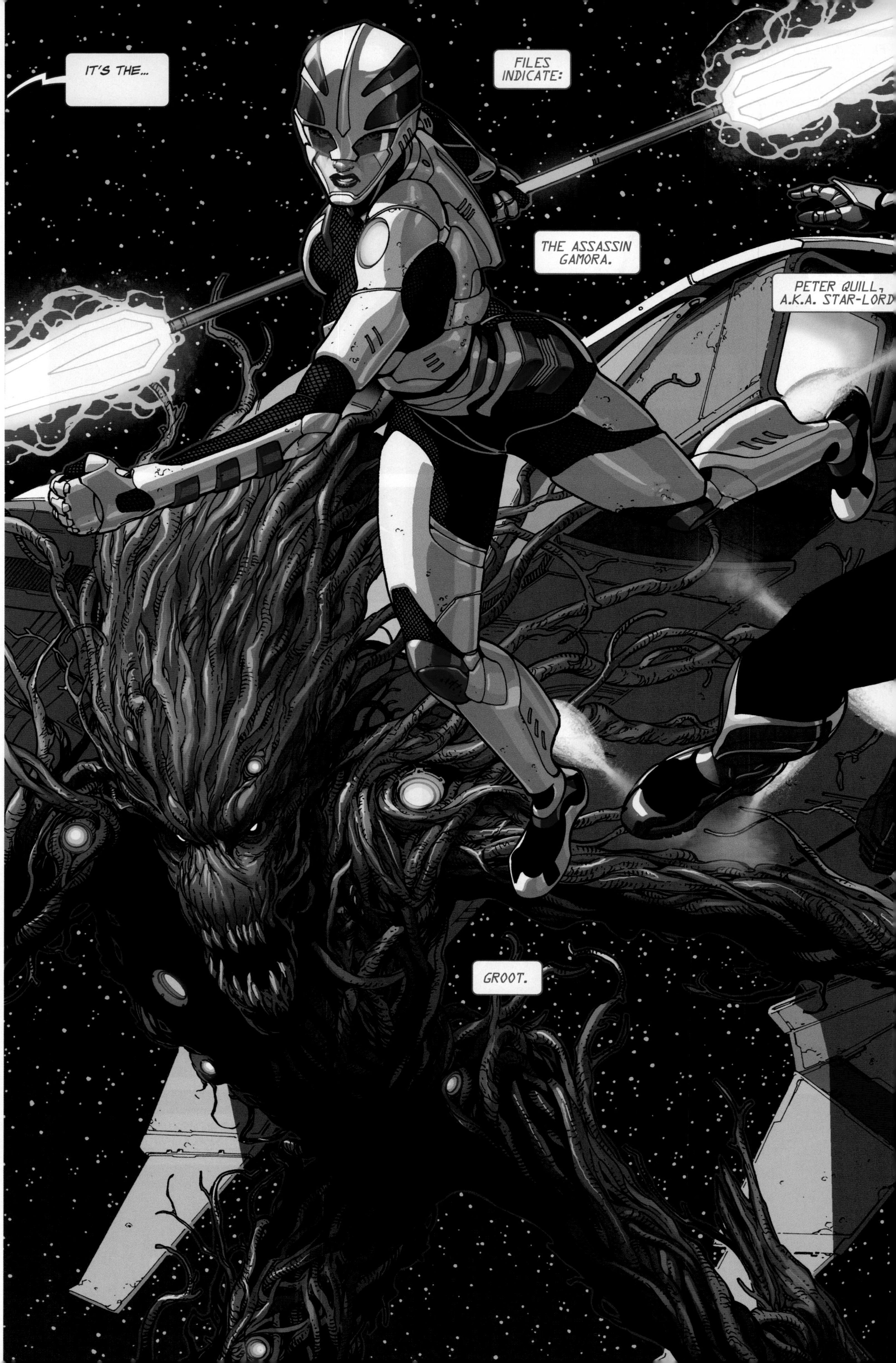

IT'S THE...
FILES INDICATE:
THE ASSASSIN GAMORA.
PETER QUILL, A.K.A. STAR-LORD
GROOT.

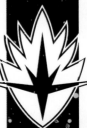

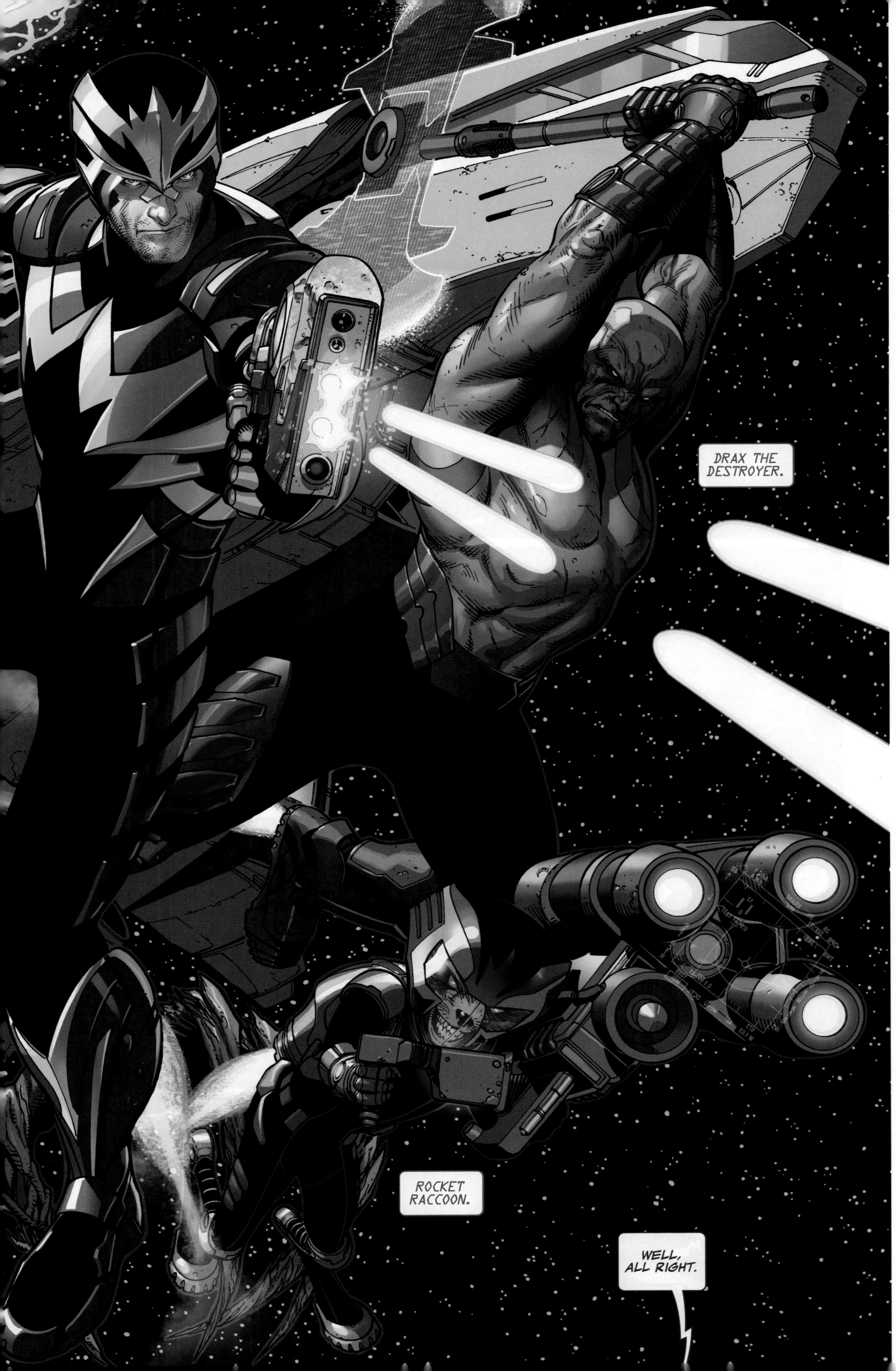
DRAX THE DESTROYER.
ROCKET RACCOON.
WELL, ALL RIGHT.

GUARDIANS OF THE GALAXY 1

(2013)

GUARDIANS OF THE GALAXY 1 (2013)

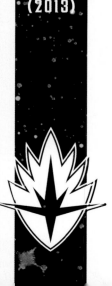

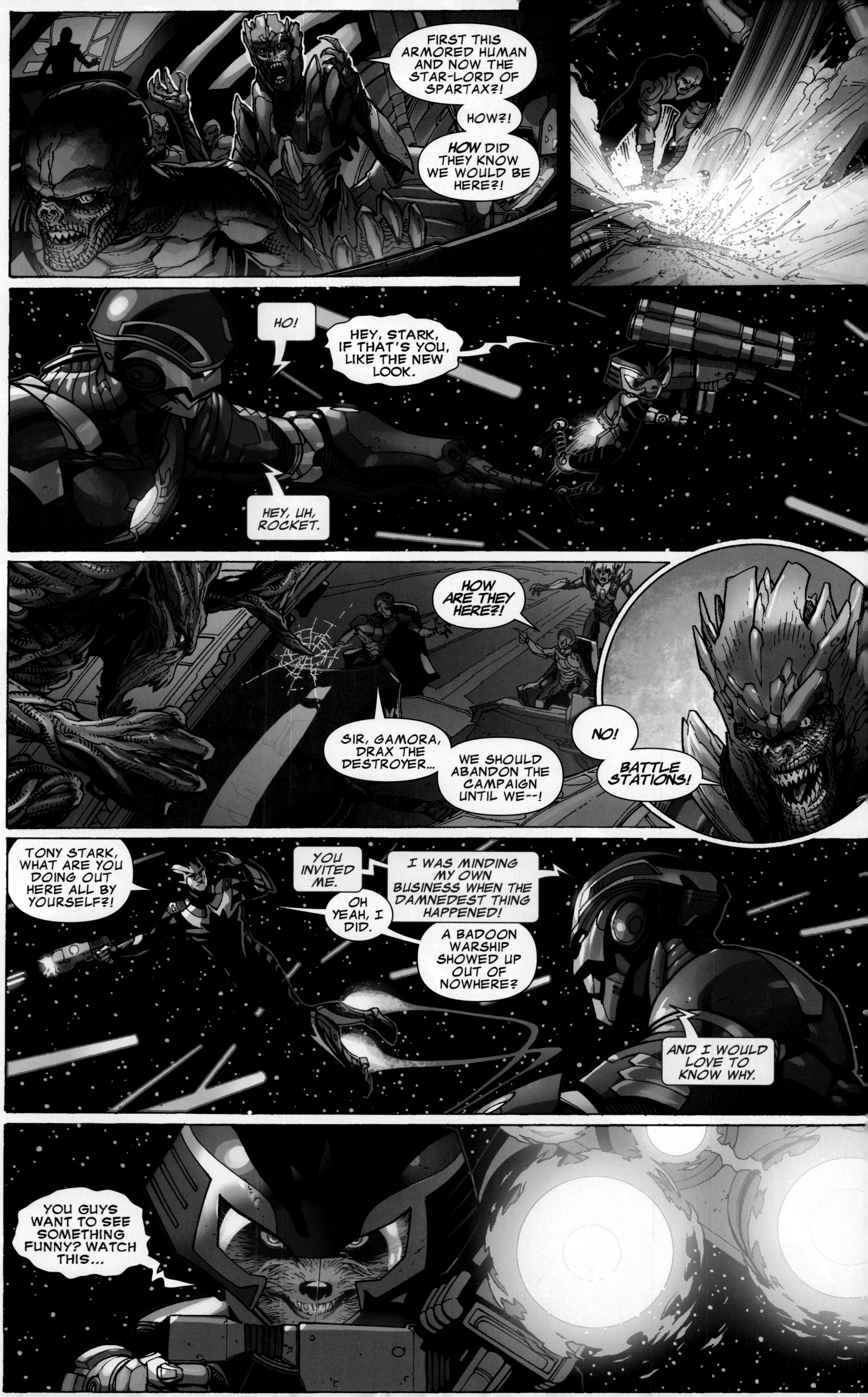
FIRST THIS ARMORED HUMAN AND NOW THE STAR-LORD OF SPARTAX?!
HOW?!
HOW DID THEY KNOW WE WOULD BE HERE?!
HO!
HEY, STARK, IF THAT'S YOU, LIKE THE NEW LOOK.
HEY, UH, ROCKET.
HOW ARE THEY HERE?!
SIR, GAMORA, DRAX THE DESTROYER...
WE SHOULD ABANDON THE CAMPAIGN UNTIL WE--!
NO!
BATTLE STATIONS!
TONY STARK, WHAT ARE YOU DOING OUT HERE ALL BY YOURSELF?!
YOU INVITED ME.
OH YEAH, I DID.
I WAS MINDING MY OWN BUSINESS WHEN THE DAMNEDEST THING HAPPENED!
A BADOON WARSHIP SHOWED UP OUT OF NOWHERE?
AND I WOULD LOVE TO KNOW WHY.
YOU GUYS WANT TO SEE SOMETHING FUNNY? WATCH THIS...

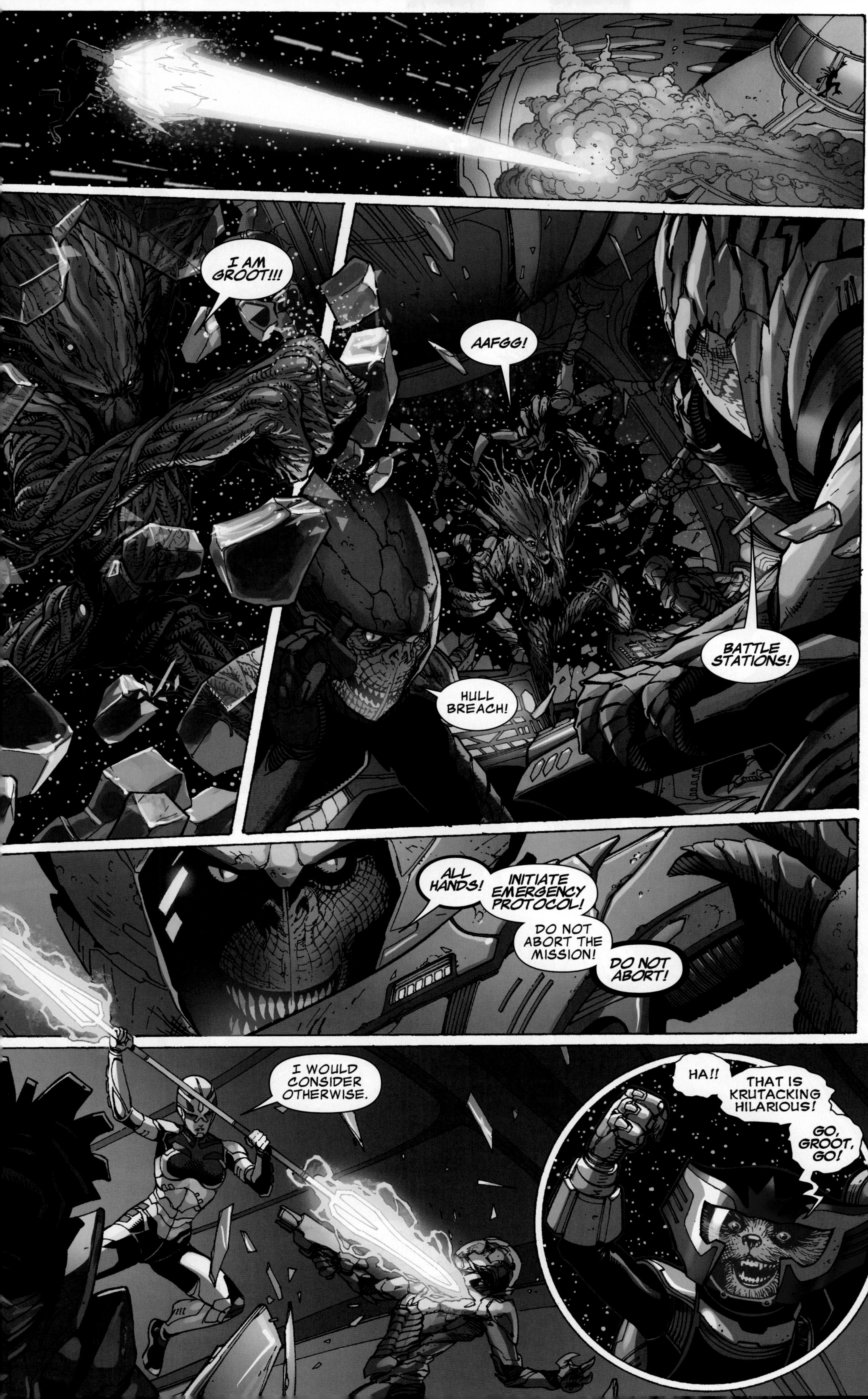
I AM GROOT!!!
AAFGG!
HULL BREACH!
BATTLE STATIONS!
ALL HANDS!
INITIATE EMERGENCY PROTOCOL!
DO NOT ABORT THE MISSION!
DO NOT ABORT!
I WOULD CONSIDER OTHERWISE.
HA!!
THAT IS KRUTACKING HILARIOUS!
GO, GROOT, GO!

GUARDIANS OF THE GALAXY 1

(2013)

GUARDIANS OF THE GALAXY 1 (2013)

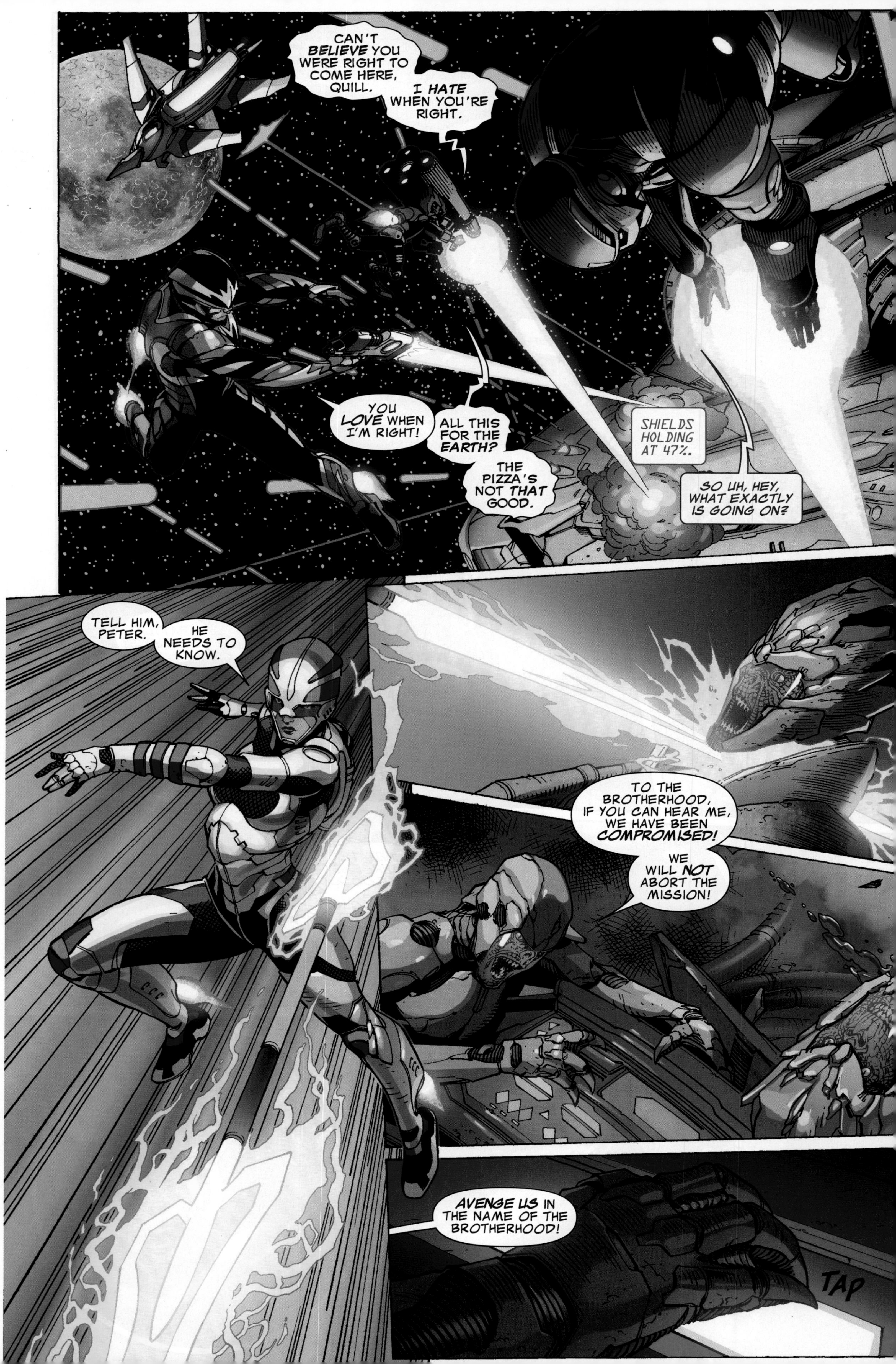

CAN'T BELIEVE YOU WERE RIGHT TO COME HERE, QUILL.
I HATE WHEN YOU'RE RIGHT.
YOU LOVE WHEN I'M RIGHT!
ALL THIS FOR THE EARTH?
THE PIZZA'S NOT THAT GOOD.
SHIELDS HOLDING AT 47%.
SO UH, HEY, WHAT EXACTLY IS GOING ON?
TELL HIM, PETER.
HE NEEDS TO KNOW.
TO THE BROTHERHOOD, IF YOU CAN HEAR ME, WE HAVE BEEN COMPROMISED!
WE WILL NOT ABORT THE MISSION!
AVENGE US IN THE NAME OF THE BROTHERHOOD!
TAP

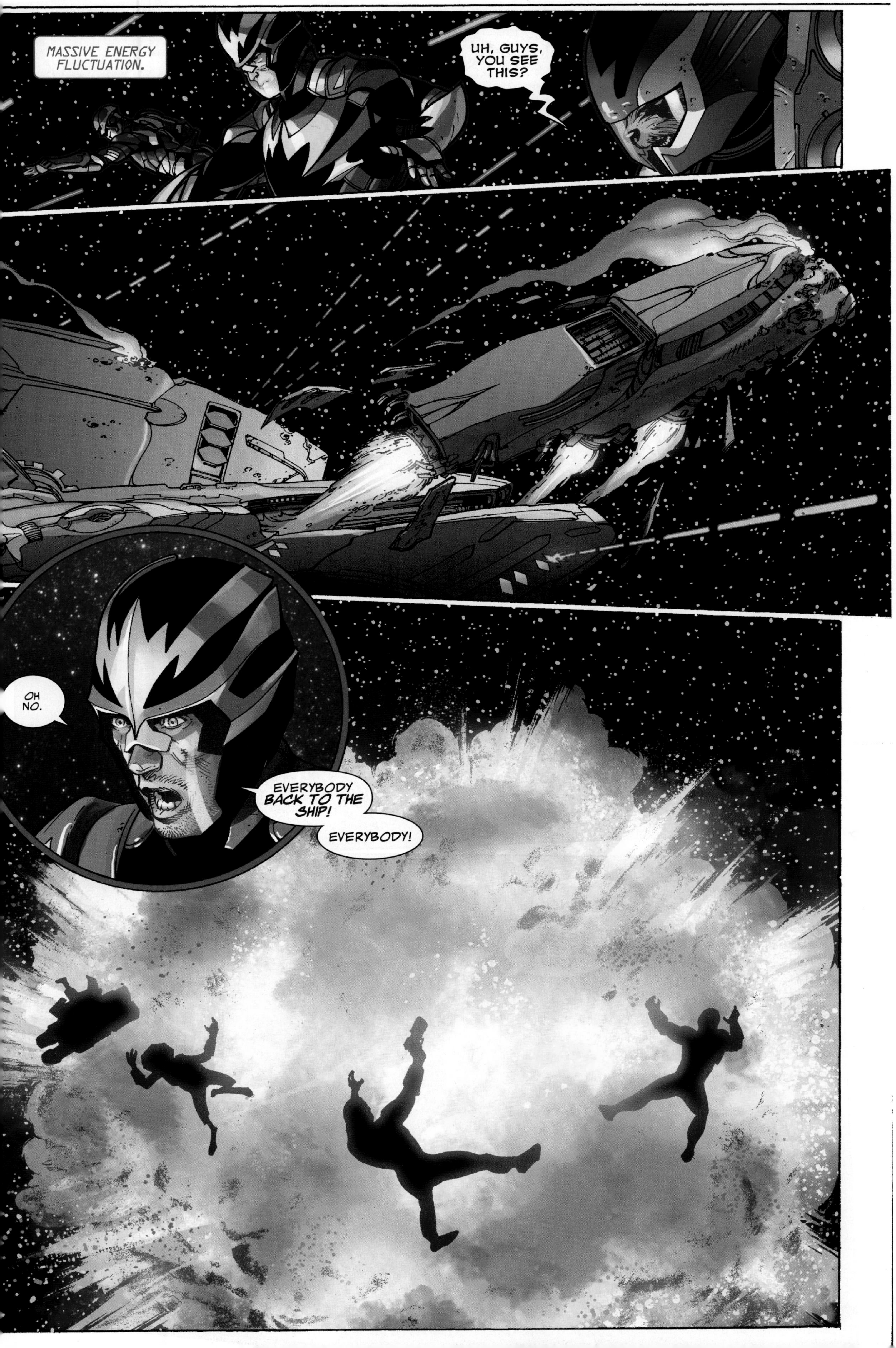
MASSIVE ENERGY FLUCTUATION.
UH, GUYS, YOU SEE THIS?
OH NO.
EVERYBODY BACK TO THE SHIP!
EVERYBODY!

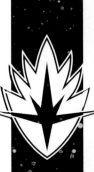

GUARDIANS OF THE GALAXY 1 (2013)

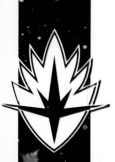

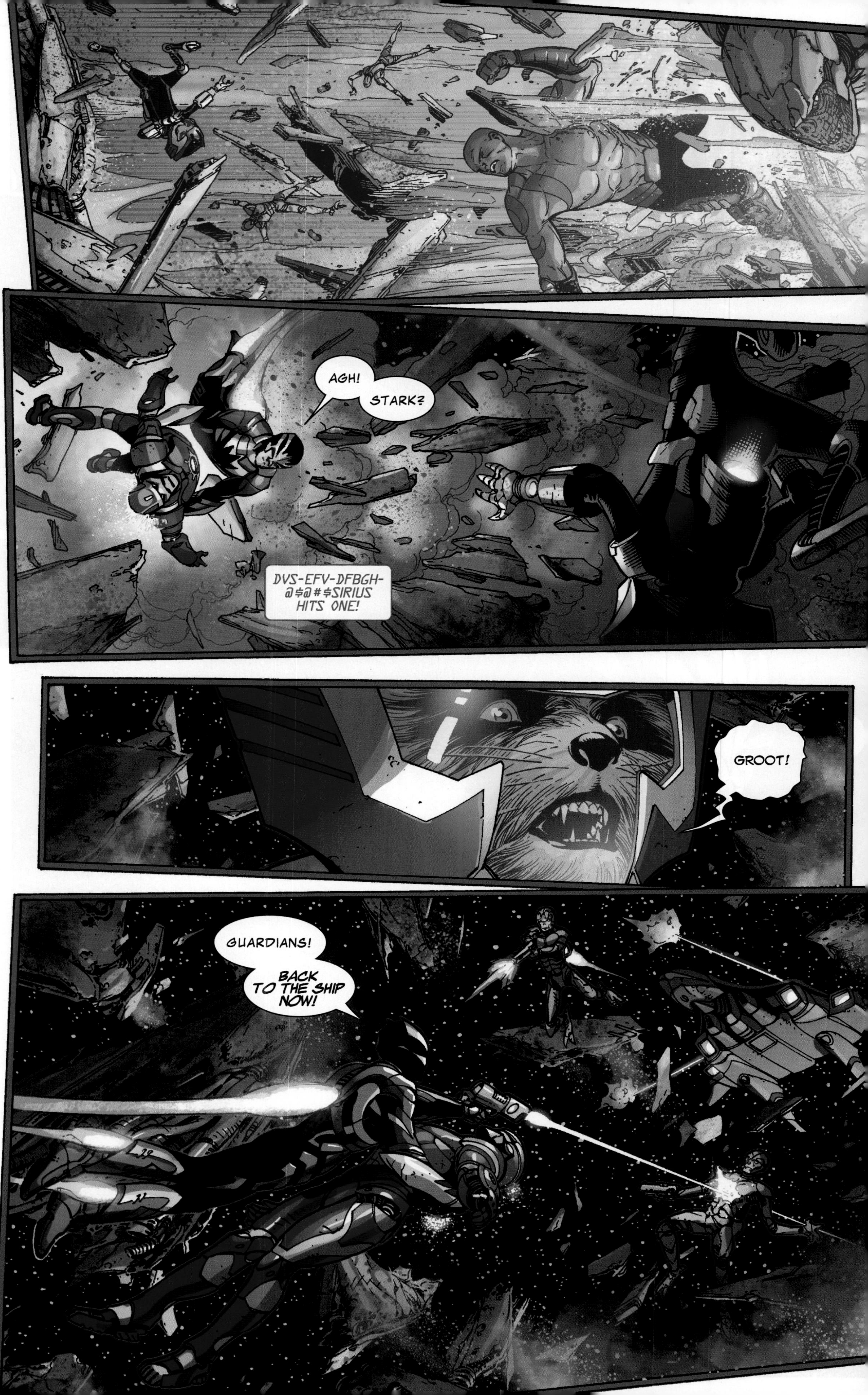
AGH!
STARK?
DVS-EFV-DFBGH-@$@#$SIRIUS HITS ONE!
GROOT!
GUARDIANS!
BACK TO THE SHIP NOW!

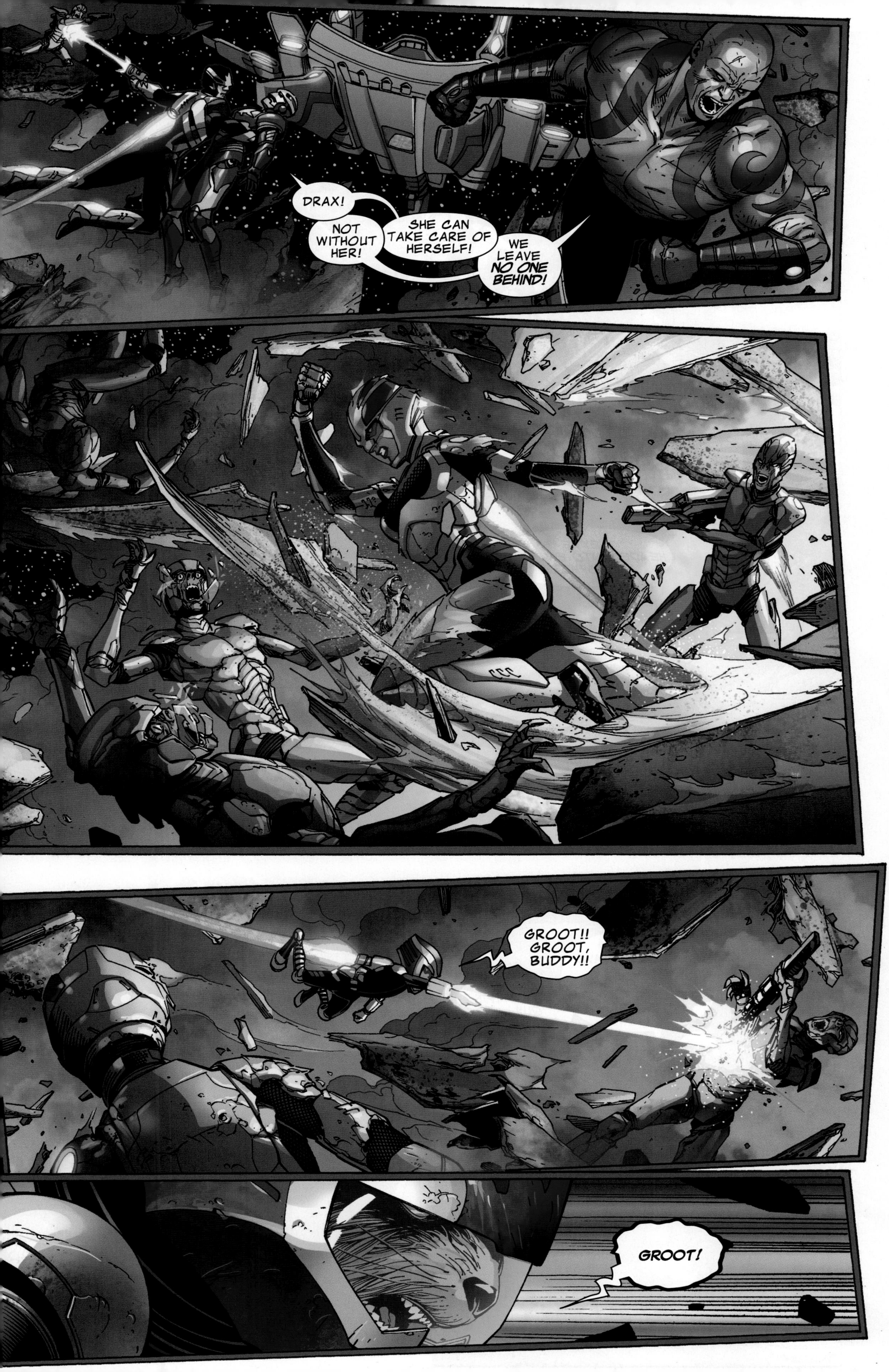
DRAX!
NOT WITHOUT HER!
SHE CAN TAKE CARE OF HERSELF!
WE LEAVE NO ONE BEHIND!
GROOT!! GROOT, BUDDY!!
GROOT!

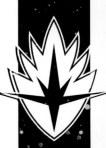

GUARDIANS OF THE GALAXY 1 (2013)

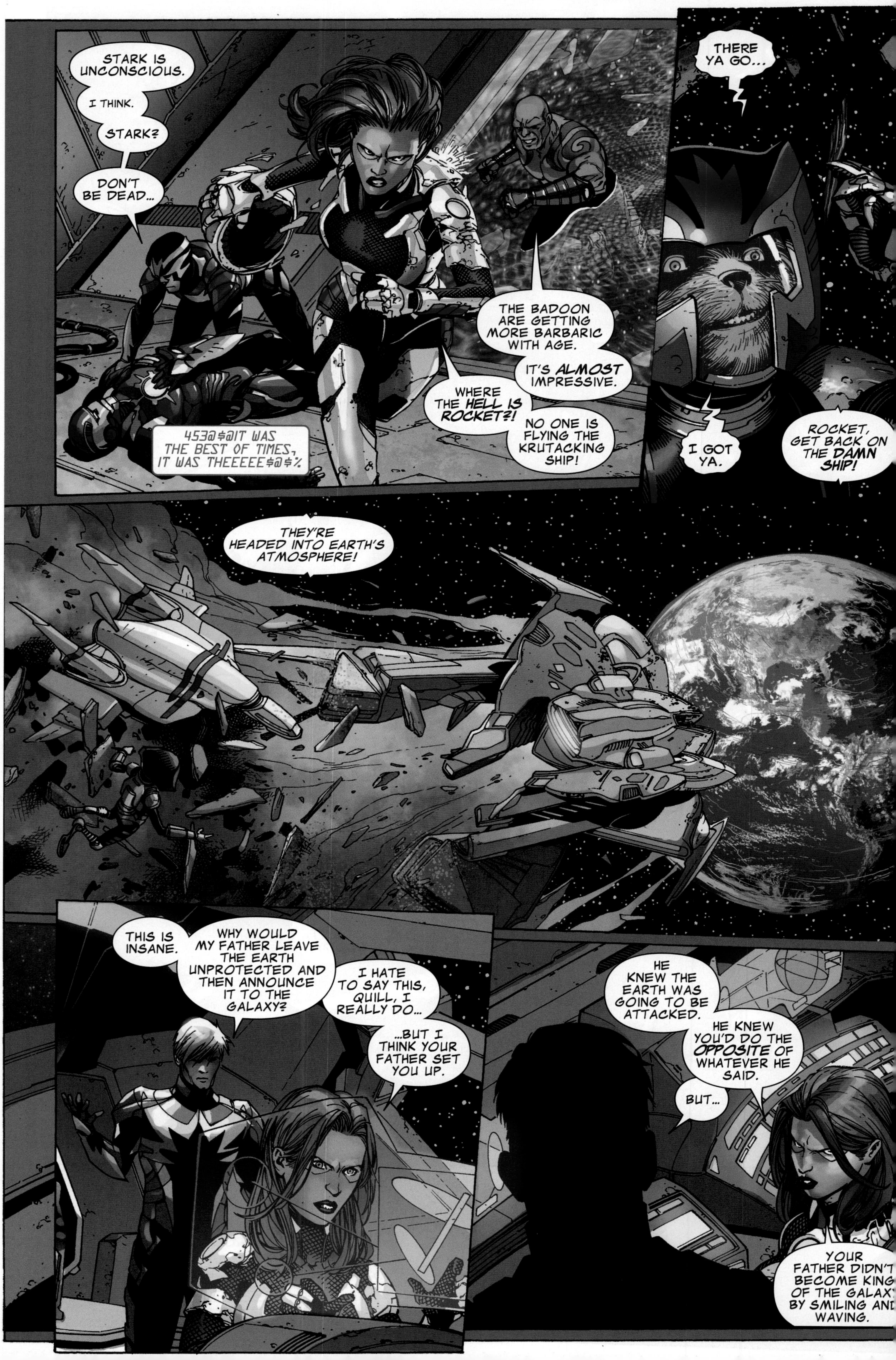

STARK IS UNCONSCIOUS.
I THINK.
STARK?
DON'T BE DEAD...
453@$@IT WAS THE BEST OF TIMES, IT WAS THEEEEE$@$%
WHERE THE HELL IS ROCKET?!
THE BADOON ARE GETTING MORE BARBARIC WITH AGE.
IT'S ALMOST IMPRESSIVE.
NO ONE IS FLYING THE KRUTACKING SHIP!
THERE YA GO...
I GOT YA.
ROCKET, GET BACK ON THE DAMN SHIP!
THEY'RE HEADED INTO EARTH'S ATMOSPHERE!
THIS IS INSANE.
WHY WOULD MY FATHER LEAVE THE EARTH UNPROTECTED AND THEN ANNOUNCE IT TO THE GALAXY?
I HATE TO SAY THIS, QUILL, I REALLY DO...
...BUT I THINK YOUR FATHER SET YOU UP.
HE KNEW THE EARTH WAS GOING TO BE ATTACKED.
HE KNEW YOU'D DO THE OPPOSITE OF WHATEVER HE SAID.
BUT...
YOUR FATHER DIDN'T BECOME KING OF THE GALAXY BY SMILING AND WAVING.

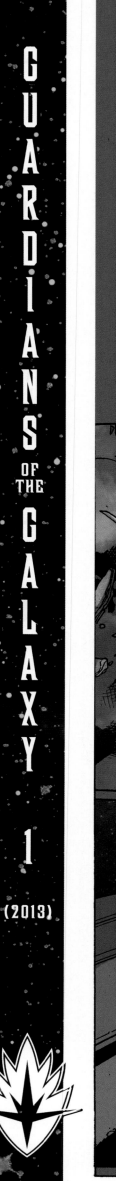

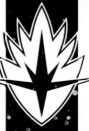

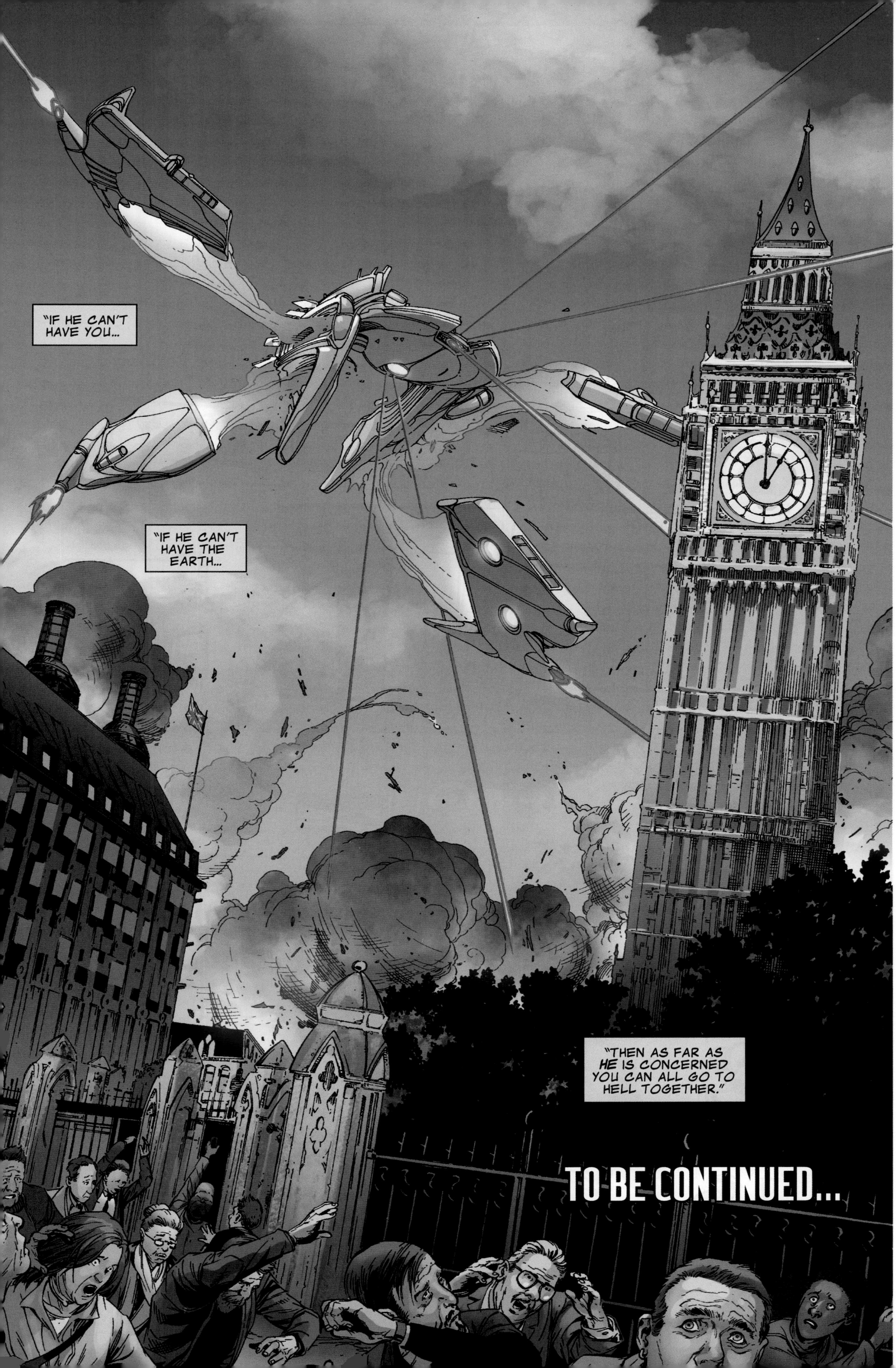
"IF HE CAN'T HAVE YOU...
"IF HE CAN'T HAVE THE EARTH...
"THEN AS FAR AS *HE* IS CONCERNED YOU CAN ALL GO TO HELL TOGETHER."
TO BE CONTINUED...

GUARDIANS OF THE GALAXY 1 (2013)

ROCKERT RACCOON #1 VARIANT BY
SKOTTIE YOUNG

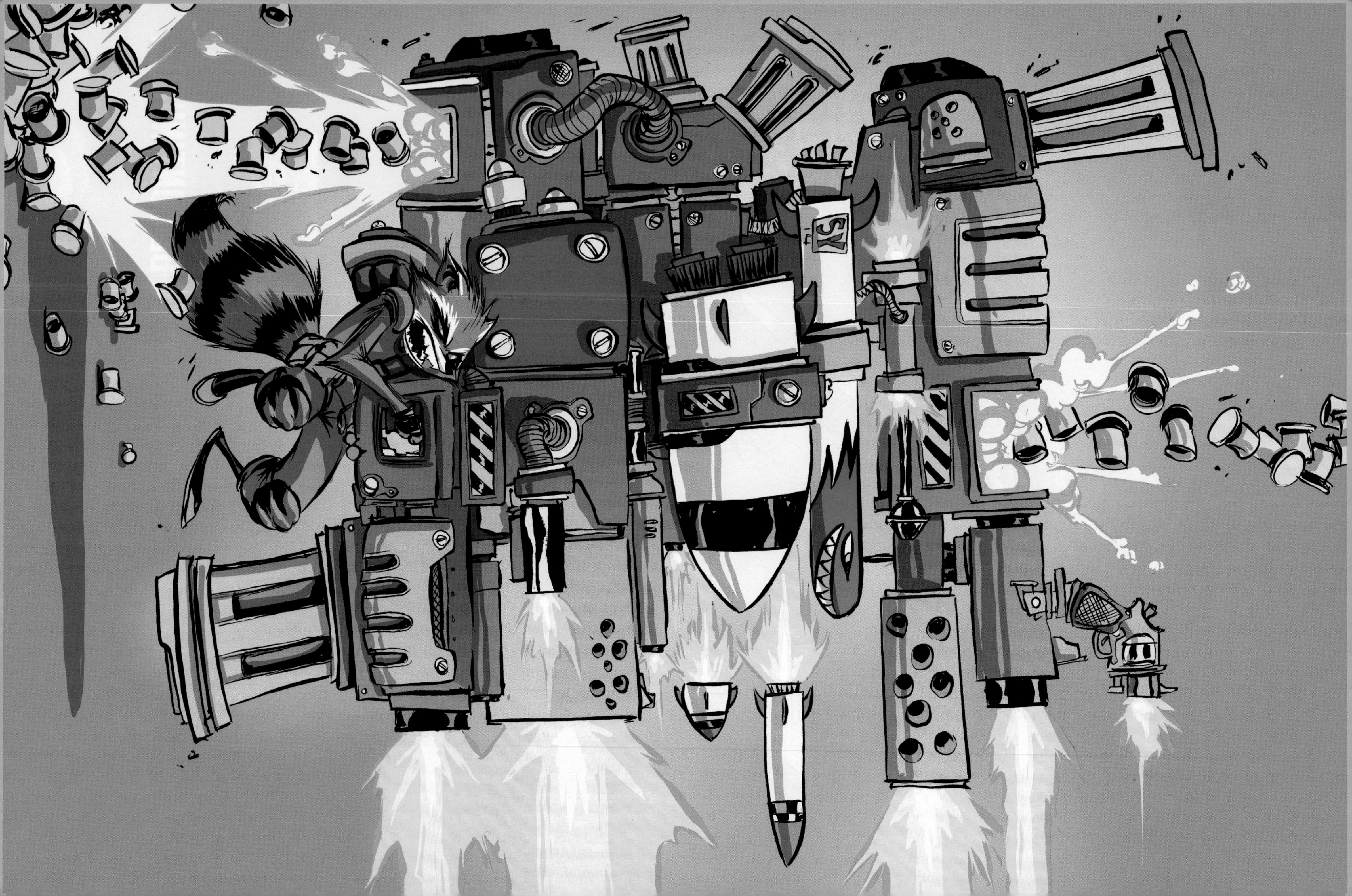
SY

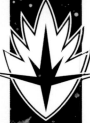

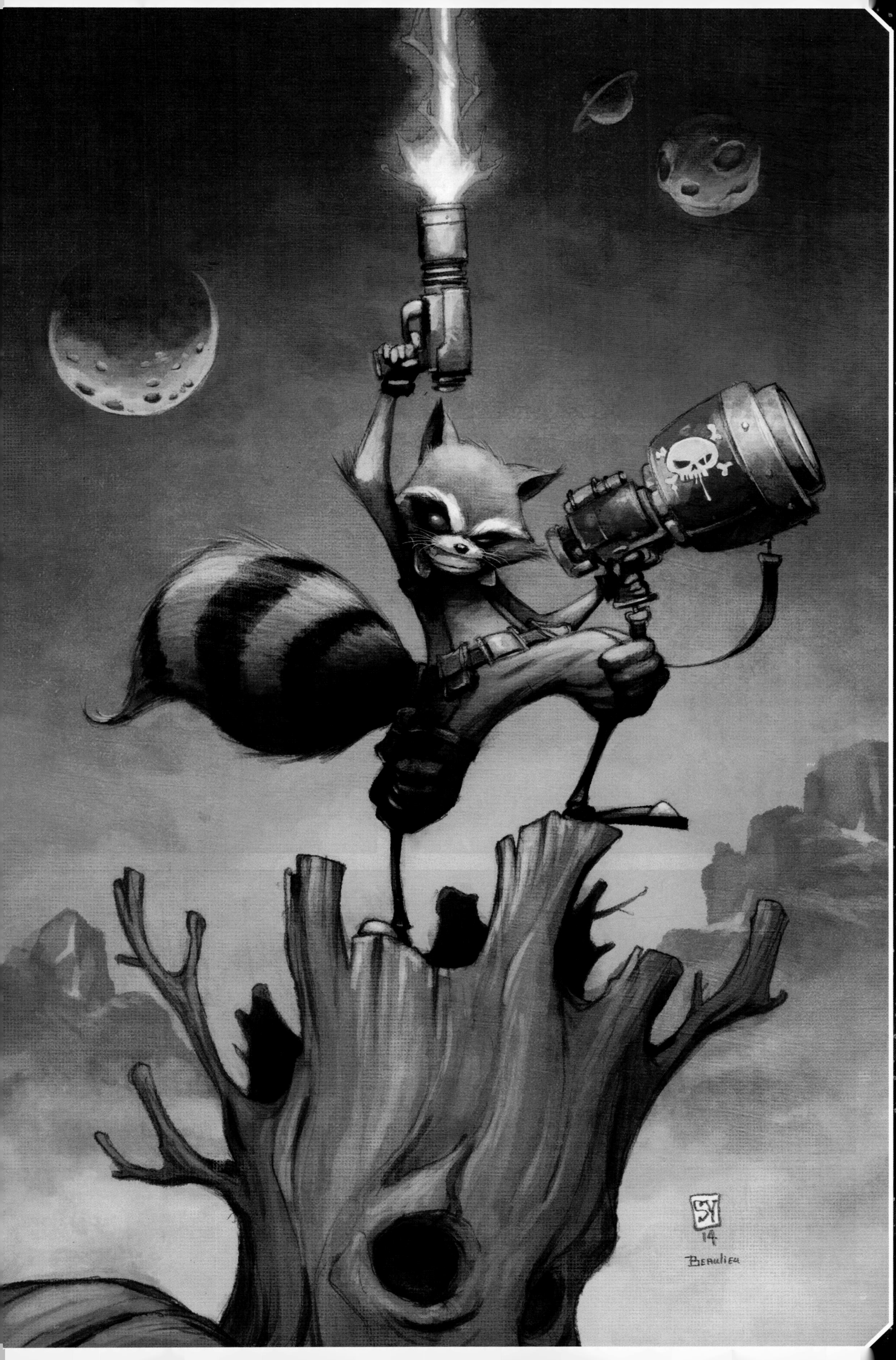
SY
14
BEAULIEU

ROCKET RACCOON 1

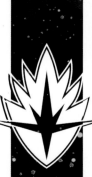

ROCKET RACCOON 1

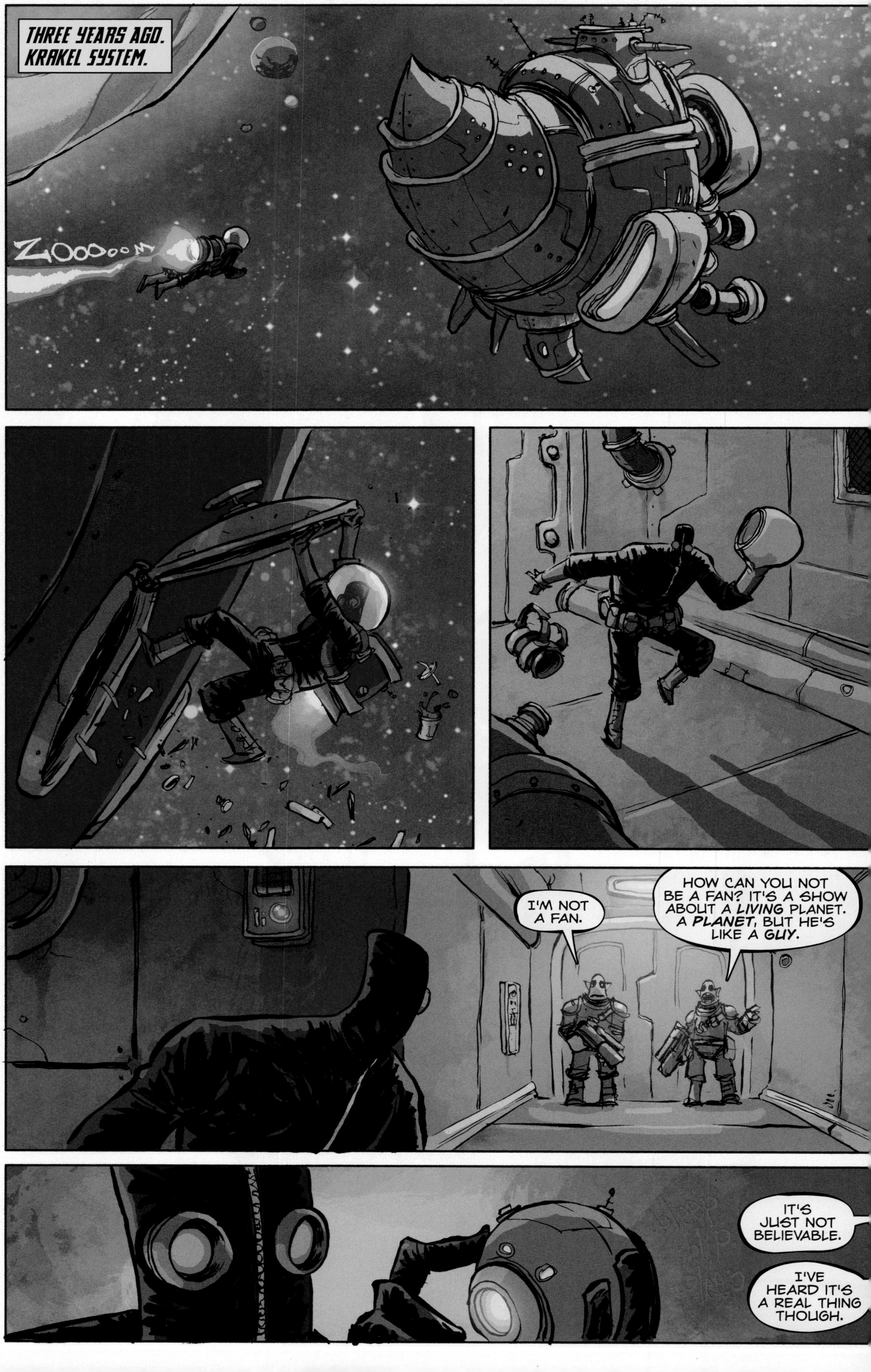
THREE YEARS AGO. KRAKEL SYSTEM.
ZOOOoom
I'M NOT A FAN.
HOW CAN YOU NOT BE A FAN? IT'S A SHOW ABOUT A LIVING PLANET. A PLANET, BUT HE'S LIKE A GUY.
IT'S JUST NOT BELIEVABLE.
I'VE HEARD IT'S A REAL THING THOUGH.

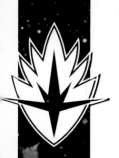

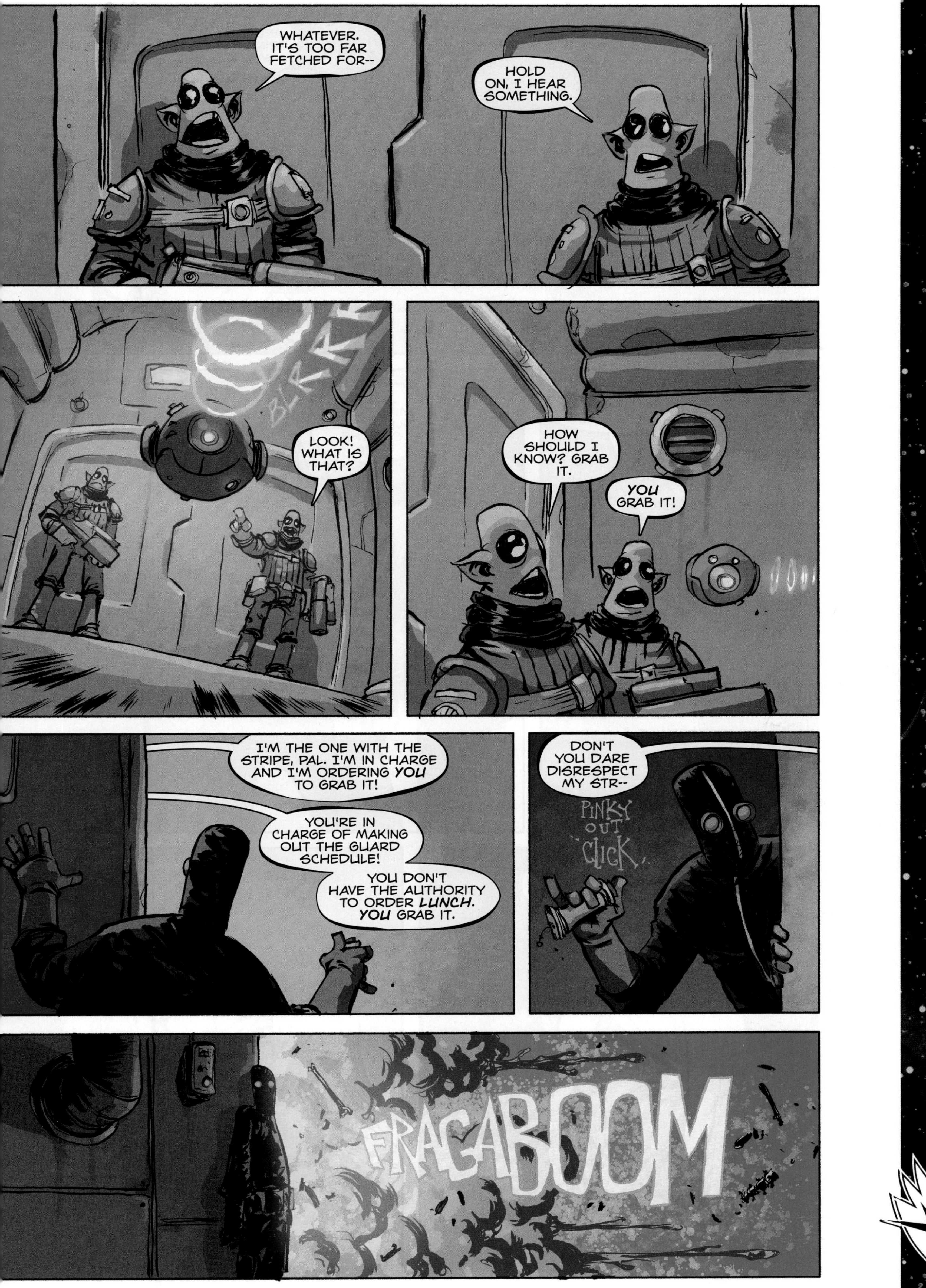
WHATEVER. IT'S TOO FAR FETCHED FOR--
HOLD ON, I HEAR SOMETHING.
BLRRR
LOOK! WHAT IS THAT?
HOW SHOULD I KNOW? GRAB IT.
YOU GRAB IT!
I'M THE ONE WITH THE STRIPE, PAL. I'M IN CHARGE AND I'M ORDERING YOU TO GRAB IT!
YOU'RE IN CHARGE OF MAKING OUT THE GUARD SCHEDULE!
YOU DON'T HAVE THE AUTHORITY TO ORDER LUNCH. YOU GRAB IT.
DON'T YOU DARE DISRESPECT MY STR--
PINKY OUT
CLICK
FRAGABOOM

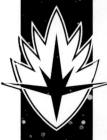

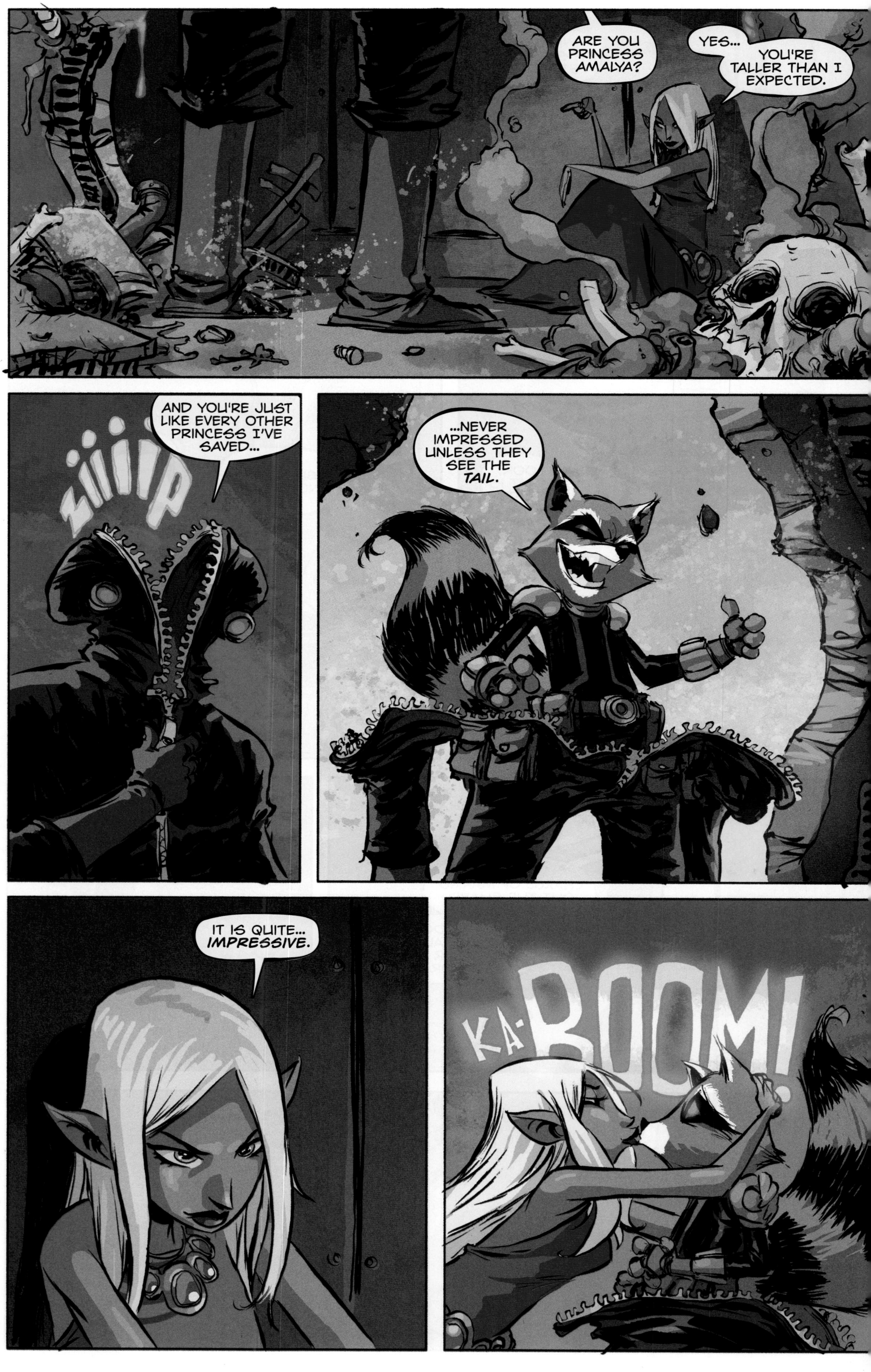
ARE YOU PRINCESS AMALYA?
YES... YOU'RE TALLER THAN I EXPECTED.
AND YOU'RE JUST LIKE EVERY OTHER PRINCESS I'VE SAVED...
ZIIIIP
...NEVER IMPRESSED UNLESS THEY SEE THE *TAIL*.
IT IS QUITE... *IMPRESSIVE*.
KA-BOOM!

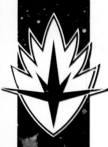

MARVEL ENTERTAINMENT PROUDLY PRESENTS

ROCKET

THE
GUNSLINGIN'
GUARDIAN
OF THE
GALAXY!

skottie young
words and art

jean-françois beaulieu
color art

jeff eckleberry
lettering

RACCOON

A CHASING TALE PART 1

skottie young, leonel castellani, david peterson,
j. scott campbell & nei ruffino, sara pichelli & justin ponsor,
jeff smith & tom gaadt, dale keown & jason keith
variant covers

skottie young
cover art

**irene y. lee &
e's clayton cowles**
production

manny mederos
logo design

devin lewis
assistant editor

sana amanat
editor

nick lowe
senior editor

axel alonso
editor in chief

joe quesada
chief creative officer

dan buckley
publisher

alan fine
executive producer

SPECIAL THANKS TO STEPHEN WACKER

ROCKET RACCOON 1

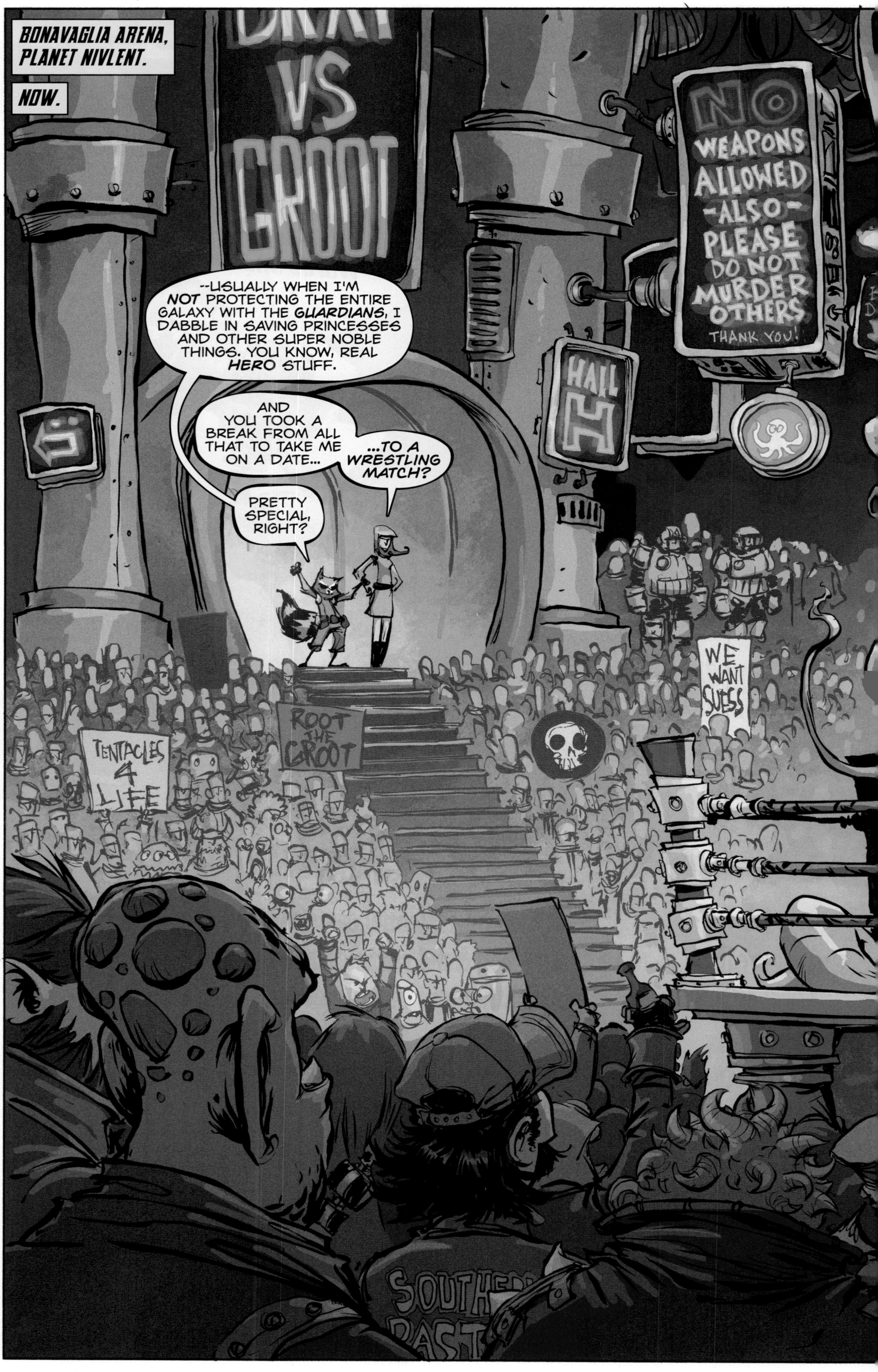
BONAVAGLIA ARENA, PLANET NIVLENT.
NOW.
VS GROOT
NO WEAPONS ALLOWED -ALSO- PLEASE DO NOT MURDER OTHERS THANK YOU!
HALL H
--USUALLY WHEN I'M NOT PROTECTING THE ENTIRE GALAXY WITH THE GUARDIANS, I DABBLE IN SAVING PRINCESSES AND OTHER SUPER NOBLE THINGS. YOU KNOW, REAL HERO STUFF.
AND YOU TOOK A BREAK FROM ALL THAT TO TAKE ME ON A DATE...
...TO A WRESTLING MATCH?
PRETTY SPECIAL, RIGHT?
WE WANT SUESS
ROOT THE GROOT
TENTACLES 4 LIFE

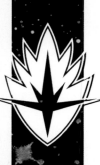

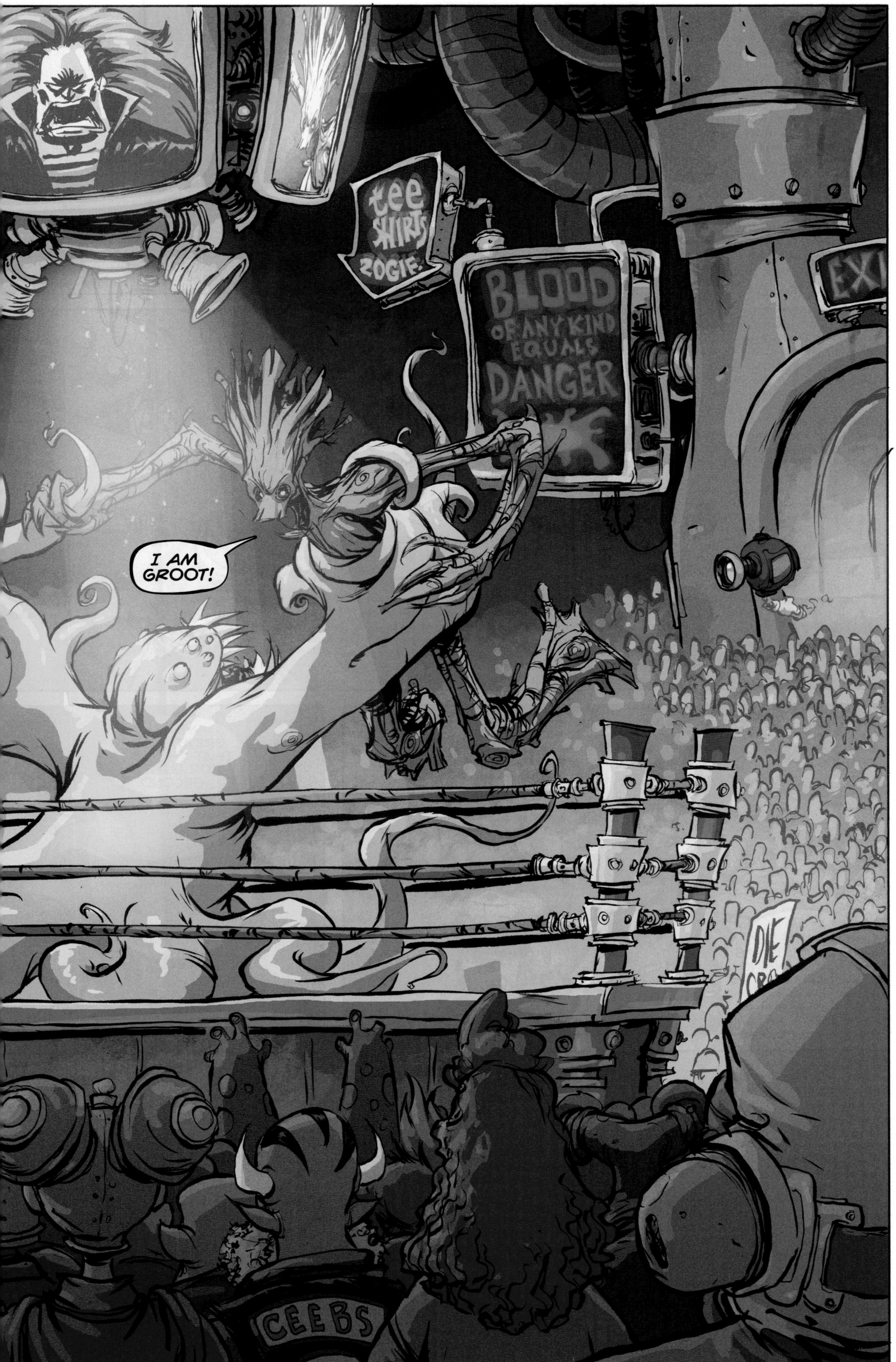
tee SHIRTS ZOGIF.
BLOOD OF ANY KIND EQUALS DANGER
I AM GROOT!
DIE
CEEBS

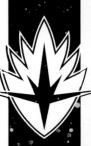

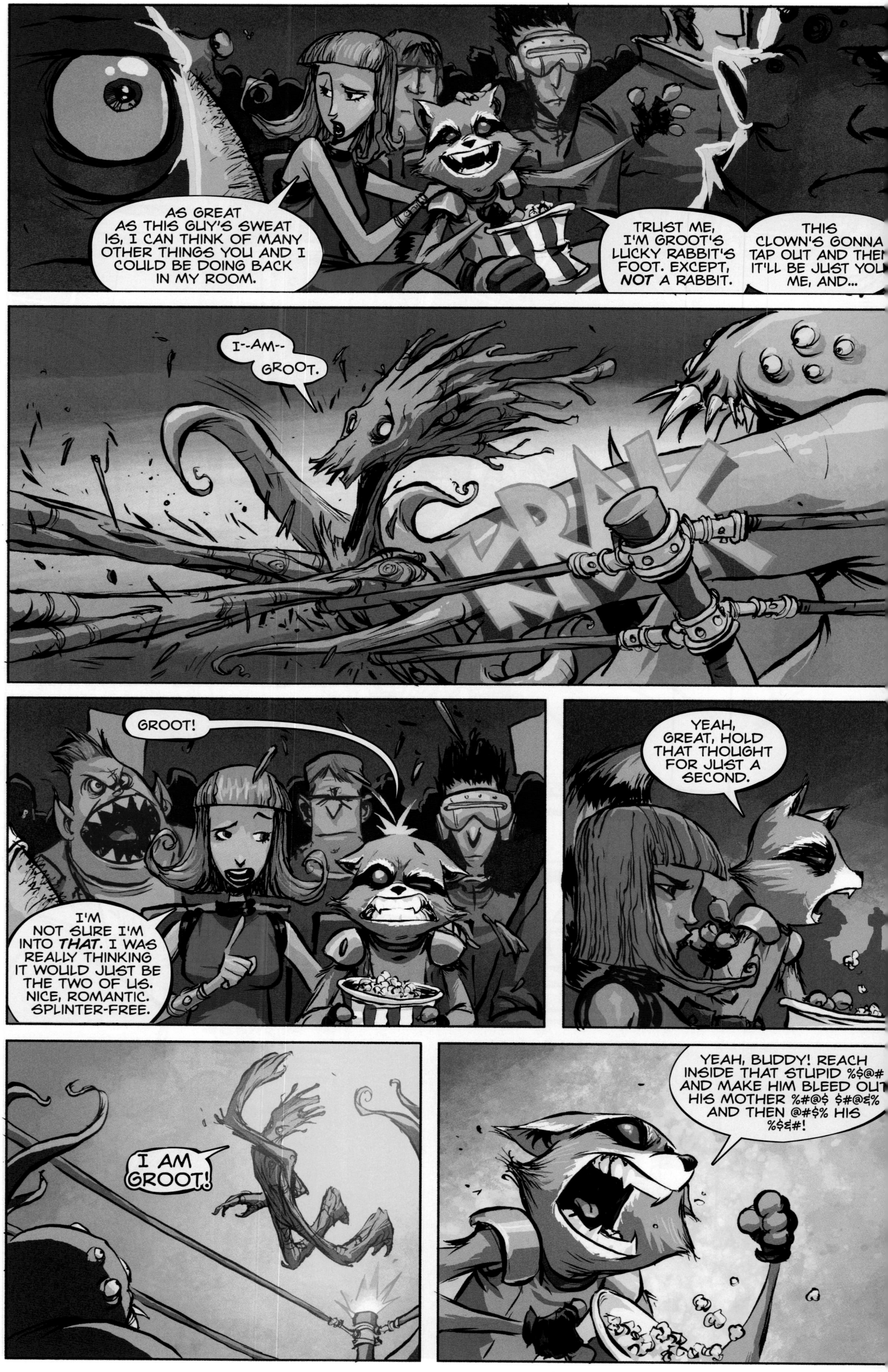
AS GREAT AS THIS GUY'S SWEAT IS, I CAN THINK OF MANY OTHER THINGS YOU AND I COULD BE DOING BACK IN MY ROOM.
TRUST ME, I'M GROOT'S LUCKY RABBIT'S FOOT. EXCEPT, NOT A RABBIT.
THIS CLOWN'S GONNA TAP OUT AND THEN IT'LL BE JUST YOU, ME, AND...
I--AM--GROOT.
KRAK
GROOT!
I'M NOT SURE I'M INTO THAT. I WAS REALLY THINKING IT WOULD JUST BE THE TWO OF US. NICE, ROMANTIC. SPLINTER-FREE.
YEAH, GREAT, HOLD THAT THOUGHT FOR JUST A SECOND.
I AM GROOT!
YEAH, BUDDY! REACH INSIDE THAT STUPID %$@# AND MAKE HIM BLEED OUT HIS MOTHER %#@$ $#@&% AND THEN @#$% HIS %$&#!

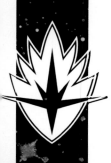

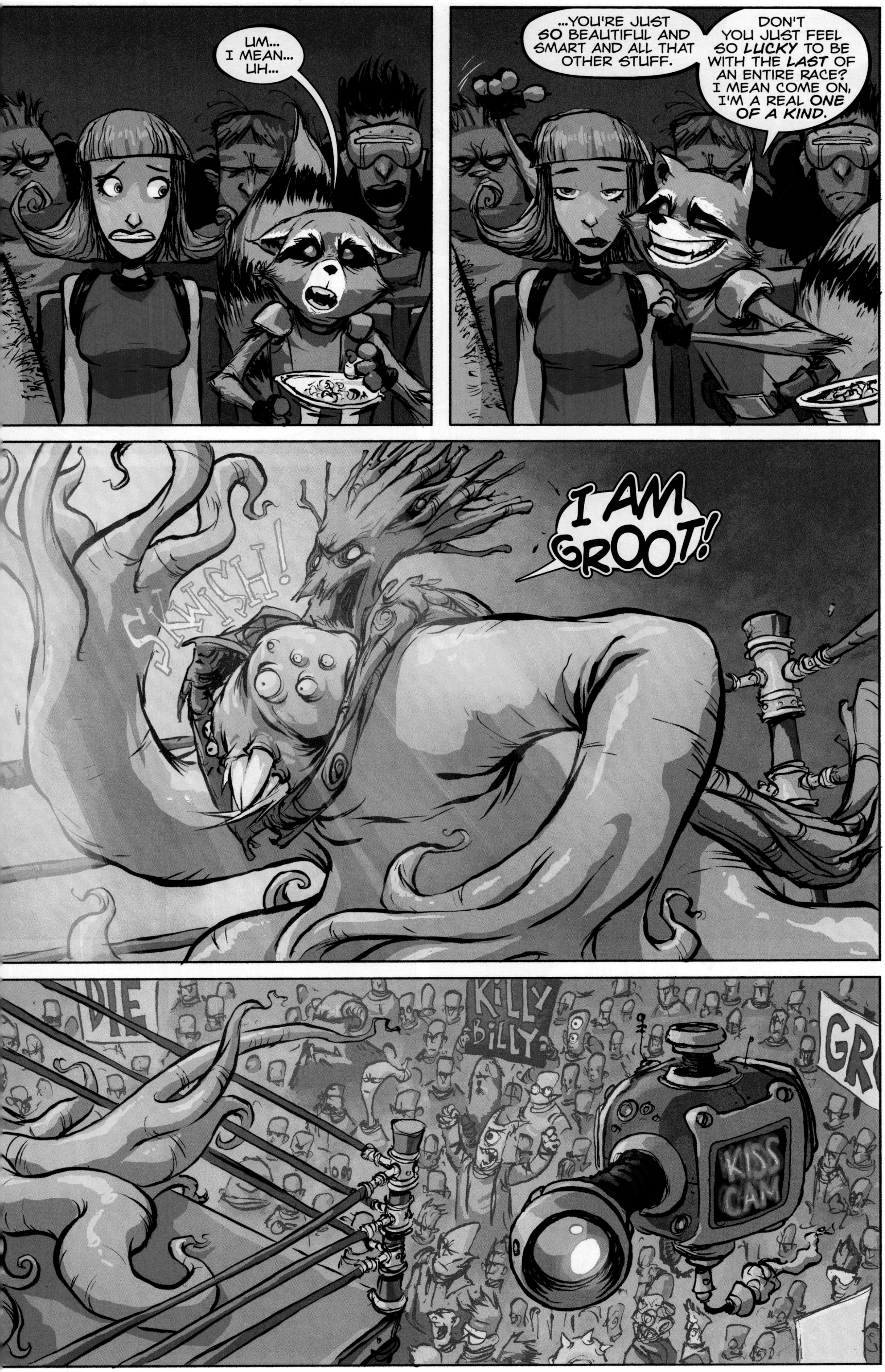
UM... I MEAN... UH...
...YOU'RE JUST SO BEAUTIFUL AND SMART AND ALL THAT OTHER STUFF.
DON'T YOU JUST FEEL SO *LUCKY* TO BE WITH THE *LAST* OF AN ENTIRE RACE? I MEAN COME ON, I'M A REAL *ONE OF A KIND.*
SWISH!
I AM GROOT!
DIE
KILLY BILLY
KISS CAM

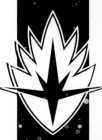

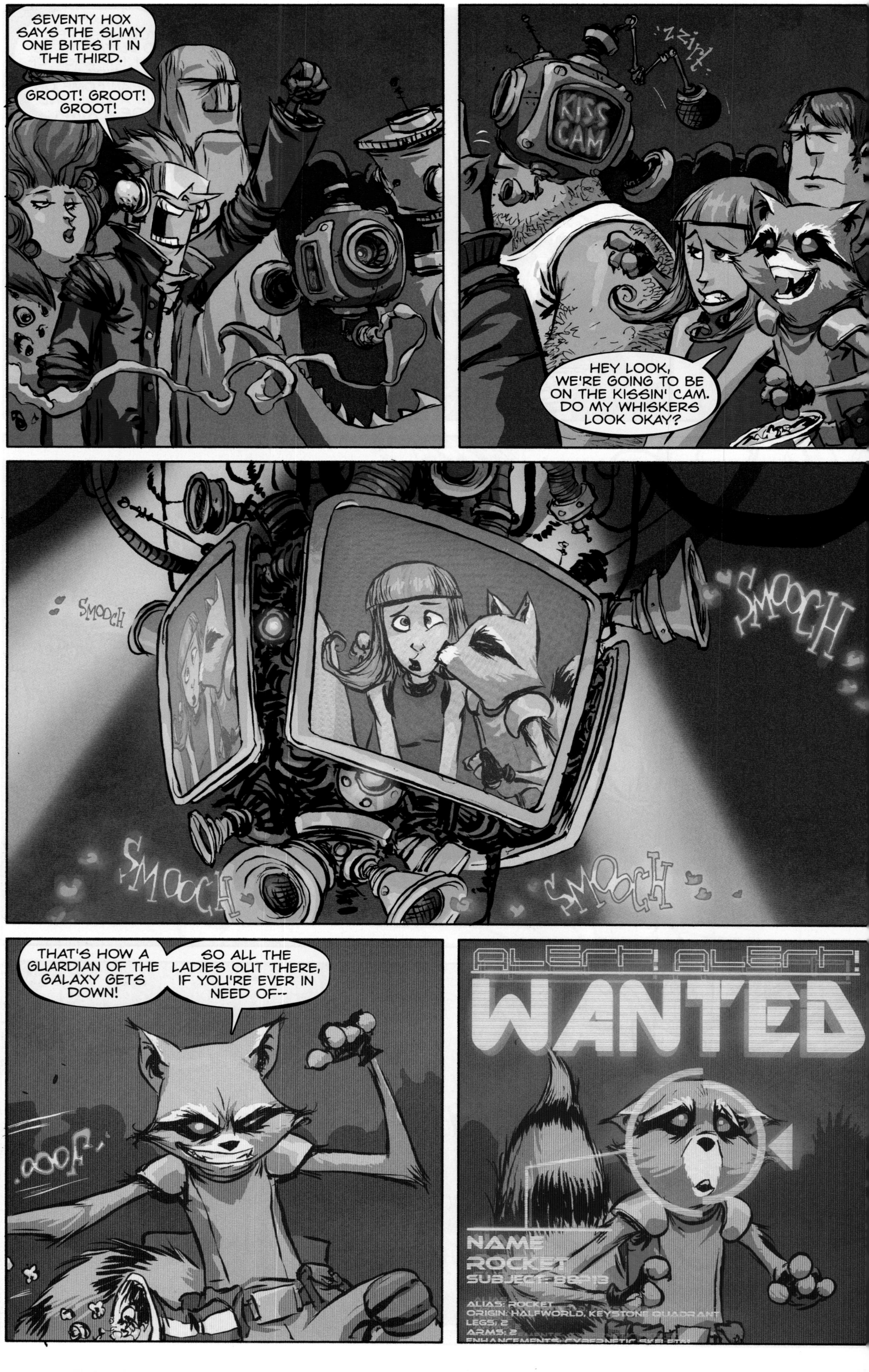
SEVENTY HOX SAYS THE SLIMY ONE BITES IT IN THE THIRD.
GROOT! GROOT! GROOT!
ZZIRT
KISS CAM
HEY LOOK, WE'RE GOING TO BE ON THE KISSIN' CAM. DO MY WHISKERS LOOK OKAY?
SMOOCH
SMOOCH
SMOOCH
SMOOCH
THAT'S HOW A GUARDIAN OF THE GALAXY GETS DOWN!
SO ALL THE LADIES OUT THERE, IF YOU'RE EVER IN NEED OF--
OOOF
ALERT! ALERT!
WANTED
NAME
ROCKET
SUBJECT: 89P13
ALIAS: ROCKET
ORIGIN: HALFWORLD, KEYSTONE QUADRANT
LEGS: 2
ARMS: 2

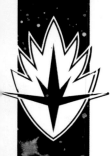

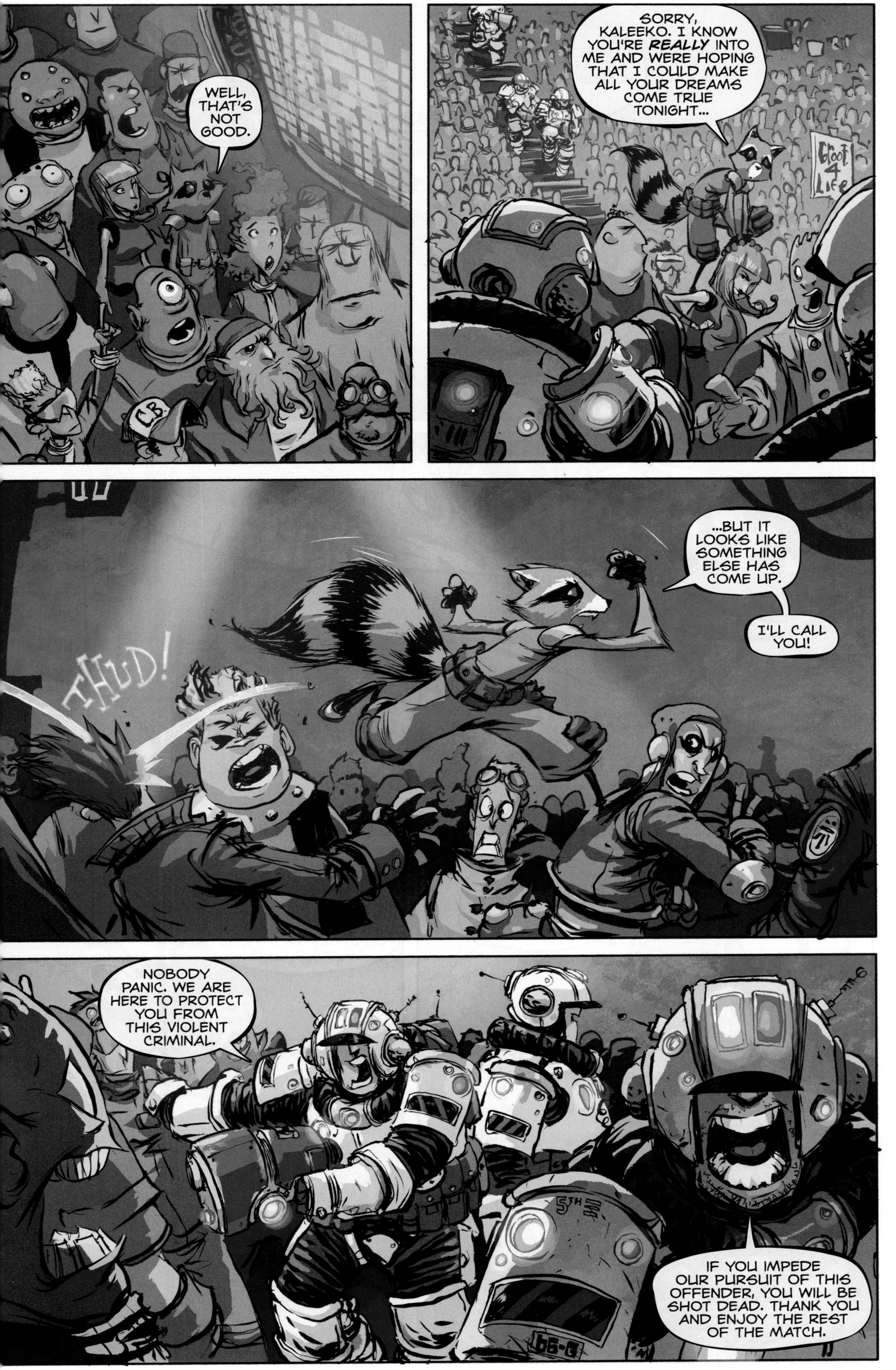
WELL, THAT'S NOT GOOD.
SORRY, KALEEKO. I KNOW YOU'RE *REALLY* INTO ME AND WERE HOPING THAT I COULD MAKE ALL YOUR DREAMS COME TRUE TONIGHT...
Groot 4 Life
...BUT IT LOOKS LIKE SOMETHING ELSE HAS COME UP.
I'LL CALL YOU!
THUD!
NOBODY PANIC. WE ARE HERE TO PROTECT YOU FROM THIS VIOLENT CRIMINAL.
IF YOU IMPEDE OUR PURSUIT OF THIS OFFENDER, YOU WILL BE SHOT DEAD. THANK YOU AND ENJOY THE REST OF THE MATCH.

ROCKET RACCOON 1

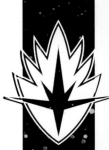

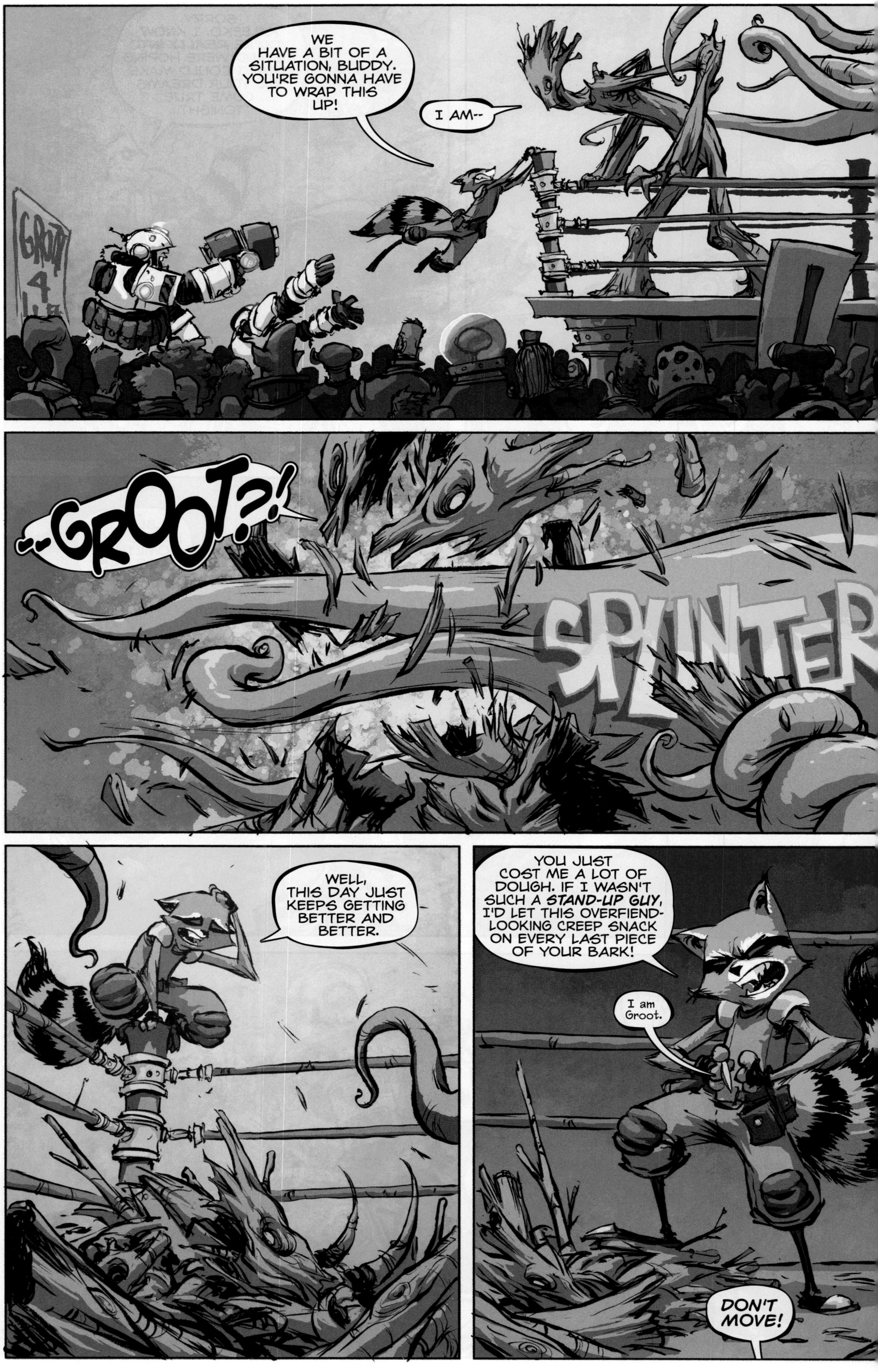
WE HAVE A BIT OF A SITUATION, BUDDY. YOU'RE GONNA HAVE TO WRAP THIS UP!
I AM--
--GROOT?!
SPLINTER
WELL, THIS DAY JUST KEEPS GETTING BETTER AND BETTER.
YOU JUST COST ME A LOT OF DOUGH. IF I WASN'T SUCH A ***STAND-UP GUY***, I'D LET THIS OVERFIEND-LOOKING CREEP SNACK ON EVERY LAST PIECE OF YOUR BARK!
I am Groot.
DON'T MOVE!

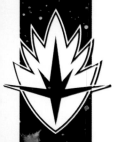

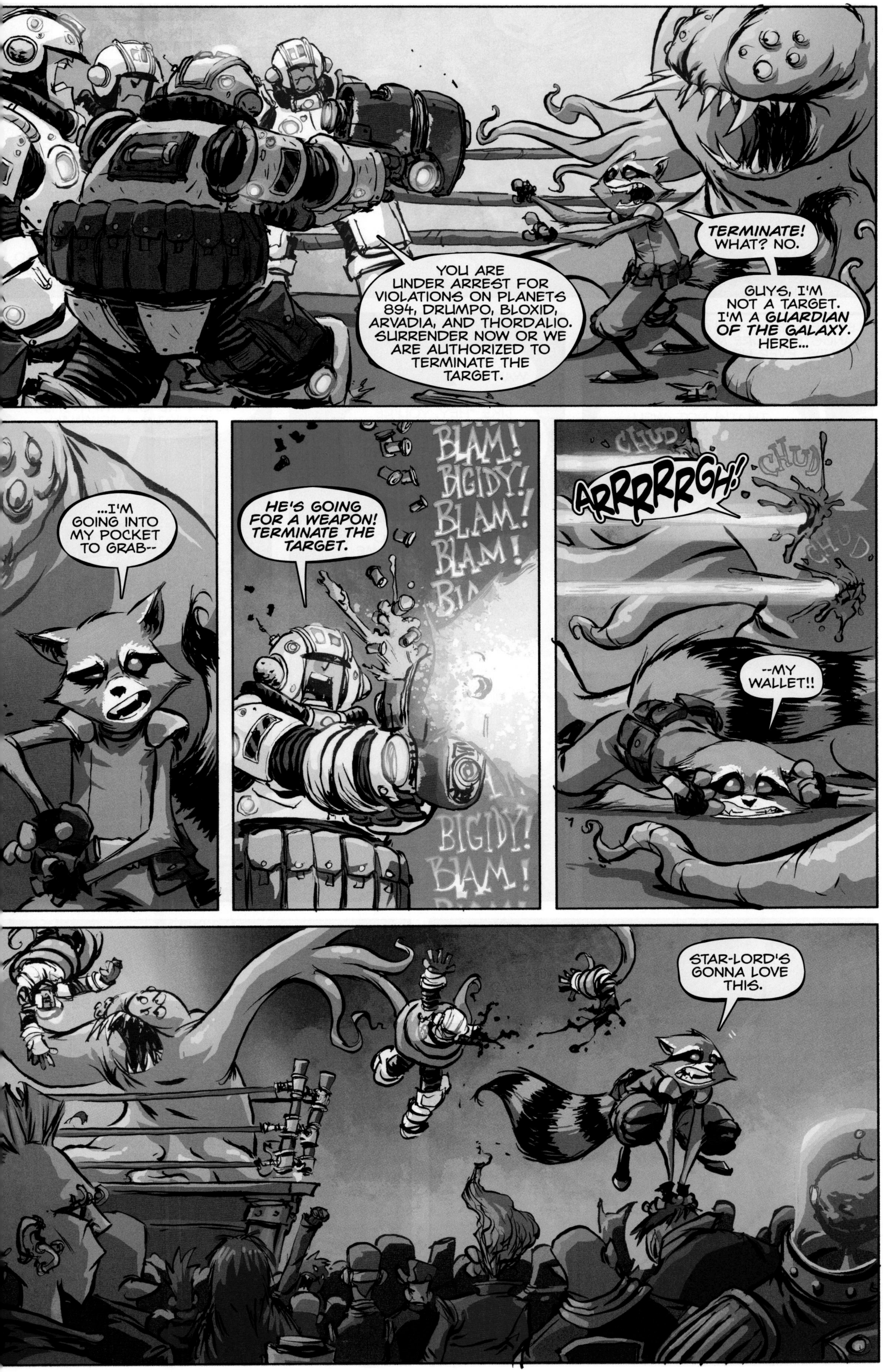
YOU ARE UNDER ARREST FOR VIOLATIONS ON PLANETS 894, DRUMPO, BLOXID, ARVADIA, AND THORDALIO. SURRENDER NOW OR WE ARE AUTHORIZED TO TERMINATE THE TARGET.
TERMINATE! WHAT? NO.
GUYS, I'M NOT A TARGET. I'M A GUARDIAN OF THE GALAXY. HERE...
...I'M GOING INTO MY POCKET TO GRAB--
HE'S GOING FOR A WEAPON! TERMINATE THE TARGET.
BLAM! BIGIDY! BLAM! BLAM!
BIGIDY! BLAM!
CHUD
CHUD
ARRRRRGH!
CHUD
--MY WALLET!!
STAR-LORD'S GONNA LOVE THIS.

ROCKET RACCOON 1

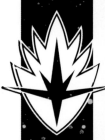

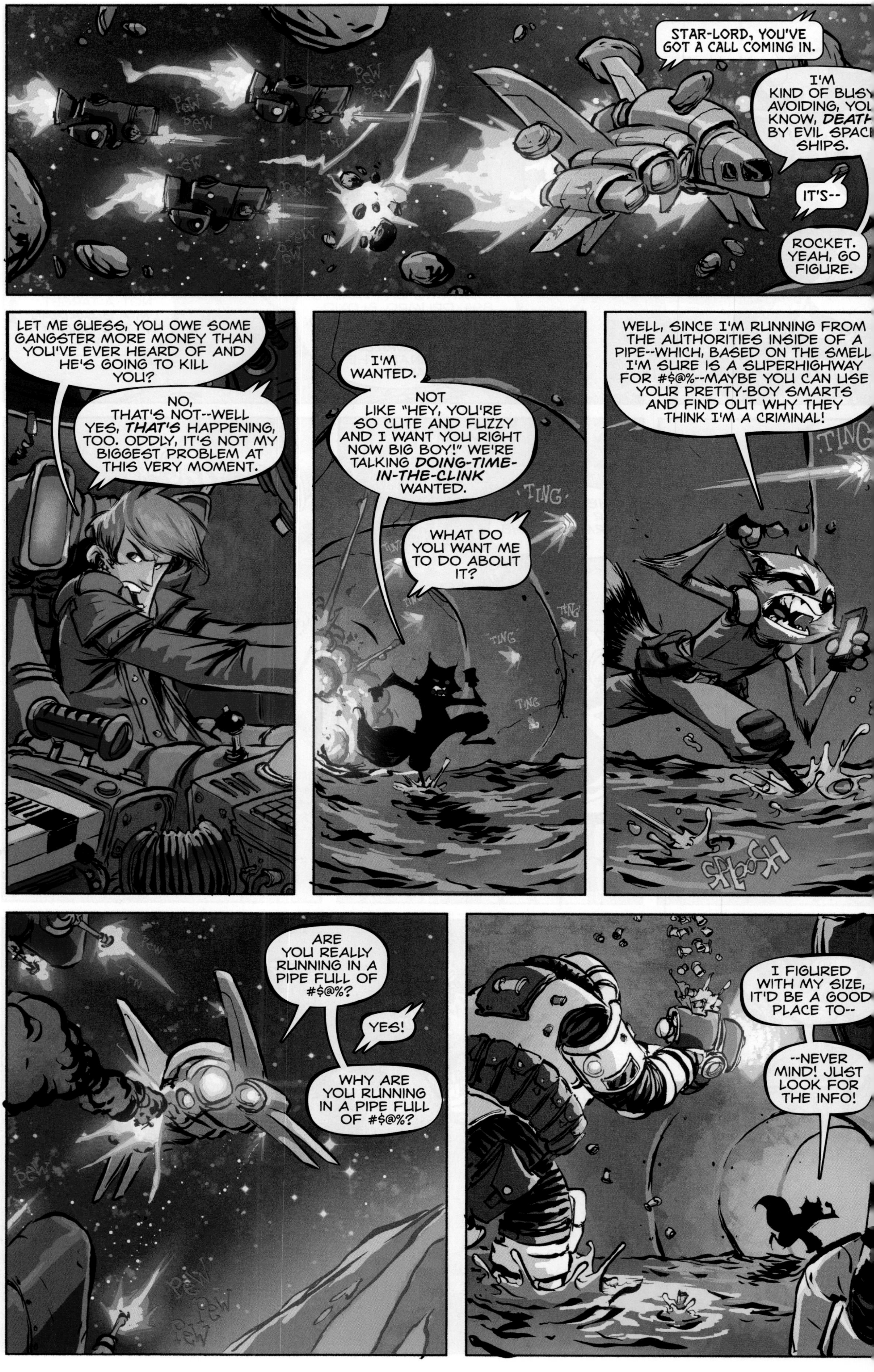
STAR-LORD, YOU'VE GOT A CALL COMING IN.
PEW PEW
I'M KIND OF BUSY AVOIDING, YOU KNOW, *DEATH* BY EVIL SPACE SHIPS.
IT'S--
ROCKET. YEAH, GO FIGURE.
LET ME GUESS, YOU OWE SOME GANGSTER MORE MONEY THAN YOU'VE EVER HEARD OF AND HE'S GOING TO KILL YOU?
NO, THAT'S NOT--WELL YES, *THAT'S* HAPPENING, TOO. ODDLY, IT'S NOT MY BIGGEST PROBLEM AT THIS VERY MOMENT.
I'M WANTED.
NOT LIKE "HEY, YOU'RE SO CUTE AND FUZZY AND I WANT YOU RIGHT NOW BIG BOY!" WE'RE TALKING *DOING-TIME-IN-THE-CLINK* WANTED.
TING
WHAT DO YOU WANT ME TO DO ABOUT IT?
TING
TING
TING
WELL, SINCE I'M RUNNING FROM THE AUTHORITIES INSIDE OF A PIPE--WHICH, BASED ON THE SMELL I'M SURE IS A SUPERHIGHWAY FOR #$@%--MAYBE YOU CAN USE YOUR PRETTY-BOY SMARTS AND FIND OUT WHY THEY THINK I'M A CRIMINAL!
TING
ARE YOU REALLY RUNNING IN A PIPE FULL OF #$@%?
YES!
WHY ARE YOU RUNNING IN A PIPE FULL OF #$@%?
PEW PEW PEW
I FIGURED WITH MY SIZE, IT'D BE A GOOD PLACE TO--
--NEVER MIND! JUST LOOK FOR THE INFO!

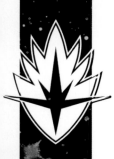

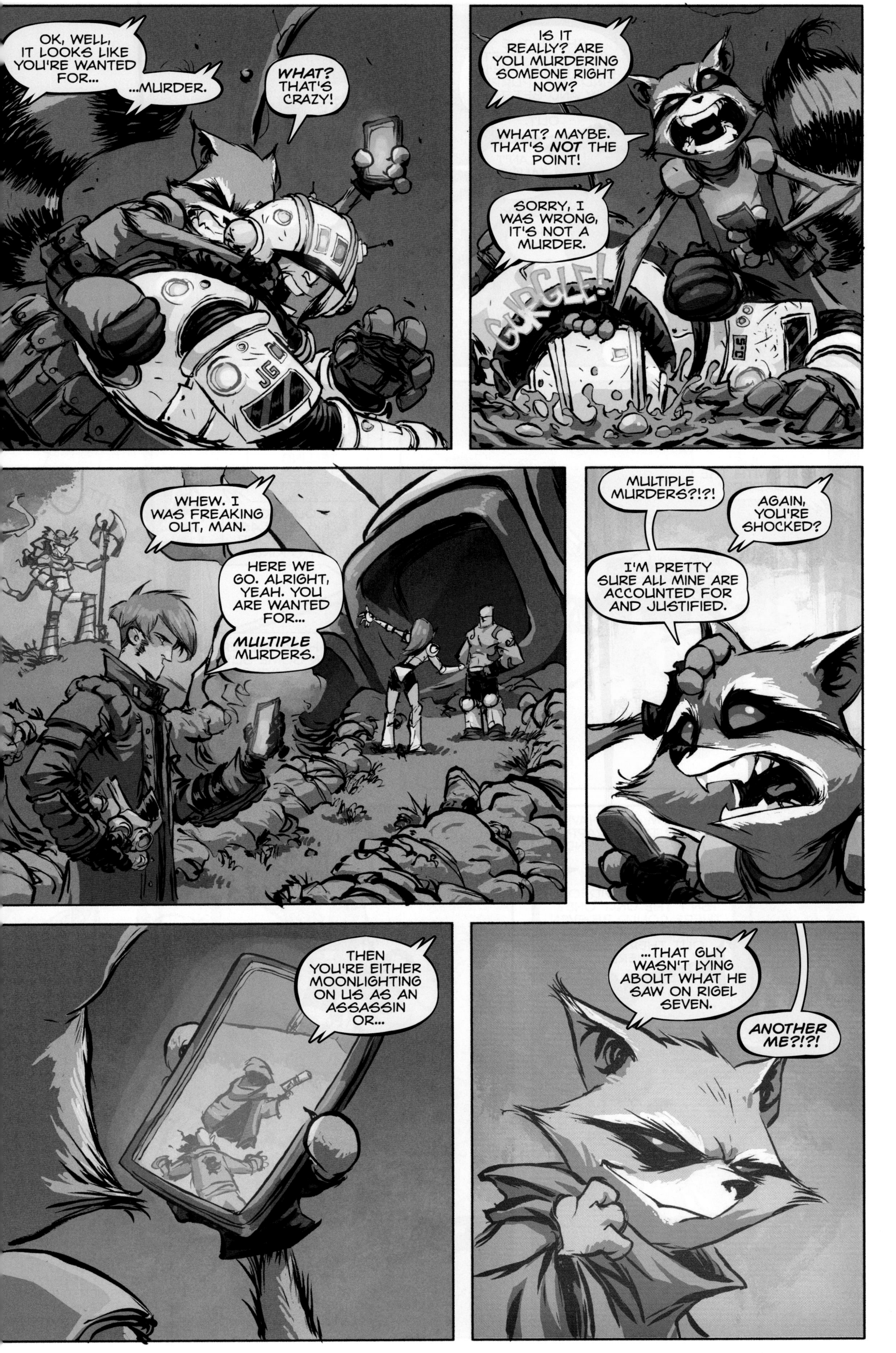

OK, WELL, IT LOOKS LIKE YOU'RE WANTED FOR...
...MURDER.
WHAT? THAT'S CRAZY!
IS IT REALLY? ARE YOU MURDERING SOMEONE RIGHT NOW?
WHAT? MAYBE. THAT'S NOT THE POINT!
SORRY, I WAS WRONG, IT'S NOT A MURDER.
GURGLE!
WHEW. I WAS FREAKING OUT, MAN.
HERE WE GO. ALRIGHT, YEAH. YOU ARE WANTED FOR... MULTIPLE MURDERS.
MULTIPLE MURDERS?!?!
AGAIN, YOU'RE SHOCKED?
I'M PRETTY SURE ALL MINE ARE ACCOUNTED FOR AND JUSTIFIED.
THEN YOU'RE EITHER MOONLIGHTING ON US AS AN ASSASSIN OR...
...THAT GUY WASN'T LYING ABOUT WHAT HE SAW ON RIGEL SEVEN.
ANOTHER ME?!?!

ROCKET RACCOON 1

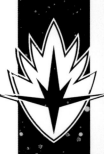

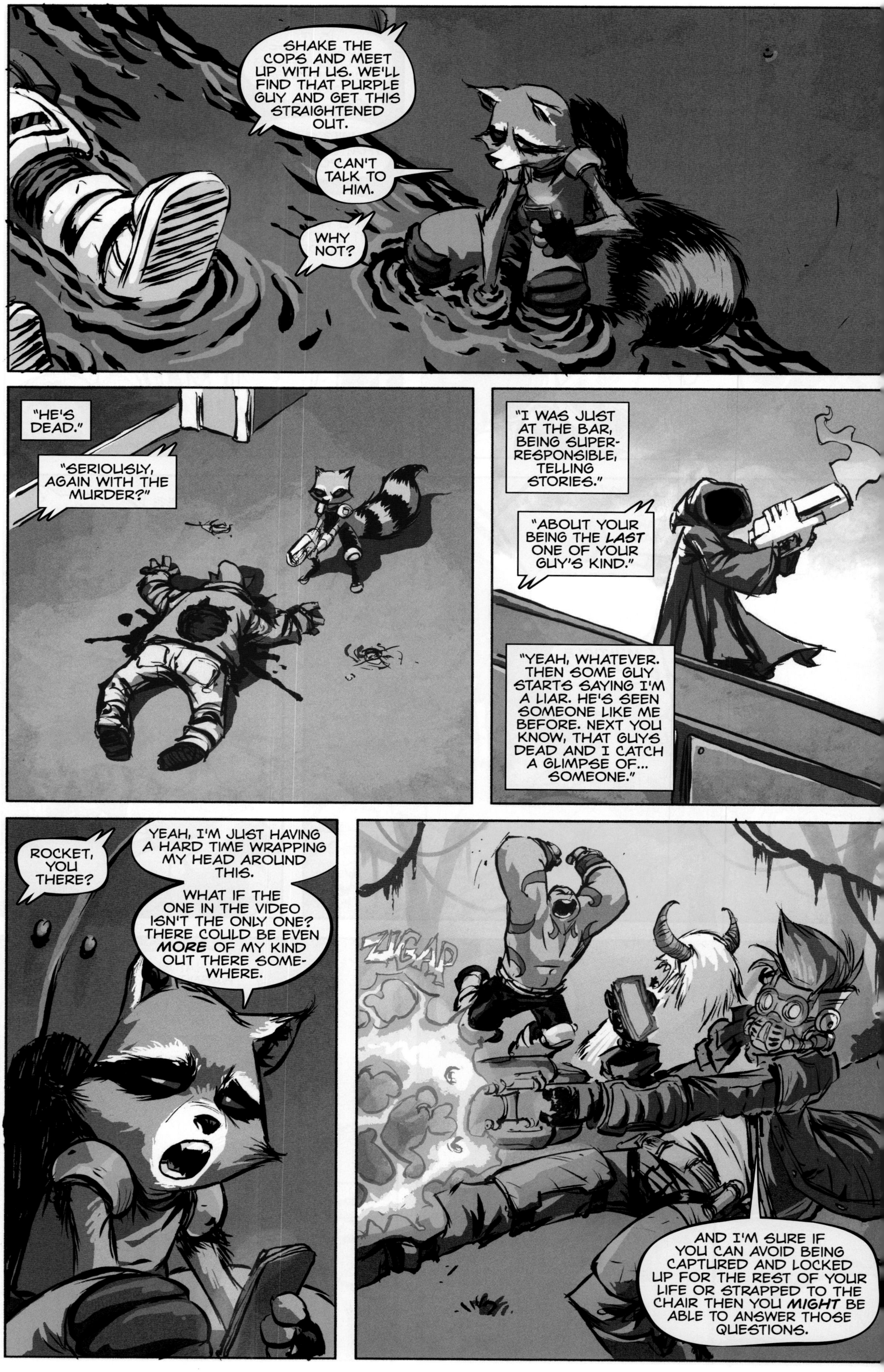
SHAKE THE COPS AND MEET UP WITH US. WE'LL FIND THAT PURPLE GUY AND GET THIS STRAIGHTENED OUT.
CAN'T TALK TO HIM.
WHY NOT?
"HE'S DEAD."
"SERIOUSLY, AGAIN WITH THE MURDER?"
"I WAS JUST AT THE BAR, BEING SUPER-RESPONSIBLE, TELLING STORIES."
"ABOUT YOUR BEING THE LAST ONE OF YOUR GUY'S KIND."
"YEAH, WHATEVER. THEN SOME GUY STARTS SAYING I'M A LIAR. HE'S SEEN SOMEONE LIKE ME BEFORE. NEXT YOU KNOW, THAT GUYS DEAD AND I CATCH A GLIMPSE OF... SOMEONE."
ROCKET, YOU THERE?
YEAH, I'M JUST HAVING A HARD TIME WRAPPING MY HEAD AROUND THIS.
WHAT IF THE ONE IN THE VIDEO ISN'T THE ONLY ONE? THERE COULD BE EVEN MORE OF MY KIND OUT THERE SOME-WHERE.
ZIGAP
AND I'M SURE IF YOU CAN AVOID BEING CAPTURED AND LOCKED UP FOR THE REST OF YOUR LIFE OR STRAPPED TO THE CHAIR THEN YOU MIGHT BE ABLE TO ANSWER THOSE QUESTIONS.

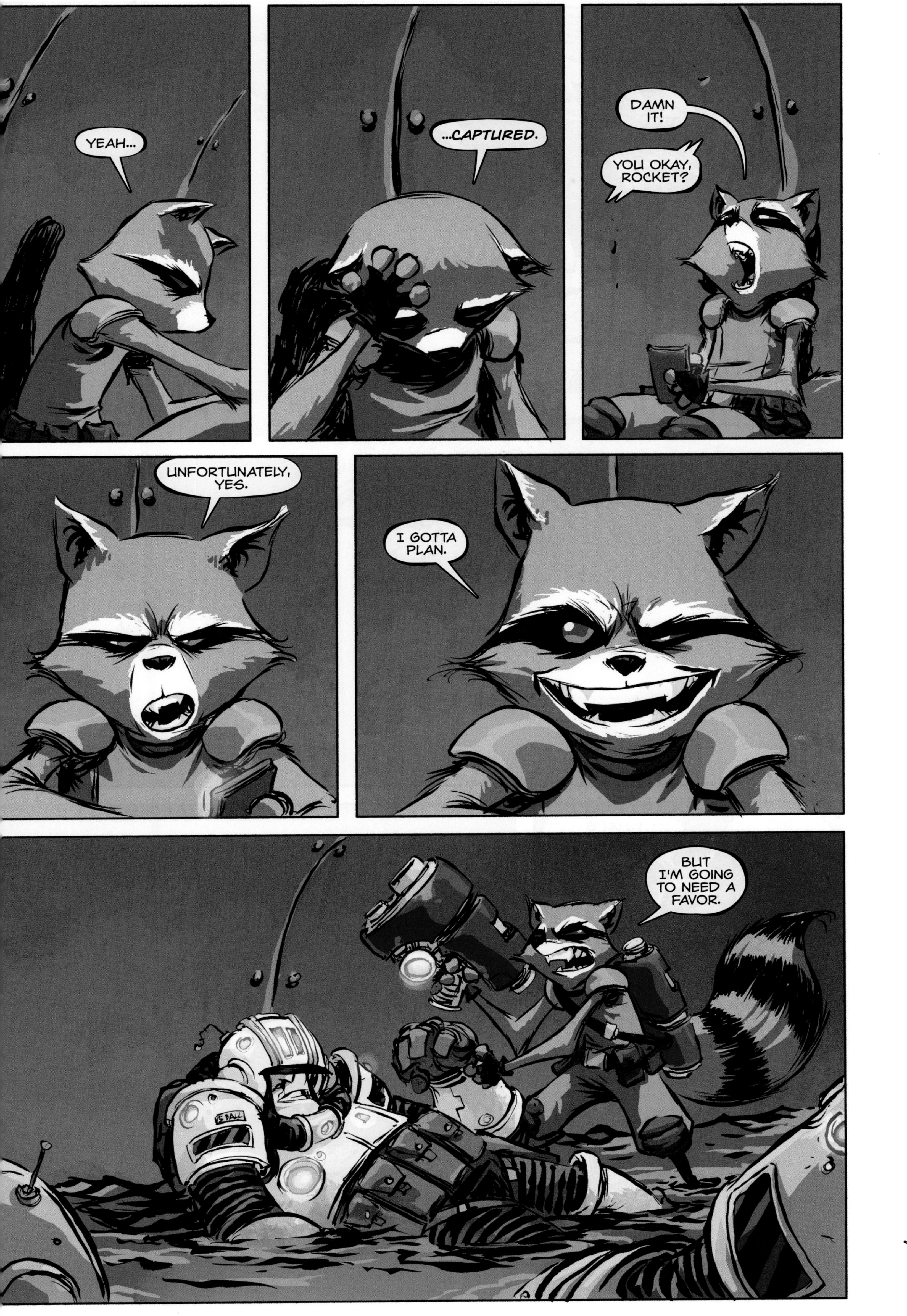
YEAH...
...CAPTURED.
DAMN IT!
YOU OKAY, ROCKET?
UNFORTUNATELY, YES.
I GOTTA PLAN.
BUT I'M GOING TO NEED A FAVOR.

ROCKET RACCOON 1

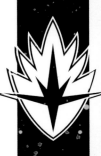

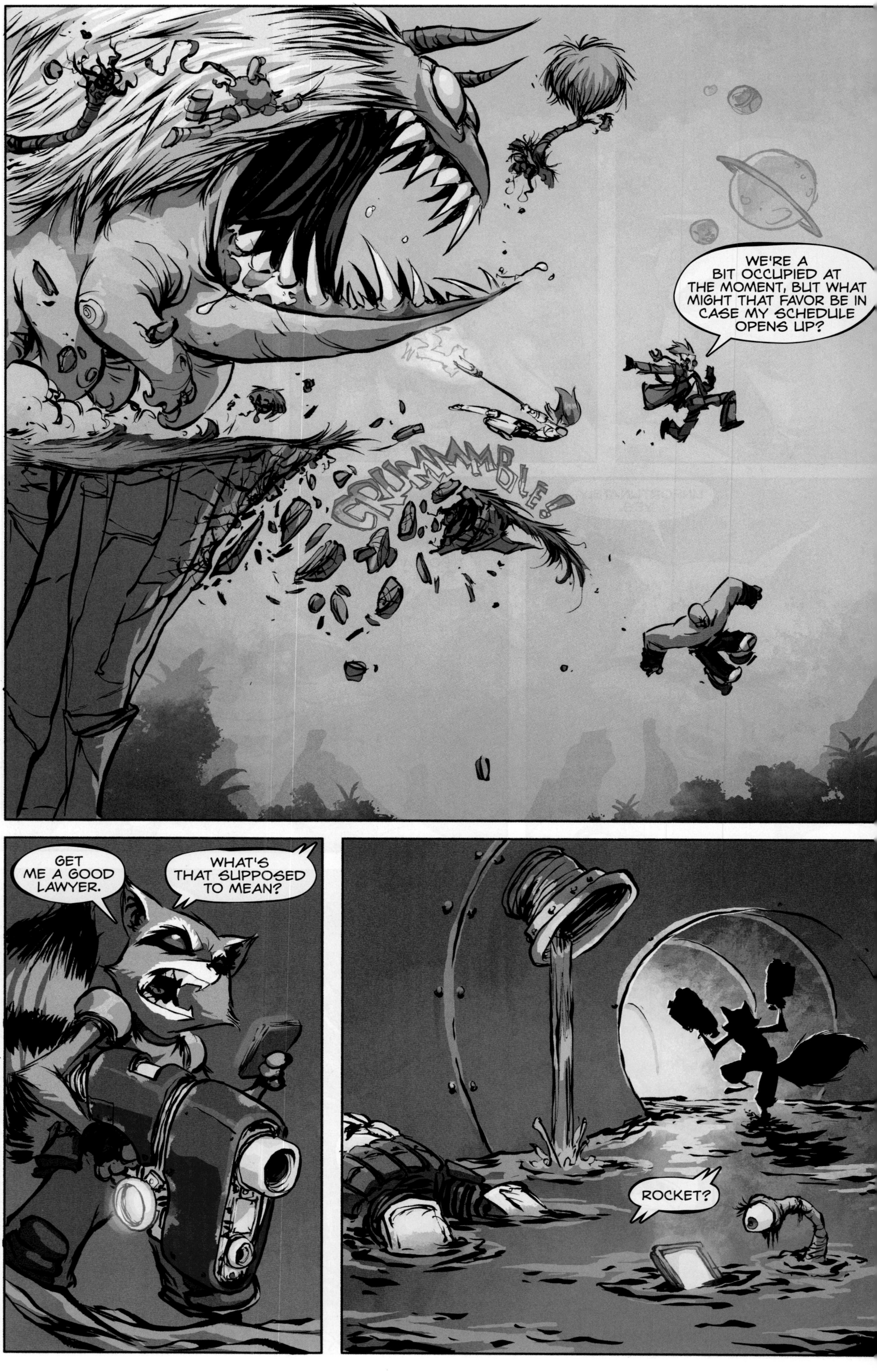
WE'RE A BIT OCCUPIED AT THE MOMENT, BUT WHAT MIGHT THAT FAVOR BE IN CASE MY SCHEDULE OPENS UP?
CRUMMMMBLE!
GET ME A GOOD LAWYER.
WHAT'S THAT SUPPOSED TO MEAN?
ROCKET?

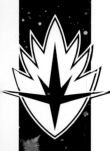

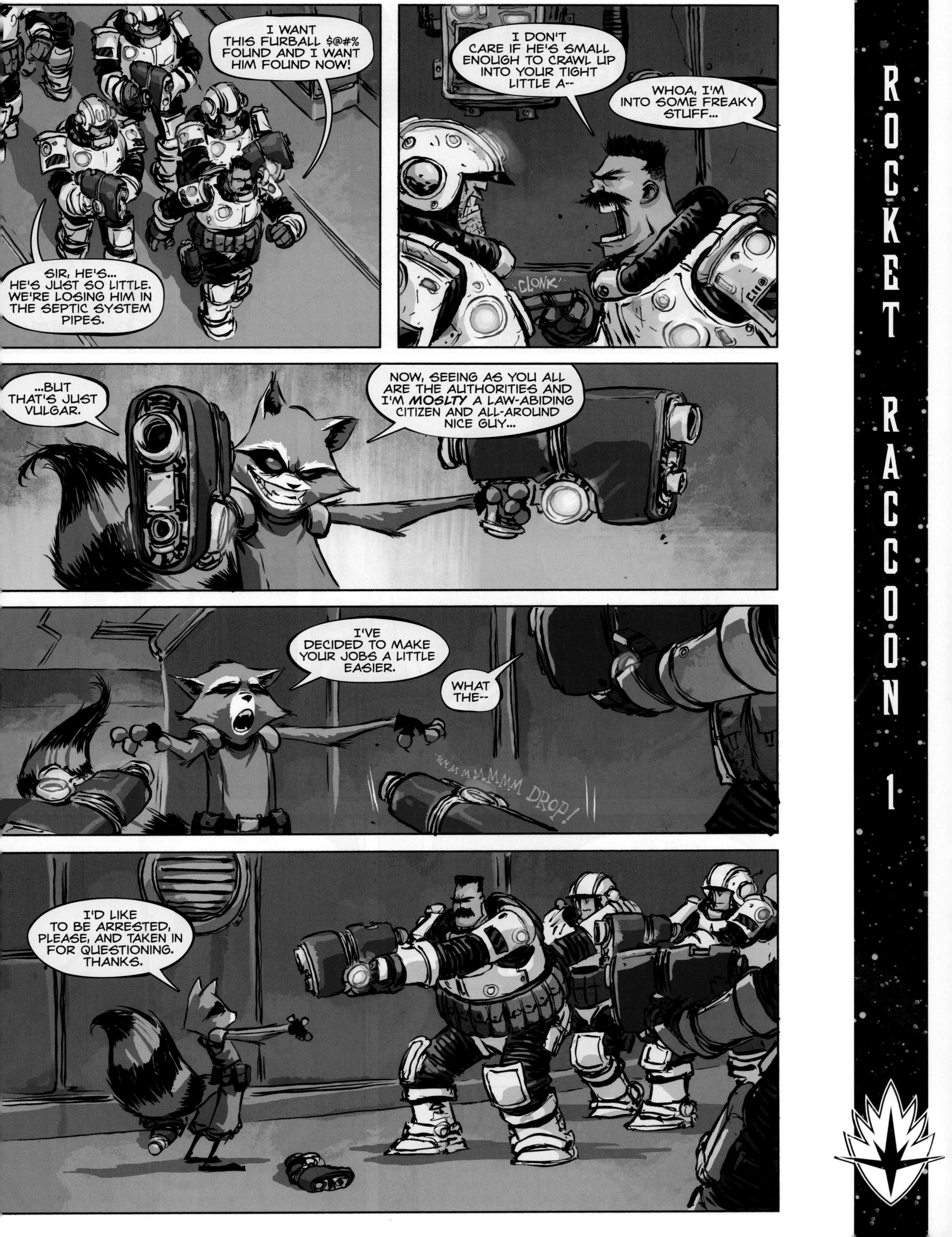
I WANT THIS FURBALL $@#% FOUND AND I WANT HIM FOUND NOW!
SIR, HE'S... HE'S JUST SO LITTLE. WE'RE LOSING HIM IN THE SEPTIC SYSTEM PIPES.
I DON'T CARE IF HE'S SMALL ENOUGH TO CRAWL UP INTO YOUR TIGHT LITTLE A--
CLONK
WHOA, I'M INTO SOME FREAKY STUFF...
...BUT THAT'S JUST VULGAR.
NOW, SEEING AS YOU ALL ARE THE AUTHORITIES AND I'M MOSLTY A LAW-ABIDING CITIZEN AND ALL-AROUND NICE GUY...
I'VE DECIDED TO MAKE YOUR JOBS A LITTLE EASIER.
WHAT THE--
MMMMMMMMMM DROP!
I'D LIKE TO BE ARRESTED, PLEASE, AND TAKEN IN FOR QUESTIONING. THANKS.
ROCKET RACCOON 1

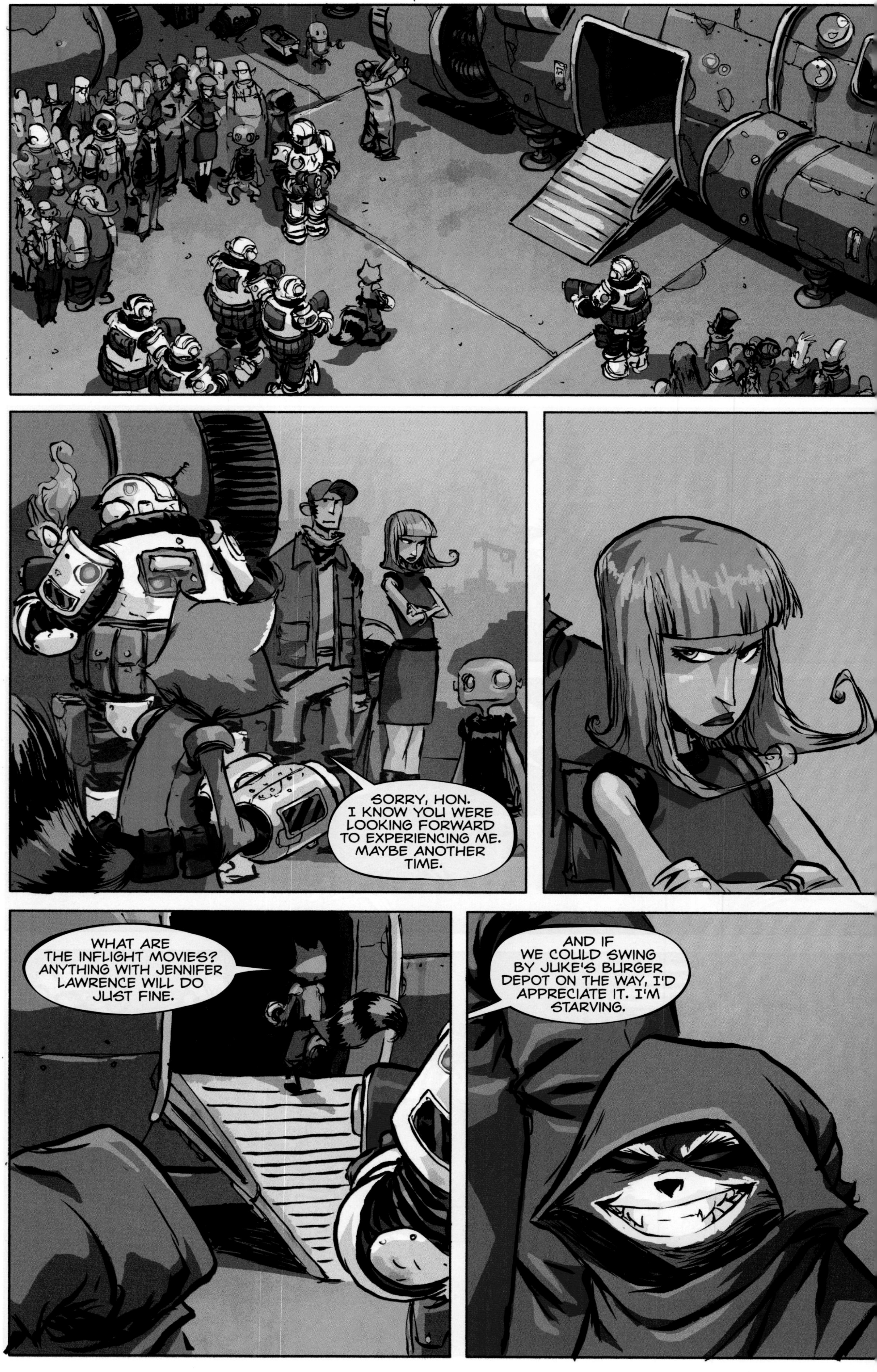
SORRY, HON. I KNOW YOU WERE LOOKING FORWARD TO EXPERIENCING ME. MAYBE ANOTHER TIME.
WHAT ARE THE INFLIGHT MOVIES? ANYTHING WITH JENNIFER LAWRENCE WILL DO JUST FINE.
AND IF WE COULD SWING BY JUKE'S BURGER DEPOT ON THE WAY, I'D APPRECIATE IT. I'M STARVING.

ROCKET RACCOON 1

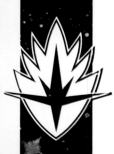

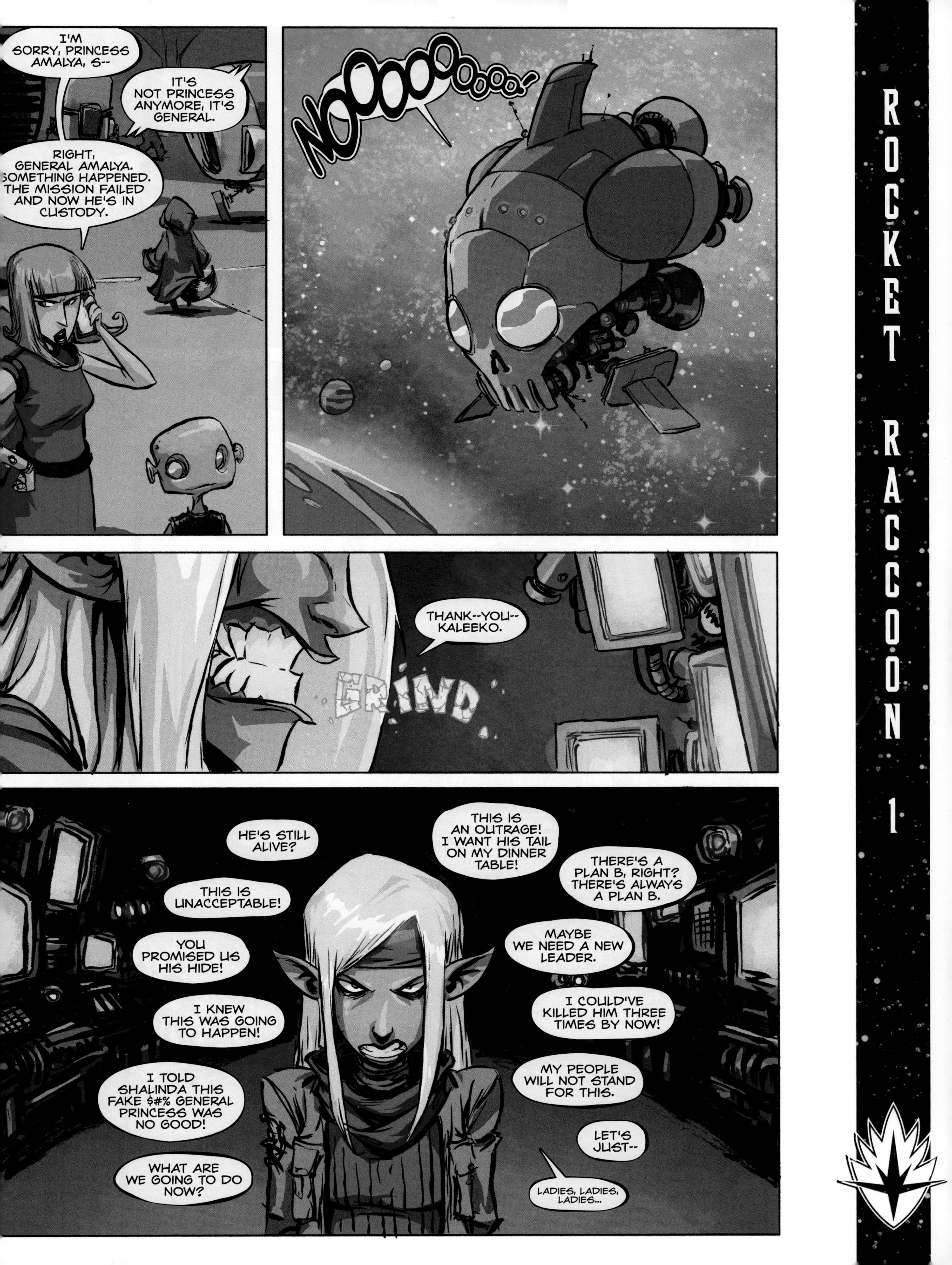
I'M SORRY, PRINCESS AMALYA, S--
IT'S NOT PRINCESS ANYMORE, IT'S GENERAL.
RIGHT, GENERAL AMALYA. SOMETHING HAPPENED. THE MISSION FAILED AND NOW HE'S IN CUSTODY.
NOOOOOooooo!
THANK--YOU--KALEEKO.
GRIND
HE'S STILL ALIVE?
THIS IS AN OUTRAGE! I WANT HIS TAIL ON MY DINNER TABLE!
THERE'S A PLAN B, RIGHT? THERE'S ALWAYS A PLAN B.
THIS IS UNACCEPTABLE!
YOU PROMISED US HIS HIDE!
MAYBE WE NEED A NEW LEADER.
I KNEW THIS WAS GOING TO HAPPEN!
I COULD'VE KILLED HIM THREE TIMES BY NOW!
I TOLD SHALINDA THIS FAKE $#% GENERAL PRINCESS WAS NO GOOD!
MY PEOPLE WILL NOT STAND FOR THIS.
LET'S JUST--
WHAT ARE WE GOING TO DO NOW?
LADIES, LADIES, LADIES...
ROCKET RACCOON 1

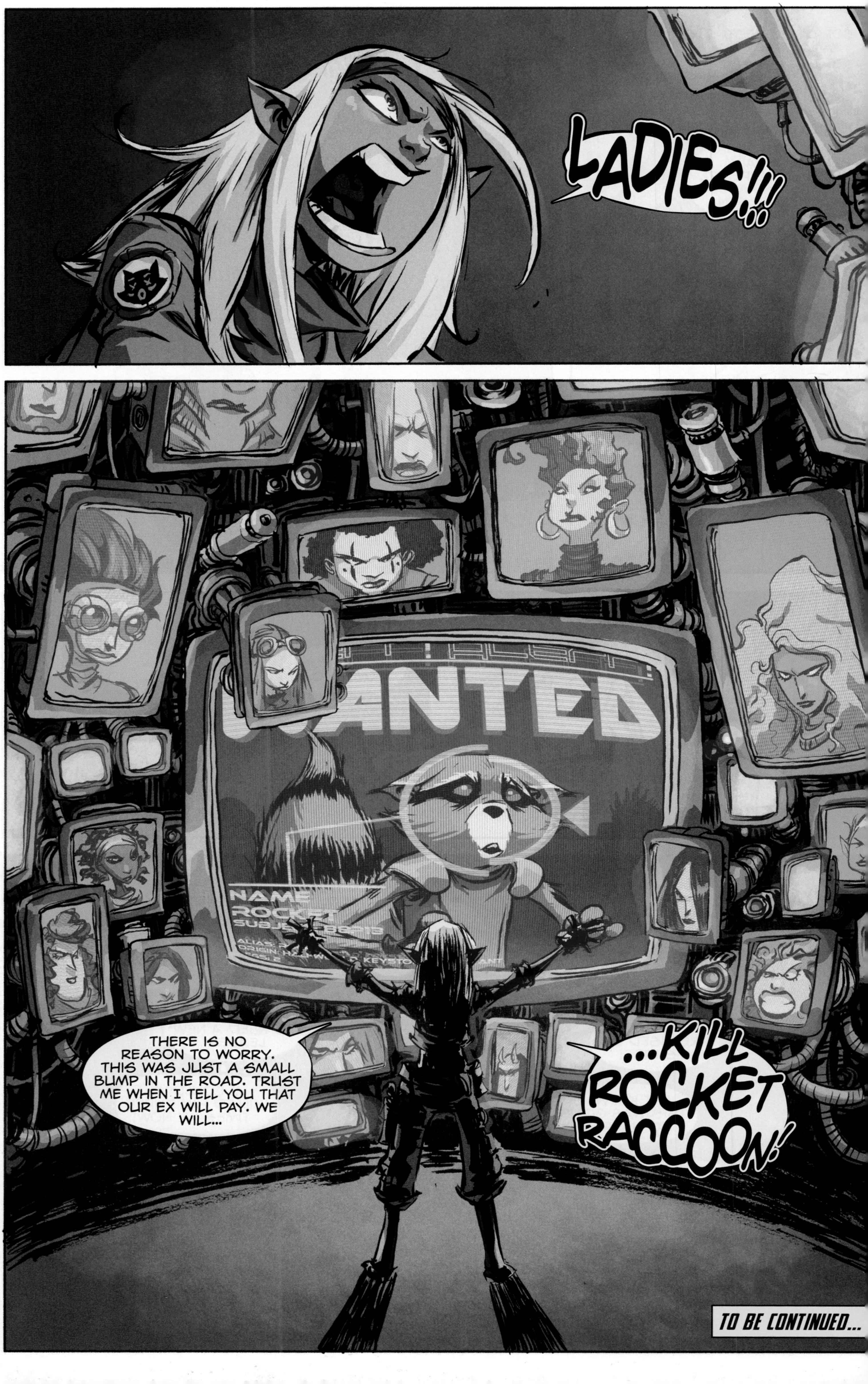
LADIES!!!
NAME
ROCKET
THERE IS NO REASON TO WORRY. THIS WAS JUST A SMALL BUMP IN THE ROAD. TRUST ME WHEN I TELL YOU THAT OUR EX WILL PAY. WE WILL...
...KILL ROCKET RACCOON!
TO BE CONTINUED...

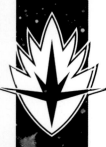

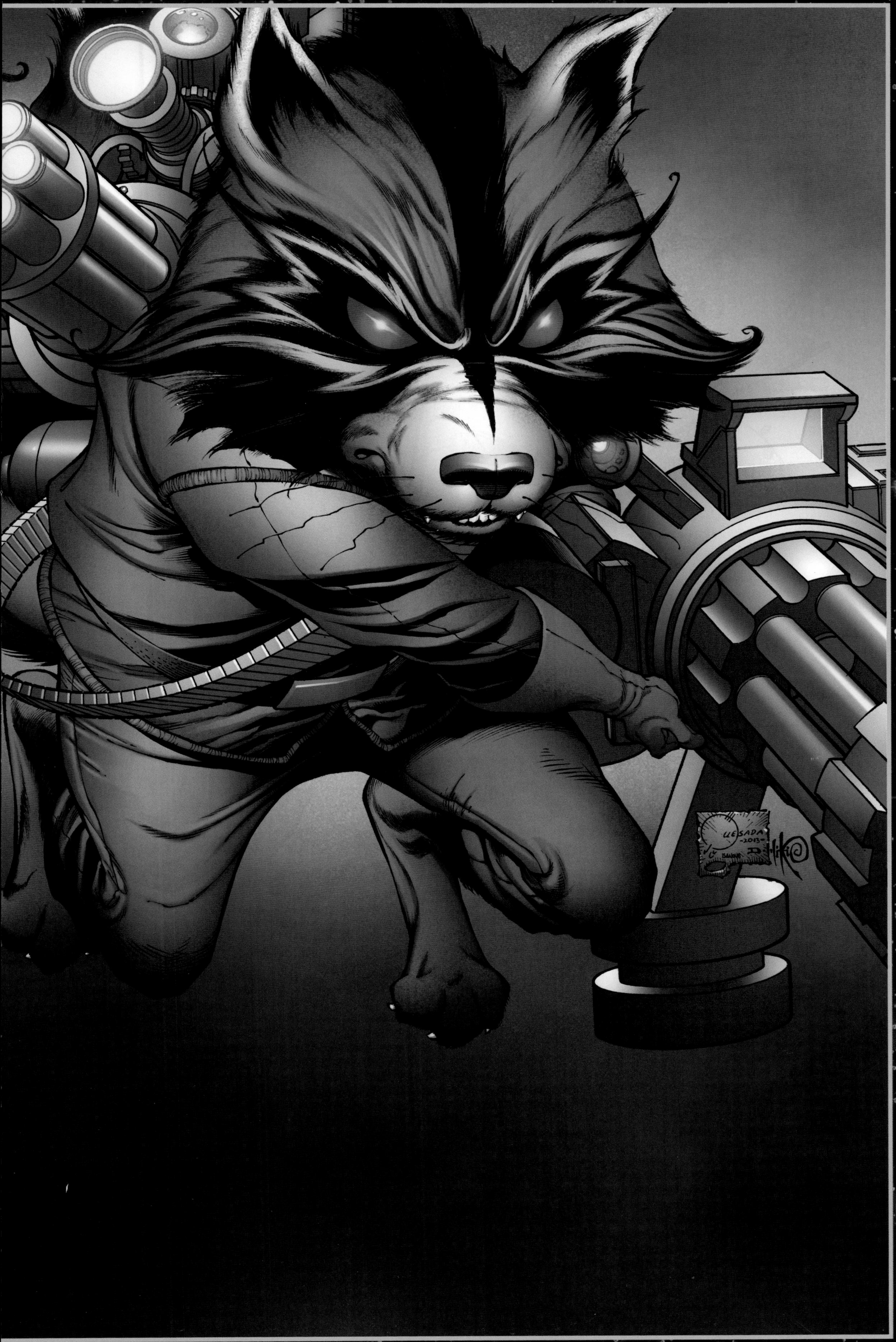

GUARDIANS OF THE GALAXY (2013) #1 VARIANT BY
JOE QUESADA, DANNY MIKI & RICHARD ISANOVE

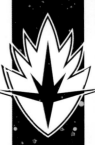

GUARDIANS OF THE GALAXY (2013) #1 VARIANT BY
SKOTTIE YOUNG

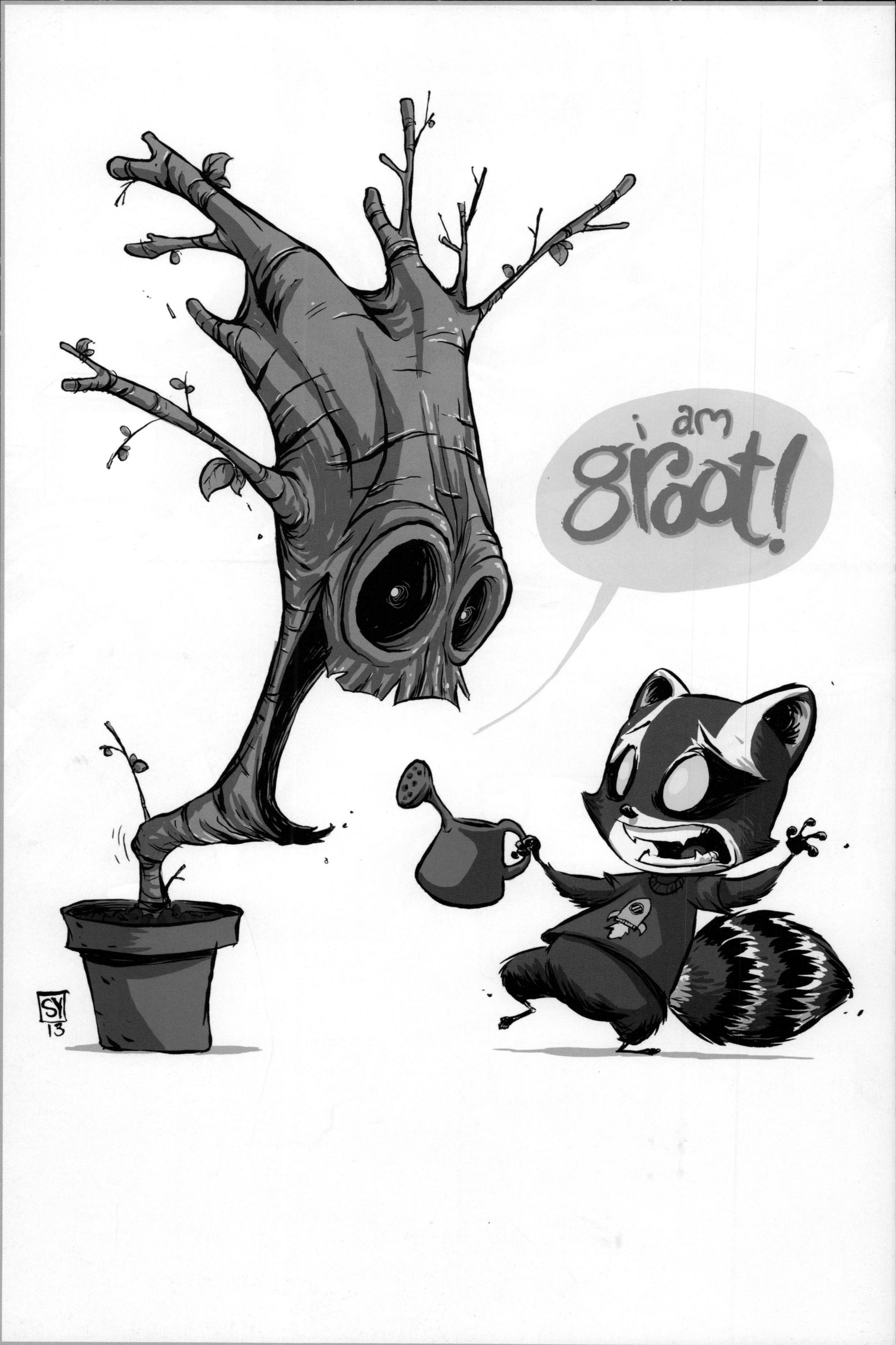
i am groot!

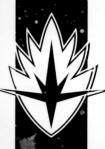

ROCKET RACCOON #1 VARIANT BY
JEFF SMITH & TOM GAADT

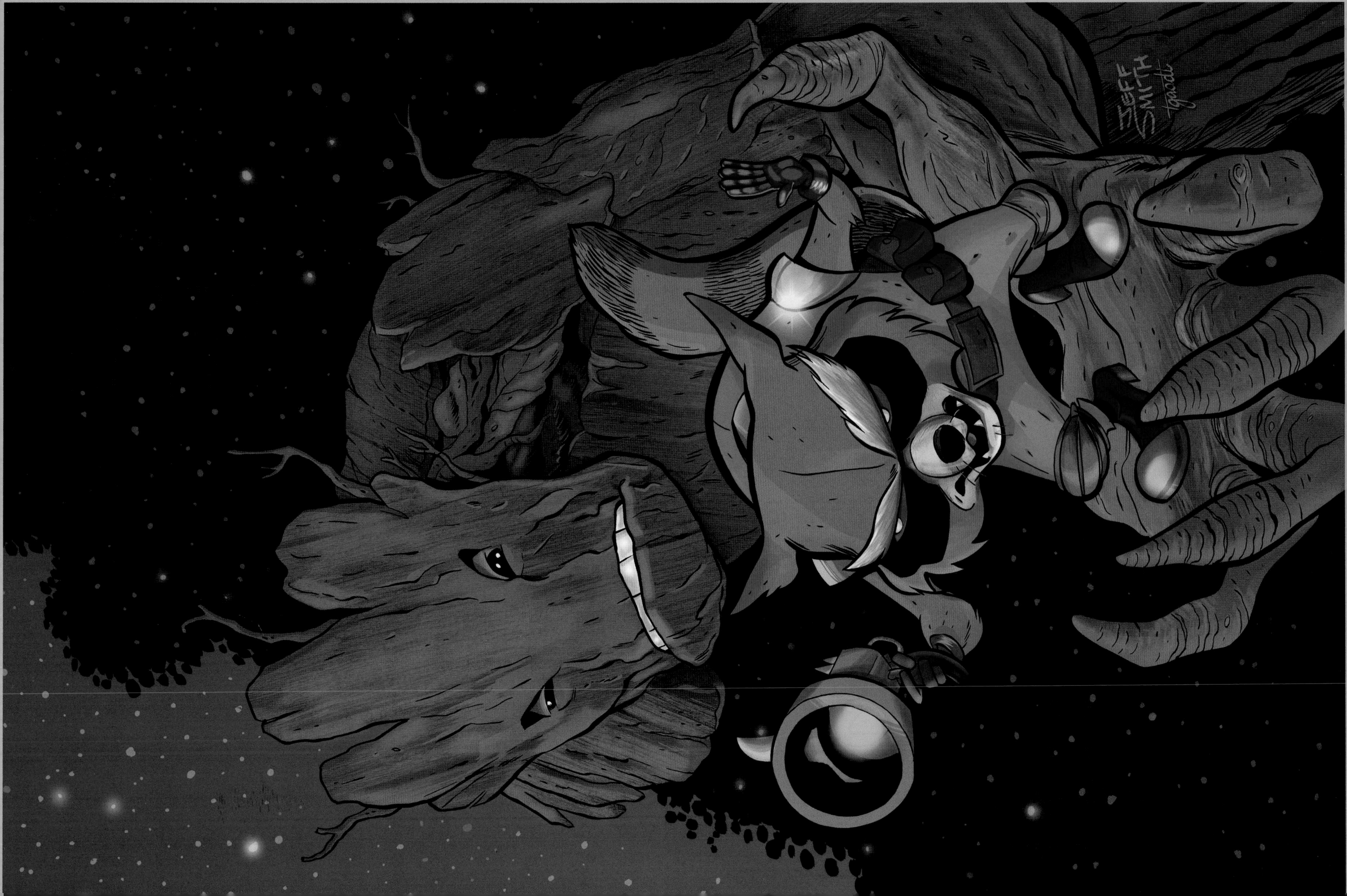
JEFF SMITH
tgaadt

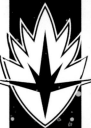

ROCKERT RACCOON #1 VARIANT BY
SARA PICHELLI & JUSTIN PONSOR

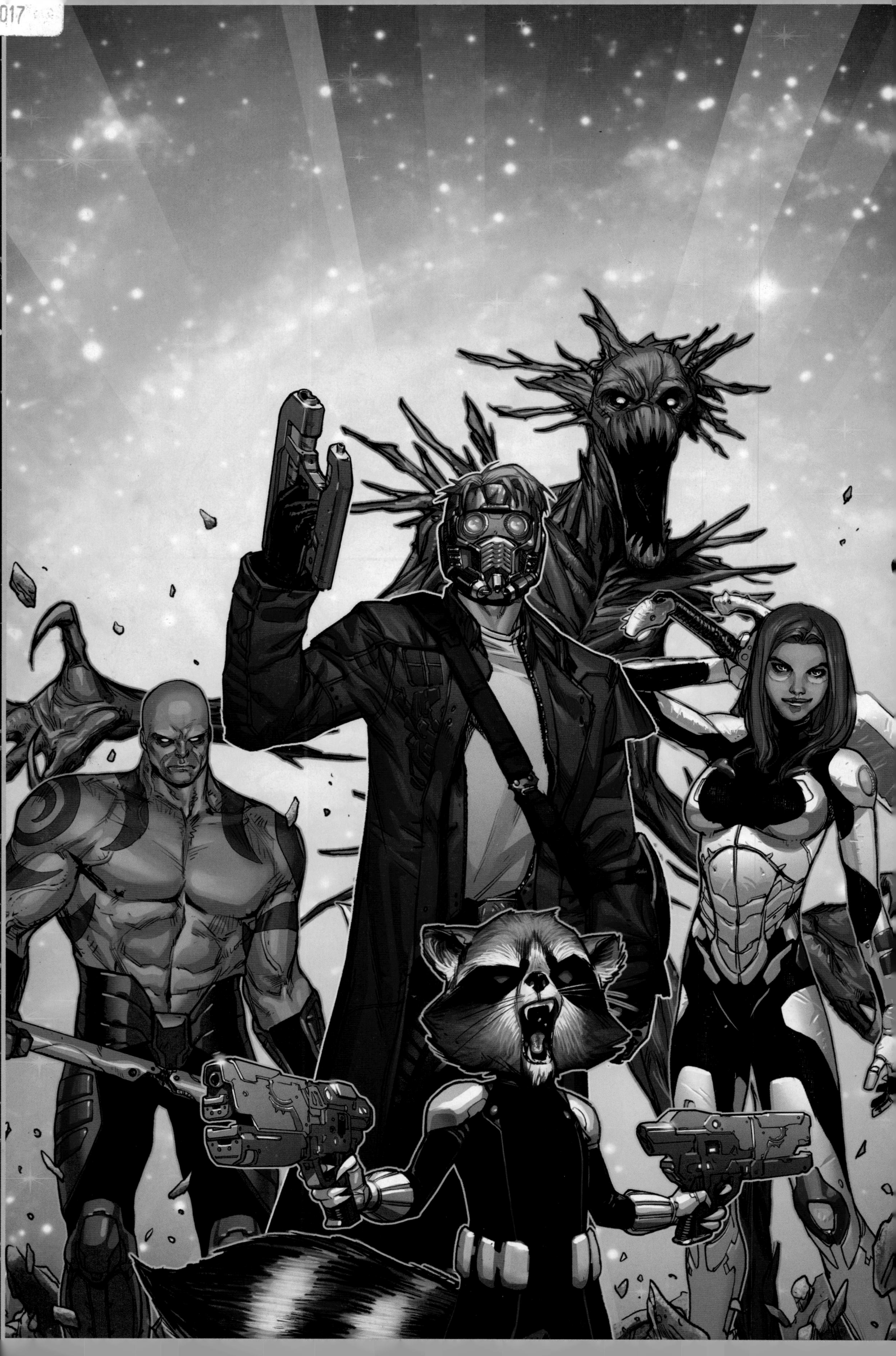